Mothers

of the

Prophets

Mothers

of the

Prophets

REVISED EDITION

LEONARD J. ARRINGTON
SUSAN ARRINGTON MADSEN
EMILY MADSEN JONES

BOOKCRAFT

SALT LAKE CITY, UTAH

For Carl and James, who share with
me the eternal blessing of being mothered and
loved by Grace Fort Arrington

—S. Madsen

To my mother, Susan: guardian, friend, and mentor

—E. Jones

Library of Congress Catalog Card Number: 00-136101

ISBN 1-57345-914-3

Printed in the United States of America   72082-6787

10   9   8   7   6   5   4   3   2   1

TABLE OF CONTENTS

Preface vii

1. Lucy Mack Smith 1

2. Abigail (Nabby) Howe Young 29

3. Agnes Taylor Taylor 40

4. Bulah Thompson Woodruff
   and Azubah Hart Woodruff 56

5. Rosetta Leonora Pettibone Snow 72

6. Mary Fielding Smith 88

7. Rachel Ridgeway Ivins Grant 110

8. Sarah Farr Smith 126

9. Jeanette Eveline Evans McKay 142

10. Julina Lambson Smith 159

11. Louisa Emeline Bingham Lee 177

12. Olive Woolley Kimball 189

13. Sarah Sophia Dunkley Benson 211

14. Nellie Marie Rasmussen Hunter 224

15. Ada Bitner Hinckley 241

PREFACE

When Leonard James Arrington, our father and grandfather, died in 1999, many paid tribute to his groundbreaking research into the lives of Latter-day Saint pioneer women. As early as 1955, and for the next four decades, Leonard wrote numerous articles and books and gave countless speeches in which he chronicled the remarkable lives and accomplishments of these faithful women, whom he often referred to as "Blessed Damozels." He brought to light the lives of the heroines of the Restoration, women who were gifted as writers, politicians, church leaders, midwives, doctors, and school teachers, among others.

In 1987, as a father-daughter project, Leonard and Susan coauthored the first edition of *Mothers of the Prophets*. This book included chapters on the lives of those women who gave birth to (and in most cases raised) a son who later became president of The Church of Jesus Christ of Latter-day Saints. The first edition included chapters on thirteen women, from Lucy Mack Smith, mother of the first president of the Church to Sarah Dunkley Benson, mother of the president of the Church at the time the book was written.

We know that Leonard is pleased that we, as a daughter-granddaughter team, have updated and revised *Mothers of the Prophets* for a second edition. It now includes two new chapters: one devoted to Nellie Rasmussen Hunter and one to Ada Bitner Hinckley. The book remains a heartfelt tribute to the little-known group of seemingly ordinary—and yet very extraordinary—

mothers of the latter-day prophets. Working on this new edition has only strengthened our conviction that the Lord chooses wisely and carefully the mothers who nurture and teach his future prophets, seers, and revelators.

Though their sons shared a common destiny, these fifteen women are very different from each other in many ways. Lucy Mack Smith, for example, was born in 1775, a year before the birth of our nation. Her life was filled with the sorrow of religious persecution as she and her family suffered at the hands of angry mobs. She is the only mother of a latter-day prophet who outlived her prophet-son.

Contrast Lucy's time with that of Nellie Rasmussen Hunter, born 110 years later in 1885, in the Sanpete Valley Mormon community of Mt. Pleasant, Utah. In spite of her own private challenges, Nellie eventually enjoyed the blessings and comforts of twentieth-century life, including penicillin, air travel, and freedom of worship.

Other differences are interesting to observe. Agnes Taylor Taylor, Mary Fielding Smith, and Jeanette Evans McKay, mothers of three latter-day prophets, were born in Great Britain and eventually walked across the plains to the Salt Lake Valley. Two other mothers were born on farms in Idaho: Louisa Bingham Lee and Sarah Dunkley Benson. The mothers of five latter-day prophets were born in Utah.

Bulah Thompson Woodruff was only twenty-six years old when she died, leaving behind her fifteen-month-old son Wilford Woodruff, and his siblings, to be raised by a stepmother. Rachel Ivins Grant, on the other hand, lived to the age of eighty-eight, having associated with every president of the Church from Joseph Smith to Joseph F. Smith. Rachel had only one child, Heber Jeddy Grant; five other mothers of latter-day prophets had eleven children each.

Several of these women contributed economically to their families, and they did so in diverse ways. Julina Lambson Smith

delivered babies as a midwife. Lucy Mack Smith sold homemade
baskets and brooms. Rachel Ivins Grant did custom sewing and
took in boarders. And Nellie Rasmussen Hunter managed apartments and pressed clothes.

Looking deep into the souls of these valiant mothers in Zion,
we can clearly see that each had difficult challenges and that each
faced those challenges with courage and great faith. Most of these
women lived at a time when the Church was still very young. They
patiently endured forced removals from their homes and the years
of pioneering in the wilderness that were necessary in those early
years. Many of them struggled with financial setbacks. Some,
including Rosetta Pettibone Snow, had difficult disagreements with
their spouses on religious matters. Several, including Abigail Howe
Young, Bulah Thompson Woodruff, Olive Woolley Kimball, and
Ada Bitner Hinckley, had serious health problems which took their
lives at a relatively young age, interrupting precious years of family
association. Two mothers, Mary Fielding Smith and Ada Bitner
Hinckley, married widowers and helped raise several children from
their husbands' previous marriages.

But one thing is clear in every case: each of the mothers of the
fifteen men who have led The Church of Jesus Christ of Latter-day
Saints has had a divine role to play. Whether they were shy or outgoing, whether they were openly affectionate or showed their love
in other ways, the Lord entrusted each of these women with a son
who would guide His Church through a particular portion of the
culminating dispensation of the gospel.

In working on this book, our own appreciation for these
women has increased enormously and our understanding of their
sons has deepened. This project has been a wonderful experience
for us and we hope it will be meaningful to readers as well.

We are grateful to descendants of each of the women for their
cooperation. Through their laughter and tears, we have sensed the
deep love they have for their noble heritage. We are also grateful to

our spouses, Dean and David, for their complete support and encouragement.

We appreciate the courtesies extended by the LDS Church Historical Library and Archives, the Utah State Historical Society, and the special collections and libraries at Utah State University, Brigham Young University, and the University of Utah. We express our gratitude, in particular, to Sheri Dew, for her endorsement of this project and her efforts in bringing about the reissuing of this book in its new edition.

Finally, we express our love for the history of The Church of Jesus Christ of Latter-day Saints. May this book confirm in the hearts and minds of those who read it, the importance of every soul in the building of the Lord's kingdom in the latter days.

Susan Arrington Madsen
Emily Madsen Jones
March 2001

I believe mothering is
the loveliest of the arts:
that great mothers
are hand-maidens of the Spirit,
to whom are entrusted God's avatars,
that no prophet is greater
than his mother.

—*Will Levington Comfort*

LUCY MACK SMITH

Blessed is my mother, for her soul is ever filled with benevolence and philanthropy; and notwithstanding her age, she shall yet receive strength and be comforted in the midst of her house. Thus saith the Lord, she shall have eternal life. —*Joseph Smith Jr.*

C hild of the frontier, nurse of two sisters who died lingering deaths, mother of four sons who died for their faith, and Mother in Israel to thousands who struggled to establish a latter-day kingdom of God, Lucy Mack Smith was a splendid exemplar of the family culture that permeated early America. Most of the schooling at that time, especially for girls, was in the home. Girls devoted much of their time to housekeeping, sewing, and looking after livestock and poultry, and children were almost entirely under the influence of their family and the small circle of acquaintances in their neighborhood. They shared their feelings and experiences with their parents and brothers and sisters, and they took great pride in the accomplishments of family members.

For many children in those days, the only book they ever read was the Bible. Similarly, with the exception of occasional revivals, the only worship service they would attend was provided by the prayers offered and hymns sung within their family unit. This was the case with Lucy Mack; it was also the case with Joseph Smith Jr., who, backed by the rich family culture of his parents, Lucy Mack and Joseph Smith Sr., emerged to become the founding prophet of The Church of Jesus Christ of Latter-day Saints.

Lucy was born in Gilsum, New Hampshire, on July 8, 1775,

Lucy Mack Smith

the last of eight children born to Solomon and Lydia Gates Mack. Solomon, a native of Lyme, Connecticut, fought in the French and Indian War (1754 to 1761), which finally culminated in the Treaty of Paris in which France ceded to Great Britain most of eastern Canada and all of the present United States east of the Mississippi except New Orleans. Solomon was also a soldier in the War of the Revolution, so he was away from home much of the time his children were growing up. An active enterpriser, he sold supplies to the army, bought and sold land, and developed properties for resale. As with many others of his day, however, he experienced several misfortunes that prevented him from prospering.

Lydia Mack, Lucy's mother, was a native of East Haddam

(Millington), Connecticut. Because of her husband's prolonged absences and lack of income, she had to raise her family under the difficult conditions prevalent in the frontier villages in New Hampshire and Vermont where they settled. Described by Lucy as "pious and affectionate," Lydia was responsible for "all the religious instructions as well as most of the educational privileges" of her eight children, all of whom turned out to be individuals of intelligence and courage. When she wrote her autobiography in her later years, Lucy devoted seven chapters to telling of her parents, grandparents, brothers, and sisters. If her manuscript is an accurate reflection, the family was public-spirited, exhibited mutual caring, and cultivated the highest religious values. Lucy and her brothers and sisters seem to have accepted that God kept a warm, personal interest in his children and would hear and answer prayers.

Gilsum, where Lucy grew up, was still a frontier region, populated at the time of her birth by perhaps thirty young to middle-aged families. It was a rocky region, with only small acreages that could grow farm and garden crops, and no orchards. Most of the land was in pasture, and the families owned milk cows, oxen, horses, and beef cattle.

The Battle of Bunker Hill had taken place just before Lucy's birth, and George Washington took command of the revolutionary army shortly thereafter. Solomon enlisted and served for a year or two, until he became ill. Back home, he was an invalid much of the time. When Lucy was a little over two, he was struck by a falling tree and almost killed. A little later he suffered from a fall and blow on the head that caused him to have periodic "fits." The family became destitute of property, and Solomon did not have the strength to furnish them a satisfactory livelihood. For a period, he and two teenage sons joined the crew of a privateer; in 1779, in a stroke of good fortune, they captured eight British vessels in Long Island Sound and received some prize money.

Solomon moved his family to Montague, Massachusetts, and remained home with them for four or five years. Then he spent four years at sea, with a fishing schooner and freighter. Shortly after he left, when Lucy was about eight, Lydia suffered a "severe fit of sickness" and became so ill that Lucy was placed in the care of her seventeen-year-old brother, Stephen. With little to show for his hard labor and enterprise, Solomon was back with his family in 1788, only to find that, through the underhanded dealing of a creditor, Lydia and the children had been evicted from their home. Solomon then moved his family to Tunbridge, Vermont; but in 1792, when Lucy was seventeen, he moved them back to Gilsum, New Hampshire, where he operated a store.

Meanwhile, Lucy's married sister, Lovisa, came down with consumption (presumably tuberculosis), and during the next five years both Lovisa and Lovina, a year younger, became seriously ill with the disease. Lucy, from age seventeen to nineteen, nursed Lovina; she carried her twenty-nine-year-old sister from bed to chair and from chair to bed. When Lovina died after two years of care, Lucy prepared to look after Lovisa, whose consumption had once more flared up. Solomon went to get Lovisa to take her to his home in Gilsum, but she died on the way. As she wrote her life history many years later, Lucy told very little of her childhood except for the illnesses and deaths that had consumed the energies of all the family. Lucy's youth was not one of happy experiences or childish adventures but of toil, frustration, sickness, and perseverance.

Depressed and melancholy after the deaths of her sisters, Lucy sought comfort in religion, seeking solace and understanding in Bible reading and prayer. There was one problem. "If I remain a member of no church," she said, "all religious people will say I am of the world, and if I join some one of the different denominations, all the rest will say I am in error." During the years she was growing up in Gilsum, there was a church, but the congregation could not afford a pastor. And whatever the religious situation in Montague, religious help was not accessible when Lucy needed it, particularly after the deaths of her sisters.

Having been especially close to her brother Stephen, Lucy

responded to his invitation to visit him in Tunbridge, Vermont, eighty miles north of Gilsum, after her sisters died. Stephen, now twenty-eight, was a partner in a mercantile and tinning establishment in Tunbridge. Among the new settlers there was Asael Smith, a selectman (county commissioner) of Tunbridge and a close friend and supporter of Stephen. It was inevitable that Lucy, an attractive woman with clear blue eyes and light brown hair, should meet Joseph Smith, Asael's second son, a strong, tall, athletic young man of twenty-three. After a year in Tunbridge, Lucy returned to her family in Gilsum, but not for long. In January 1796 she returned to Tunbridge and married Joseph Smith.

Joseph and Lucy Smith, ages twenty-five and twenty, respectively, began life under favorable circumstances. Asael gave them part ownership in a handsome farm, and Stephen Mack and his partner presented Lucy with one thousand dollars, money that she laid away as a cash reserve. Joseph and Lucy set to work on their farm. Their first child, a son, died in childbirth. Two years after their marriage Lucy bore a second son, Alvin, and two years later a third son, Hyrum.

In 1802, after six years of farming in Tunbridge, Joseph and Lucy rented their farmhouse and land and moved to Randolph, a larger village seven miles to the west, where they opened a store. Joseph had heard that enormous profits could be made by freighting ginseng root to China, where it was prized for its ability to prolong life and restore virility. As a part of their new enterprise, he set about collecting the root, probably buying or trading for it from local farmers. After the root was crystallized, he took it to New York and contracted to have it shipped to China on consignment. He stood to make $4,500. But the son of a Royalton, Vermont, merchant who sailed with the cargo apparently pocketed the entire proceeds and escaped to Canada. Joseph pursued him, but in vain. He was financially ruined. He could not cover the cost of the inventory for his store and was forced to sell his farm. Lucy contributed her thousand dollar wedding gift to keep the family going. As she

Joseph Smith Sr.

described it, they had crossed the line from "embarrassment of debt" to "embarrassment of poverty."

As a propertyless family, the Smiths began a cycle of renting farms that were later sold and then having to move on to another. During the next fourteen years they moved seven times—at first to farms around Tunbridge, Royalton, and Sharon, Vermont; then to Lebanon, New Hampshire; then back to Norwich, Vermont; and finally to western New York State. During these years Lucy gave birth to Sophronia in 1803, Joseph Jr. in 1805, Samuel Harrison in 1808, Ephraim in 1810 (he died ten days after birth), William in 1811, Catherine in 1812, and Don Carlos in 1816. By the time the family moved to New York in 1816, Lucy was forty-one and had given birth to ten children, of whom eight were living. She would bear an additional daughter, Lucy, in 1821 in New York.

During these years of farming and moving, Joseph Sr. occasionally taught school during the winter to bring in extra income. In addition, the family received help from both Joseph's and Lucy's parents, and especially from Lucy's brother Stephen. There was work, but there was also family caring. Lucy remembered these years as full of joy and satisfaction. As she wrote, "We looked around us and said what do we now lack? There is nothing which we have not a sufficiency of to make us and our children perfectly comfortable both for food and raiment as well as that which is necessary to a respectable appearance in society both at home and abroad." The family had morning and evening prayers and sang hymns together. The children went to school, and they all pitched in to work on winter nights, making their own clothing and small handicraft items to sell. Still, the family was not able to accumulate enough to buy land or to provide security for the future.

In 1812, while they were in Lebanon, New Hampshire, a typhoid fever epidemic swept through the region, leaving six thousand dead. All of the Smith children were stricken. Sophronia, the worst affected, was ill for three months and was finally left motionless, with eyes fixed as if in death. Joseph and Lucy clasped hands, knelt, and uttered a desperate prayer. Then Lucy grabbed her up in a blanket, pressed her close, and paced back and forth until the child finally sobbed and began to breathe. None of the children died.

Nevertheless, Joseph Jr., seven years of age at the time, was left with an infection that refused to heal. At first the sore was in his armpit; then it moved down to his left shin and ankle. The local surgeon opened the wound to release the infection, and when the wound failed to heal, he made another incision. Finally he consulted surgeons at Dartmouth Medical College, and they proposed amputation. When seven doctors (perhaps some were medical students) descended on the Smith home to perform the operation, Lucy refused to permit amputation. She insisted that they could cut out the diseased portion of bone but must leave the healthy bone

intact. This they reluctantly agreed to do. It was an agonizing operation, done without any kind of painkiller, with the boy held
tightly in the arms of his father. Not able to bear the sight, Lucy
walked out to the fields. Fortunately, the doctor who operated was
the one professional in New England who could perform such an
operation, and it was a success. After three months of constant pain
the leg began to heal, but convalescence required three years, during which time Joseph was either in bed or on crutches. To the end
of his life he had a slight limp.

As these episodes reveal, Lucy was a resolute and determined
woman. She paced the floor with Sophronia; she carried Joseph
back and forth from his bed to his chair in front of the fire or to
the table in the kitchen; she covenanted with God to preserve her
family; and she comforted her children in their sufferings and
problems.

But Lucy, who had a high-strung temperament, had her own
health problems. In 1803, when she was twenty-eight and before
Joseph Jr. was born, she had come down with a cold, then a fever,
which the doctor diagnosed as consumption. She was very ill, fearful of death, and felt unprepared to meet God. She had not experienced the kind of conversion that born-again Christians of her day
felt was an essential precursor of salvation. So ill that her husband
and her mother, who was looking after her, despaired of her life,
Lucy pleaded with God to spare her so that she might bring up her
children and be a comfort to her husband. She wrote:

"My mind was much agitated during the whole night.
Sometimes I contemplated heaven and heavenly things; then my
thoughts would turn upon those of earth—my babes and my companion. During this night I made a solemn covenant with God, that
if He would let me live I would endeavour to serve him according
to the best of my abilities. Shortly after this I heard a voice say to
me, 'Seek, and ye shall find; knock, and it shall be opened unto
you. Let your heart be comforted; ye believe in God, believe also in

me.'" A few minutes later, she wrote, "my mother came in and, looking upon me, said, 'Lucy, you are better.'"

As she recovered her health, Lucy still felt troubled about religion. She had conversations with visiting ministers and with religious neighbors, but she could not find the godliness or heavenly spirit that she sought. "I therefore determined to examine my Bible and, taking Jesus and His disciples for my guide, to endeavour to obtain from God that which man could neither give nor take away." Finally she was baptized, but not into any specific religious denomination.

Later, when the Smiths moved to Tunbridge, Lucy attended Methodist meetings, but she did not feel a desire to affiliate with them. Her husband had a dream in 1811 that he related to her, and which she took seriously enough to record verbatim. The dream was filled with symbolism, but Lucy wrote that her husband concluded from it that church members knew no more of the kingdom of God than did those who made no profession of religion whatever. She yearned for association with a church, yet she remained alienated, partly by her husband's skepticism. Although they had regular prayers and sang hymns, he joined no church until his own son organized the restored Church of Christ in 1830.

The medical bills from the operation and subsequent recovery of young Joseph kept the Smiths impoverished. They moved to Norwich, Vermont, where they rented a farm from Squire Moredock and operated a kind of store out of their home. Lucy learned to paint oil tablecloths to sell; her husband peddled homemade baskets and brooms, root beer, cakes, boiled eggs, gingerbread, fruit, and other items. But their crops failed for two successive years.

When, after the spring planting of 1816, the frost continued through a summer highlighted by snow and ice, Joseph Sr. felt that he had had enough; he decided to move the family south to New York State. Leaving Lucy behind to supervise the move, he looked for new land in the Genesee region. A Mr. Howard was going to

Palmyra and offered to accompany the rest of the Smith family.
With the help of her mother, Lucy and the older boys assembled
the provisions and clothing they needed. As they were about to
depart, some creditors, who had held back until this crucial time
to get a better settlement, presented their claims. By the time she
had settled with everyone, Lucy was left with less than eighty
dollars.   .

Lucy and the eight children left Norwich in the late fall of
1816. Snow was on the ground, and they traveled by sleigh to
Royalton, where they left Lucy's mother with her son. In an unfortunate accident, Lydia Mack, who had been living with Lucy's family for some time, was injured by an overturning wagon; she had a
premonition that she would not live to see them again. Her first
concern was that her daughter's family remain religious. She
declared: "I must soon exchange the things of this world for those
which pertain to another state of existence, where I hope to enjoy
the society of the blessed; and now as my last admonition, I
beseech you to continue faithful in the service of God to the end
of your days, that I may have the pleasure of embracing you in
another and fairer world above." She died two years later as a result
of her injuries.

Transferring their goods from the sleigh to a wagon, Lucy and
her children headed for Palmyra, three hundred miles to the west.
They had trouble with Caleb Howard, their driver. He refused to
allow Joseph Jr. to ride, preferring to have some girls in an accompanying family ride next to him. Since Joseph, now ten, had just
discarded his crutches and was still lame, Alvin and Hyrum tried
to intercede in his behalf, but Howard knocked them down with
the butt of his whip.

When Lucy ran out of money near Utica, almost one hundred
miles from their destination, Howard threw the Smiths' goods out
into the street and drove off with their team and wagon. Lucy
found him some time later in a bar and, before a company of travelers, accused him of robbing and leaving her destitute with eight

children. When Howard attempted to drive off, Lucy grabbed the reins, the children mounted the wagon, and they resolutely drove on with bystanders cheering. With no money, by the end of the trip Lucy paid innkeepers with clothing and yards of cloth. The family arrived in Palmyra, Lucy recalled, with "a small portion of our effects, and barely two cents in cash." Joseph Sr. was waiting for them. "We all now sat down," she wrote, "and counselled together relative to the course which was best for us to adopt in our destitute circumstances."

Palmyra was a booming town with perhaps three thousand inhabitants. Most of the trades and professions were represented, and there was a bookstore, a tannery, a harness shop, a distillery, and a drugstore, as well as four taverns. To obtain cash with which to buy land, Lucy once more painted oil tablecloths, members of the family sold refreshments from a small shop and peddled them by cart when crowds gathered for celebrations and revivals, and the older boys worked for farmers needing extra hands for harvesting, digging wells, and landscaping. After two years of this labor, Lucy and Joseph were able to buy a farm two miles south of Palmyra in what would later become the township of Manchester. There they built, to use Lucy's words, "a snug log-house, neatly furnished." The four-room home provided sleeping space for ten people: six boys from two to nineteen, two girls six and fifteen, and the parents.

Family members now devoted most of their effort to clearing the land and preparing it for the planting of crops. According to Lucy, the men's labor was prodigious—they cleared thirty acres the first year. This enabled them to sell potash and pearl ash from the burnt trees, considerable cordwood, and some maple sugar. They apparently grew corn for the family and animals on the first land they cleared. They also sold brooms, baskets, cakes, maple sugar, and molasses, and very likely they fished, trapped, and hunted. They were also making many friends. Lucy was proud of her family. She wrote, "We began to rejoice in our prosperity; our hearts glowed with gratitude to God for the manifestations of His favor that surrounded us."

The Smiths were not caught up with material concerns to the exclusion of spiritual anxieties. Joseph Sr. continued to have dreams and visions that were impressive enough for him to relate them to Lucy and the family. Each of the dreams dwelt on the search for healing, for salvation, for beauty. It is also apparent that the parents and the older children were affected by the enticements of the local Presbyterian, Methodist, Baptist, and Quaker churches and the frequent revivals in the area. Indeed, Lucy, Hyrum, Sophronia, and Samuel decided to join the Presbyterian church, but Joseph Sr. and the other sons held back. Among these was Joseph Jr., who in 1820 was so infused by religious feelings that he went to a clearing in the nearby woods to pray. "A pillar of light" came down and rested upon him, he later told his parents, and he was "filled with the Spirit of God." "I saw the Lord and he spake unto me," he said. The message he received in this vision was one of forgiveness and redemption; but in response to his question concerning which church to join, he was told he should join none of them. He must wait for the Lord to accomplish His purposes.

The round of work continued. The family cleared and fenced additional land and planted an orchard, and some of the sons worked for farmers in the vicinity. With the threat of losing their farm over their heads, they held school in their own house and, under Lucy's direction, studied the Bible. Alvin, who was now twenty-three, began to build a large wood frame house. This was rendered all the more necessary when a new baby, Lucy, was born to Lucy in 1821. But in November 1823, before the house was finished, Alvin died. Lucy wrote that he had been given an overdose of medicine by a drunken doctor.

Shortly before Alvin's death, Joseph Jr. had another experience that significantly altered the lives of the Smiths. On September 21, 1823, when he was seventeen, Joseph waited until the others had gone to sleep and then began an intense supplication to God.

While he was praying, he felt the room growing lighter and lighter. Suddenly, a person appeared in the light, standing above the floor. Joseph recalled: "He had on a loose robe of most exquisite whiteness. It was a whiteness beyond anything earthly I had ever seen, nor do I believe that any earthly thing could be made to appear so exceedingly white and brilliant. His hands were naked, and his arms also, a little above the wrist; so also were his feet naked, as were his legs, a little above the ankles. His head and neck were also bare. I could discover that he had no other clothing on but this robe, as it was open so that I could see into his bosom. Not only was his robe exceedingly white, but his whole person was glorious beyond description and his countenance truly like lightning."

The being, who identified himself as Moroni, assured young Joseph that he (Joseph) enjoyed the acceptance of God, that God had a work for him, and that his mission would be quite unlike any that he had dreamed of. He told Joseph about a book "written upon gold plates, giving an account of the former inhabitants of this continent and the source from whence they sprang. . . . The fulness of the everlasting gospel was contained in it, as delivered by the Savior to the ancient inhabitants." He also told Joseph about two stones in silver bows: "The possession and use of these stones were what constituted seers in ancient or former times," Joseph later wrote, adding that "God had prepared them for the purpose of translating the book." More was said, and Joseph understood that he was destined to play an important role in preparing for the return of Christ.

After delivering the message, the angel disappeared. But while the startled Joseph was trying to grasp the meaning of it all, the room began to brighten again. Moroni reappeared, and he repeated every word he had said before. Then he ascended a second time, only to appear a third time to repeat the same message.

Dawn broke shortly after the third message, and the family began to stir to do their morning chores. That morning, as he and his father and older brother worked at harvesting wheat, young

Joseph stopped, as if in deep thought. Urged on by his brother, he resumed work, but he soon stopped again. Noticing Joseph's pallor, his father sent him back to the house; but while he was attempting to climb the fence, he fainted, and for a time he lay unconscious. As he came to, he saw Moroni standing over him once more. The angel repeated the message a fourth time, this time directing Joseph to tell his father. Joseph returned to the field and related to his father what had transpired. Joseph Sr. accepted his son's story and told him that he must be careful to follow the instructions of the angel.

The plates the angel had described lay in a hill about three miles southeast of the Smith farm. Having seen the hill in vision the night before, Joseph Jr. knew just where to look for them. He dug away the earth and uncovered a stone box which contained the plates, the Urim and Thummim, and a breastplate. Considering the indigent circumstances of the Smith family, it is easy to see why Joseph could hardly avoid thinking of their worth and what they would bring on the market. That this thought should occur to the young man angered Moroni, who once more appeared, rebuked him for impure motives, and told him that, as Joseph reported, "the time for bringing them forth had not yet arrived." Joseph was to go to the hill the next year for further instructions. According to Lucy, he had to wait "until he had learned to keep the commandments of God—not only till he was willing but able to do it."

That evening young Joseph told his family about the angel and the plates. They all believed, convinced that God was about to give them "a more perfect knowledge of the plan of salvation and the redemption of the human family. This caused us greatly to rejoice." Lucy added, "the sweetest union and happiness pervaded our house, and tranquility reigned in our midst."

In the winter evenings that followed, Lucy wrote, "Joseph would occasionally give us some of the most amusing recitals that could be imagined. He would describe the ancient inhabitants of this continent, their dress, mode of traveling, and the animals upon which they rode; their cities, their buildings, with every particular; their mode of warfare; and also their religious worship. This he would do with as much ease, seemingly, as if he had spent his whole life with them."

But the portents of the future were not happy ones. Lucy later remembered that Joseph warned the family after he first saw the plates that they must not mention them outside the home, for people "would try to take our lives; and . . . our names would be cast out as evil by all people." All these things proved to be true.

In the Smith household and on the farm, work went on. To raise money to help complete a new frame house, Joseph, Lucy, and their children continued working for established farmers and businesses. Joseph Jr. married Emma Hale in January 1827. Finally, in September 1827, after four annual visitations of the angel, Joseph brought back to his parents' home a box containing the gold plates and placed it under the hearthstones in the west room. Lucy wrote that after he returned from the hill, her son said, "Do not be uneasy, mother, all is right—see here, I have got a key." Lucy said the "key," presumably the Urim and Thummim, consisted of "two smooth, three-cornered diamonds set in glass, and the glasses were set in silver bows, which were connected with each other in much the same way as old-fashioned spectacles." Joseph also showed her the breastplate, wrapped in a muslin handkerchief thin enough to allow the glistening metal to be seen. With metal straps for fastening to hips and shoulders, it was apparently made for a person of extraordinary size.

Because of the interference of neighbors—their insistence on seeing the plates, their repeated attempts to steal them, and their demands that the plates be sold and the revenue shared with them—Joseph Jr. later took them to Harmony, Pennsylvania, to the home of his wife's parents, where he began the systematic process of translation. During those months Lucy and Joseph Sr. took occasion to visit their son and daughter-in-law in Harmony. They remained for nearly three months, visiting not only their children but Emma Smith's parents as well.

In 1829 the manuscript of the Book of Mormon, described by Lucy as "a record of the origin of aborigines of ancient America," was copyrighted and submitted to a printer for publication. Lucy, in her history, devotes a whole chapter to describing the efforts of persons in the region to prevent the printing. In fact, she insisted on keeping one copy of the final manuscript in a chest under the head of her bed so that if the other copy were stolen or destroyed, no disaster would ensue. Then, confident that the printing would proceed without interruption, she relaxed and became pensive. She wrote:

"When I meditated upon the days of toil, and nights of anxiety, through which we had all passed for years previous, in order to obtain the treasure that then lay beneath my head; when I thought upon the hours of fearful apprehensions which we had all suffered on the same account, and that the object was at last accomplished, I could truly say that my soul did magnify the Lord, and my spirit rejoiced in God my Savior. I felt that the heavens were moved in our behalf, and that the angels who had power to put down the mighty from their seats, and to exalt them who were of low degree, were watching over us; that those would be filled who hungered and thirsted after righteousness, when the rich would be sent empty away; that God had helped his servant Israel in remembrance of his promised mercy, and in bringing forth a Record, by which is made known the seed of Abraham, our father. Therefore, we could safely put our trust in him, as he was able to help in every time of need."

The book was published by the end of March 1830.

On April 6, 1830, the Smiths and perhaps fifty or sixty others who were persuaded that the Book of Mormon was of divine origin, and that young Joseph (now twenty-five) had been instructed to establish the restored church, gathered at the home of Peter and Mary Whitmer in Fayette, New York, to organize the Church of

Christ. During the day there was a solemn sacrament service, singing, baptisms in nearby Seneca Lake, and the exercise of heavenly gifts. Among those baptized were Joseph Smith Sr. and Lucy. Lucy wrote: "When Mr. Smith [Joseph Sr.] came out of the water, Joseph [Jr.] stood upon the shore, and taking his father by the hand, he exclaimed, with tears of joy, 'Oh, my God! have I lived to see my own father baptized into the true Church of Jesus Christ!'" From that date, Joseph Sr. was a "Father in Israel," and Lucy was a "Mother in Israel." Their lives were inextricably tied up with their prophet-son and with the tumultuous history of the infant Church of Jesus Christ that had been organized that day.

In the meantime, Lucy and Joseph Sr., unable to make the annual payments on their farm, had sold it and were staying with their oldest living son, Hyrum, in Manchester. Warned by Joseph Jr. that his life was in danger there, Hyrum moved to Colesville, some twenty miles distant, where he moved in with Newel and Sally Knight. Joseph likewise urged his father and mother to leave Manchester to avoid harassment from the local people, telling them that they should move to Waterloo, near the Whitmer family.

When Hyrum departed for Colesville, Lucy and Joseph Sr. and their youngest child, Lucy, were left alone, for Don Carlos, Catherine, and William were away, and Samuel was on a missionary assignment. That night Joseph Sr. fell ill. Early the next morning a Quaker gentleman came to collect on a note for fourteen dollars that Joseph Sr. had signed. Normally, collectors would give fair warning, but the Quaker was insistent. "If thou dost not pay me immediately," Lucy remembered him saying, "thou shalt go forthwith to the jail, unless . . . thou wilt burn up those Books of Mormon; but if thou wilt burn them up, then I will forgive thee the whole debt." Lucy offered her gold beads and Joseph tried to settle for the six dollars he had on him, but the intruder went to the door and beckoned to a constable. The lawman ordered Joseph into the police wagon without even permitting him to eat the porridge Lucy had prepared for him.

Other creditors came the next day. That evening a stranger
pounded on the door, demanding to see Hyrum. He was followed
by a second, a third, and a fourth. They searched the house and
threatened to take some corn stored in an upstairs room. While
they were searching, Lucy glanced out the window and saw the
heads of men in every direction, "some on foot, some on horseback, and the rest in wagons." Obviously, a mob of "bandits, religious bigots, and cutthroats," as Lucy referred to them, had
gathered. Alone with little Lucy, she knelt and begged the Lord to
save her children. At that moment her son William bounded into
the house. He sized up the situation, grabbed a large fire iron, ran
upstairs to chase the four intruders out, and, still brandishing the
iron lever, went outside to confront the crowd. At his appearance,
the mob fled.

Samuel returned early the next morning and set forces in
motion to achieve the release of his father. He then helped Joseph
and Lucy move to Waterloo. Their reception there was friendly,
and they were soon holding evening meetings for singing and
prayer. But forces were underway that would make that home
temporary. At a church conference held in January 1831, Joseph
Smith Jr. announced a revelation that directed that the Church, to
"escape the power of the enemy," should move to northern Ohio.
The gathering of Israel would commence.

Throughout the late winter and early spring of 1831, one hundred or so members of the Church in New York made their way
west to Kirtland, Ohio. Joseph Smith Sr. and his sons Samuel and
Hyrum went ahead to join Joseph Jr., leaving their families to
follow. Lucy left in early May, taking charge of a group of about fifty
persons. They boarded a canal boat from a dock on the Seneca
River, then followed the Cayuga and Erie canals to Buffalo. Heavy
ice on Lake Erie blocked further passage. While they waited for the
ice to break, Lucy boarded her party onto a steamboat and told
them to "lift their hearts in prayer to God." Suddenly the ice

miraculously parted, leaving space enough for the boat to pass through; then, just as suddenly, it closed behind them.

The immigrants finally reached Fairport, eleven miles from Kirtland, and were in Kirtland by the middle of May. The Smith farmhouse in New York, the Peter Whitmer farm where the Church had been organized, the places of worship in Waterloo and Colesville—all had been left behind. Lucy, now fifty-five, and Joseph Sr., sixty, had left their old lives behind and expected to spend the rest of their days in association with members of the Church of Christ.

Shortly after moving to Kirtland in the spring of 1831, Lucy paid a visit to the wife of her brother Stephen, Temperance Mack, who now lived in Pontiac, Michigan. Stephen had moved from Tunbridge, Vermont, to Detroit in 1807 to open a general merchandise store. He served with the Michigan Volunteers during the 1812 war against England, moving to Pontiac, twenty-six miles north of Detroit, in 1818. He died in 1826.

Accompanying Lucy were her son Hyrum and a few other Latter-day Saints. They were cordially received by Temperance. During the four-week visit Lucy, now an enthusiastic missionary for the new faith, told Temperance the good news about the Book of Mormon and the restored gospel. Temperance was converted and remained a faithful member the rest of her life. During the visit Lucy was introduced to the minister of a Protestant church in Pontiac. "So you are the mother of that poor, foolish, silly boy, Joe Smith, who pretended to translate the Book of Mormon," he mused. In writing of the experience later, Lucy says she shook her finger in his face, stoutly proclaimed the truth of Joseph's work, and prophesied that within three years the Latter-day Saints would have a third of his church, including the deacon. The minister laughed, but the prediction came true in two years. In 1838 Temperance moved to Kirtland to be with her daughter Almira, who also became an ardent Latter-day Saint, and to be close to Lucy.

In 1833 Lucy's ever busy workload was increased by her husband's ordination as patriarch of the Church. Blessing feasts were a common festivity at the time in Kirtland. Held in the homes of various members, these activities occasionally featured full meals, at other times cake and cider or fruit juice. Then Father Smith gave patriarchal blessings to all who attended. Lucy helped in the preparations and entertaining that accompanied these meetings, which were often held at the Smith home and which attracted so many that latecomers had to be turned away. After the Kirtland Temple was completed in 1836, the meetings were held there. Mary Fielding Smith, who was present at one of them, described the marvelous blessings given by her future father-in-law: "The hearts of the people were melted and the Spirit & power of God rested down upon us in a remarkable manner. Many spake in tongues & others prophesied & interpreted. . . . [It was] a time of love & refreshing. The Bretheren as well as the Sisters were all melted down and we wept and praised God together."

In Kirtland, the leaders of the Church began to erect a meetinghouse-schoolhouse. It was not finished before they had to go to Missouri in the spring of 1834 to assist the Saints who had been driven out of their homes there. They left Reynolds Cahoon in charge of completing the building, but he said he had neither the time nor the means to finish it. Impatient for the building's completion, Lucy told her husband that she would try to raise the means herself. Within two weeks she had raised sufficient funds and employed carpenters and cabinetmakers. The building was completed in time for use that fall.

While Lucy's sons Joseph and Hyrum were in Missouri, they fell deathly ill from cholera. They prayed to be healed, and finally Hyrum sprang to his feet and exclaimed, "I have had an open vision, in which I saw mother kneeling under an apple tree; and she is even now asking God, in tears, to spare our lives, that she may again behold us in the flesh. The Spirit testifies, that her prayers, united with ours, will be answered." "Oh, my mother!" the

Prophet exclaimed upon his return, "how often have your prayers been the means of assisting us when the shadows of death encompassed us."

Considering the responsibilities of Joseph Smith Sr. as patriarch, as well as Lucy Smith's motherly and neighborly instincts which often prompted her to invite travelers to stay with them, the Smiths were almost in the position of running a free hotel. Lucy wrote in her memoirs, "How often I have parted every bed in the house for the accommodation of the brethren, and then laid a single blanket on the floor for my husband and myself, while Joseph and Emma slept upon the same floor, with nothing but their cloaks for both bed and bedding."

In 1835, Joseph Jr. invited his parents to move into an upper room of his own house. They accepted the invitation. Lucy wrote that she hoped to devote most of her time to the study of the Bible, the Book of Mormon, and the Doctrine and Covenants. However, a sudden accident prevented her from doing so. One day, as she was going downstairs to dinner, she slipped on a stick near the top of the stairs and plunged down the steps head first. The accident crippled her to some extent and also blinded her; she was in bed several weeks and the doctors were unable to help her. Finally she called on the elders to bless her so she could see to read. They did so, and, she recalled, "when they took their hands off my head, I read two lines in the Book of Mormon." So well was she healed that she did not wear glasses until after she was seventy, some ten years later.

In September 1837, Joseph Smith Sr. was sustained as an assistant counselor in the First Presidency of the Church; he continued to serve also as patriarch. That fall and throughout the winter, the Saints in Kirtland were severely persecuted by angry mobs and forced to flee to Missouri. Joseph and Lucy left in early 1838, moving to a small log hut near their son Joseph's home in Far West, Missouri.

But in Missouri the Saints continued to have difficulties with older settlers. Finally they were presented with an order to either leave Missouri or be exterminated. When a militia came to see that the order was carried out, Lucy and Joseph heard frightful screams and loud shouting. They assumed that their son, the Prophet, had been killed. That proved untrue, but the militia did forcibly arrest both Joseph and Hyrum, as well as several other Church leaders. As he was being taken to prison, the Prophet asked for a few moments to say good-bye to his family, but this was denied. However, Lucy managed to slip through the guard and to extend her hand under the wagon cover to touch her sons. She felt Joseph seize her hand and kiss it, and heard him shout, "God bless you, my dear mother!" Joseph Sr. did not get to see his sons at all.

The Saints abandoned their homes and fields in Missouri and headed for Illinois, first to Quincy and then to Commerce, which they renamed Nauvoo. Some five months later Joseph and Hyrum and their associates escaped from their captors and joined their families in Nauvoo. There the Prophet built a home for his parents near his own.

The Smith family gathered at the home frequently. On one occasion when all of the family were present, Joseph Sr. gave each of them a special blessing. Then he addressed Lucy, telling her, "Mother, do you not know that you are one of the most singular women in the world?" "No," she replied, "I do not." "Well, I do," he continued. "You have brought up my children for me by the fireside and, when I was gone, you comforted them. You have brought up all my children, and could always comfort them when I could not. . . . Do not mourn, but try to be comforted. Your last days shall be your best days." Shortly thereafter, in September 1840, he died. He was sixty-nine.

After the death of her husband, Lucy continued to bear her testimony, attend meetings, visit her children and grandchildren and nurse them when they were sick, and comfort and assist many who had suffered as the result of the exodus from Missouri. The year after her husband's death, her youngest son, Don Carlos, also died.

Though only twenty-five, he had been the editor of the Church magazine, the *Times and Seasons,* and a brigadier general in the Nauvoo militia.

In 1843 Lucy moved into the home of Joseph Jr. and Emma. Many visitors came to Nauvoo, the City Beautiful, desiring to meet not only the Prophet, but his mother as well. To show these visitors the items connected with Mormon history and doctrine that she had saved and collected, Lucy established a small, private museum. The articles on exhibit included not only Church magazines, newspa-

Lucy Mack Smith's home in Nauvoo, Illinois

pers, pamphlets, and books, but also various historical artifacts and antiquities. Among the most talked-about items were four Egyptian mummies, which were connected with some papyrus scrolls that the Prophet used in writing the Book of Abraham.

Another of Lucy's activities was connected with the Nauvoo Female Relief Society, organized on March 17, 1842. She became a member at the second meeting, held a week after its organization, and all of her daughters and daughters-in-law living in the region became members, as did Temperance Mack and her daughter Almira. Lucy was always referred to in the society's discussions in almost reverential terms, and prayers were offered that her days should be prolonged so that she should "enjoy much in the society of sisters, and shall hereafter be crowned a mother of those that shall prove faithful!" On the day she was voted in, the minutes show that Lucy arose and said she rejoiced in what was being done. Then she wept, hoping that "the Lord would bless and aid the Society in feeding the hungry and clothing the naked."

Lucy's greatest moment of anguish was in June 1844, when she went to view the dead bodies of Joseph and Hyrum after their assassination in Carthage Jail. Her account of the experience is as follows:

"After the corpses were washed and dressed in their burial clothes, we were allowed to see them. I had for a long time braced every nerve, roused every energy of my soul and called upon God to strengthen me; but when I entered the room and saw my murdered sons extended both at once before my eyes, and heard the sobs and groans of my family and the cries of 'Father! Husband! Brothers!' from the lips of their wives, children, brothers and sisters, it was too much. I sank back, crying to the Lord in the agony of my soul, 'My God, my God, why hast thou forsaken this family!' A voice replied, 'I have taken them to myself, that they might have rest.' Emma was carried back to her room almost in a state of insensibility. Her oldest son approached the corpse and dropped upon his knees, and laying his cheek against his father's, and kissing him, exclaimed, 'Oh, my father, my father!' As for myself, I was swallowed up in the depths of my afflictions, and though my soul was filled with horror past imagination, yet I was dumb until I arose again to contemplate the spectacle before me. Oh! at that moment how my mind flew through every scene of sorrow and distress which we had passed together, in which they had shown the innocence and sympathy which filled their guileless hearts. As I looked upon their peaceful, smiling countenances, I seemed almost to hear

them say, 'Mother, weep not for us, we have overcome the world
by love; we carried to them the gospel, that their souls might be
saved; they slew us for our testimony, and thus placed us beyond
their power; their ascendancy is for a moment, ours is an eternal
triumph.'"

Not long after this, her son Samuel, who had managed to evade
the mob in bringing the bodies back from Carthage, complained of
an illness brought on by overexertion and exposure. He lingered
on for a month and died in July. He had gone, to use Lucy's words,
"to join his brothers, and the ancient martyrs, in the Paradise of
God." Lucy, who was now sixty-nine and burdened by "the cruelty
of an ungodly and hard-hearted world," to use her words, had
endured the deaths of her husband and five of her six sons who
had lived to manhood—Alvin, Hyrum, Joseph Jr., Samuel, and Don
Carlos.

After she was able to quiet her feelings, Lucy decided that the
most important contribution she could make to the memory of her
husband and sons, as well as to the church they had been agents in
establishing, would be to tell the complete story of her family and
of the restoration of the gospel. With the encouragement of
Brigham Young and the Council of Twelve Apostles, she secured
the help of Martha Jane Knowlton Coray, a schoolteacher. During
the winter of 1844–45, she dictated her reminiscences to Sister
Coray in an almost stream-of-consciousness narration. The reminiscences were written in some eighteen notebooks and bore the
tentative title "History of Mother Smith, by Herself." Under the
direction of Lucy and Sister Coray, this was then edited and refined
to produce the preliminary manuscript of a book. Finally, with the
addition of other material that occurred to Lucy as she went
through the preliminary manuscript, a "final" manuscript, now in
the Church Archives in Salt Lake City, was copied out by Sister
Coray.

When Orson Pratt, an apostle of the Church, was in England
as president of the British Mission and publisher of the *Latter-day*

Saints Millennial Star, he was able to acquire the manuscript. He published it in Liverpool in 1853 under the title *Biographical Sketches of Joseph Smith the Prophet, and His Progenitors for Many Generations.* The book is 296 printed pages in length and covers the period from the birth of Lucy's father in 1735 to the assassination of her sons in 1844. She concludes her history by bearing testimony to the truth of her account of her prophet-son and the divine work in which he was engaged. It continues to be the principal source for the inspiring story of the early life of the Prophet and the family in which he was reared. The book, as well as copies of surviving letters she wrote, including one as early as 1829, show Lucy to have been an articulate person—intelligent, fluent, and with a remarkable memory.

By the time Lucy finished her history, the Saints had determined to leave Illinois and migrate to the Great Basin of the Rocky Mountains. In the conference at which the exodus was announced, Lucy was invited to address the congregation. The clerk of the conference recorded her address as follows (changing the third person of the clerk into first person, as she would have delivered it):

"I am truly glad that the Lord has let me see so large a congregation. I had a great deal of advice to give, but Brother Brigham Young has done the errand, he has fixed it completely. . . . I raised up eleven children, seven of them boys. I raised them in the fear and love of God. When they were two or three years old I told them I wanted them to love God with all their hearts. I told them to do good. I want all you to do the same. God gives us our children and we are accountable. . . . I presume there never was a family more obedient than mine. I did not have to speak to them but once. I want you to teach your little children about Joseph in Egypt and such things, and when they are older they will love to read their Bible. Set your children to work; protect their health. Remember that I love children, young folks, and everybody. Now, brothers and sisters, if you consider me a Mother in Israel, I want you to say so."

At this point Brigham Young put the question: "All who consider Mother Smith as a Mother in Israel, signify it by saying yes!" One universal "Yes" ran through the hall, according to the clerk. Lucy then remarked that eighteen years had passed since Joseph Smith the Prophet had become acquainted with the contents of the plates. She recalled scenes of Church history—the trials and privations, the persecutions and suffering—and expressed confidence in the future, declaring:

"I feel that the Lord will let Brother Brigham take the people away. Here, in this city, lie my dead—my husband and children. If the rest of my children go with you (and I would to God they may all go), they will not go without me; and if I go I want my bones brought back in case I die, so they may be deposited with my husband and children."

Brigham Young made a solemn promise that should she be in the West when she died, her bones would be returned to Illinois. This proved not to be necessary. For reasons of health and age, Lucy decided to remain in Nauvoo with her daughter Lucy Milliken. Two years later she went to live with her daughter-in-law, the Prophet's widow, Emma Smith Bidamon. Lucy died at Emma's home on May 5, 1855, age seventy-nine, fully confident that the celestial crown of glory awaited her in eternity. She was buried beside her husband and sons in the family burial ground in Nauvoo.

SOURCES

The best single sources on the life of Lucy Mack Smith are Lucy Mack Smith, *Biographical Sketches of Joseph Smith the Prophet and His Progenitors for Many Generations* (Liverpool, England, 1853), and Richard L. Bushman, *Joseph Smith and the Beginnings of Mormonism* (Urbana and Chicago: University of Illinois Press, 1984). Biographies of Joseph Smith that tell of his parentage include Edward W. Tullidge, *Life of Joseph the Prophet* (Plano, Illinois: Board of Publication of the Reorganized Church of Jesus Christ of Latter Day Saints, 1880); John Henry

Evans, *Joseph Smith: An American Prophet* (New York: Macmillan, 1933); Preston Nibley, *Joseph Smith the Prophet* (Salt Lake City: Deseret News Press, 1944); Donna Hill, *Joseph Smith, the First Mormon* (New York: Doubleday, 1977); and Francis M. Gibbons, *Joseph Smith, Martyr, Prophet of God* (Salt Lake City: Deseret Book, 1977).

The lives of Lucy's grandparents and their influence on Lucy and her family are traced in Mary Audentia Smith Anderson, *Ancestry and Posterity of Joseph Smith and Emma Hale* (Independence, Missouri: Herald House Publishing, 1929), and Richard Lloyd Anderson, *Joseph Smith's New England Heritage: Influences of Grandfathers Solomon Mack and Asael Smith* (Salt Lake City: Deseret Book, 1971). A biography of Lucy's sister-in-law is John and Audrey Cumming, *The Pilgrimage of Temperance Mack* (Mount Pleasant, Michigan, 1967).

Short sketches on the life of Lucy include "Lucy Mack Smith," in Emma M. Phillips, *33 Women of the Restoration* (Independence, Missouri: Herald House Publishing, 1960), pp. 11–17; "Lucy Mack Smith," in Richard S. Van Wagoner and Steven C. Walker, *A Book of Mormons* (Salt Lake City: Signature Books, 1982), pp. 309–13; Jaynann M. Payne, "Lucy Mack Smith: Faith in the Family," in *Joseph Smith, Sr., Family Reunion, 18–19 August 1972, Nauvoo, Illinois;* "Lucy Smith" in Andrew Jenson, *Latter-day Saint Biographical Encyclopedia* 1:690–92; "Lucy Mack Smith," in Brigham Young University, *Dedication and Naming of 22 Buildings* (Provo, Utah, May 26, 1954), pp. 26–27.

Other sources include "George A. Smith, Obituary of Lucy, the Mother of the Prophet," published in *The Mormon* (New York), July 12, 1856; Vida E. Smith, "Character Sketch of Lucy Mack Smith," *Journal of History* 1 (1908): 406–12; Edward W. Tullidge, *The Women of Mormondom* (New York, 1877), pp. 6–9, 297–300; Heman C. Smith, "Distinguished Women: Lucy Mack Smith," *Journal of History* 12 (1919): 103 ff.; Mary Salisbury Hancock, "The Three Sisters of the Prophet Joseph Smith," *The Saints Herald,* January 11, 1954, pp. 10–12; Richard Lloyd Anderson, "Joseph Smith's Home Environment," *Ensign* 1 (July 1971): 56–59; and Linda King Newell and Valeen Tippetts Avery, *Mormon Enigma: Emma Hale Smith* (Garden City, New York: Doubleday, 1984), esp. p. 265.

Abigail (Nabby) Howe Young

Of my mother—she that bore me—I can say, no better
woman ever lived in the world than she was. I have the
feelings of a son toward her: I should have them—It is
right; but I judge the matter pertaining to her from the
principles and the spirit of the teachings I received
from her. Would she countenance one of her children
in the least act that was wrong according to her traditions? No, not in the least degree. —*Brigham Young*

In October 1785, when she was twenty years old, Abigail
(Nabby) Howe received a proposal of marriage from John
Young. John, two years older than Nabby and a veteran of the
Revolutionary War, was a "small, nimble, wiry man" who had
worked for Colonel John Jones, a well-to-do landowner in
Hopkinton, Massachusetts, a farming community about twenty-five
miles southwest of Boston. John's father had died when he was six,
and following colonial practice, the death of the father meant the
dissolution of the family. John and some of his brothers and sisters
were "bound out" to families that would take them in and raise
them. A virtual servant, and frequently whipped, John ran away to
volunteer for George Washington's army when he was sixteen; he
served in three campaigns.

Nabby, with a "doll-like face, blue eyes, and yellowish brown hair folded in natural waves and ringlets," was popular in the social set of the town, a good singer, and thought to be "a good catch." She had a gentle disposition and a pleasing personality, and was pious. She also came from a family of some substance; her relatives included Elias Howe Jr., who later invented the sewing machine, and Samuel Gridley Howe, the educator and reformer who was the husband of Julia Ward Howe, author of "The Battle Hymn of the Republic."

Nabby's parents thought her foolish to marry "the little orphan" whose future was so uncertain. But Nabby liked John, saw real potential in his energy and personality, and went ahead with the marriage. After she had accepted John's proposal, one can imagine that on some night before the wedding, he dared to sing to her the jolly song of the Revolution:

> "O soldier, soldier won't you marry me, with your musket,
>   fife, and drum?"
> "Oh, no, sweet maid, I cannot marry thee, for I have no
>   coat to put on."
> Then up she went to her grandfather's chest
> And got him a coat of the very very best,
> She got him a coat of the very very best,
> And the soldier put it on.

And by the time John had got the soldier into a hat, boots, and gloves—with the help of grandfather's chest and three more verses—the last verse was laughed through with gusto as Nabby joined in:

> "For I have a wife of my own."

The ceremony was held on October 31, 1785, in Christ Church (Congregational) in Hopkinton. There, Nabby and John started life together on a farm.

Nabby was born on May 3, 1765, in Hopkinton, the third of eleven children born to Phineas and Susanna Goddard Howe. She bore difficulties with good nature, handled tensions with laughter, and was prepared to achieve her identity by mothering and nurturing. Nabby's father was active in town affairs, signed at least one letter from the Hopkinton town fathers to the Continental Congress, and cast a skeptical eye toward higher authorities, whether political or ecclesiastical. Her mother was religious, accepting biblical statements as being literal and supporting evangelical revivals. She was also frugal: she carefully preserved her one silk dress to wear throughout her life. She and Phineas had their children christened at Christ Church and sent them to subscription school, singing school, and church socials.

Nabby continued these family traditions. One contemporary referred to her as "quite a reformer." Presumably, she meant by this that Nabby was always willing to help others do the right thing. She was sometimes sought by neighboring families to give counsel to newlyweds; she was a methodical and orderly person; and she had a lively sense of humor. She was pretty, had a good social sense, and encouraged the singing of hymns in her home.

After three years and the birth of two girls, Nancy and Fanny, in Hopkinton, John and Nabby moved to Durham, south of Albany, Greene County, New York, in the Platauva District on the eastern side of the Catskills. This was described as "a vast wilderness where fish and game were plentiful." A number of Revolutionary War veterans had moved there. John's older brother William had died there, and John may have taken up his land or independently acquired his own. The Youngs probably moved there during the winter of 1788–89. The wagon roads, such as there were, were too muddy to travel in spring or fall and too dusty during the summer. No doubt John wanted to get to his land by early spring in order to clear it and begin planting. Nabby was pregnant with her third child, Rhoda, who was born the following September in Durham.

Two years later Nabby and John were back in Hopkinton. Perhaps the Durham country was wilder than John anticipated; perhaps they returned in response to the pleadings of the Howes. At

Abigail's five sons in 1856.
From left: Lorenzo, Brigham, Phinehas, Joseph, and John

any rate, they were greeted warmly on their return. "All the family flew out to receive us," wrote Fanny, who at the time was only three, "and caught the three children (one older and one younger than myself) in their arms while grandmother and mother wept." The Youngs established themselves again on the south slope of Sadler's Hill in Hopkinton. In May 1791, their first son, John Jr., was born. They remained on their Hopkinton farm for another ten years, during which Nabby, Susannah, Joseph, and Phinehas were added to the family.

Eight children, all of them reasonably healthy, must have put a strain on both John and Nabby. John worked exhaustingly to provide enough to eat. He was quick to be tender but also quick to be angry. Just as Colonel Jones's wife had whipped him as a child, so John was not hesitant to discipline his own children. As his son Brigham later said, "It was a word and a blow with him but the blow came first." Nabby was calmer; free with counsel and correction, she bore their trials with good cheer.

Because of their poverty and John's heavy workload, Nabby found herself having to teach her children to read and write and do simple arithmetic. She often sang as she performed household tasks, and she led the children in their prayers and Bible reading. In the evening, John entertained the family with stories of his experiences during the war of liberation and subsequently on Colonel Jones's "plantation."

Two events had occurred in Durham that had lasting effects on the family. The first was that Nabby came down with consumption (what we later came to call tuberculosis), and her strength and resistance gradually wore down. Ultimately, much of her housework had to be done by her children, and eventually she would die when she was only fifty.

The other event was the conversion of Nabby and John to Methodism. Methodist circuit riders often called at the cabins of new settlers and baptized, conducted funerals, held revivals, and in other ways looked after the spiritual welfare of those on the frontier. John, who believed that a person might hold to an orthodox creed and yet be a meager Christian, just as one might "keep inside of statute law and yet be a meager citizen," was attracted to their fiery revivals, their orderly habits, and the warm spirit they exhibited. Religion was not something to be taken for granted and left to wither on the vine. Impatient with predestination and limited atonement, and above all with the theological quibbling of the various churches, John and Nabby believed in inner conversion—the "witness of the spirit" and "Christian perfection." So warmly did Nabby and John embrace Methodism that John himself, three of his sons, and eventually one of his sons-in-law became itinerant Methodist preachers.

In 1801 John and Nabby decided to move to southern Vermont. Just north of the Massachusetts border, at a place called Whitingham, a few settlers had begun to move in to cultivate the land and organize a town. On November 18, 1800, John bought a fifty-acre farm from his sister's wealthy husband, and in January 1801 the Young family went by ox-sled and horsesled (one sleigh for Nabby and the children, the other for their transportable family possessions) to the new destination. By then John was thirty-seven; Nabby, thirty-four; Nancy, fourteen; Fanny, thirteen; Rhoda, eleven; John Jr., nine; Nabby, seven; Susannah, five; Joseph, three; and Phinehas, one. For some unexplained reason, perhaps to console Nabby's parents, they left Rhoda behind with the Howes.

John and Nabby apparently stayed in the cabin of an earlier migrant until they could build their own home. They were probably assisted by neighboring settlers in the "log raising" of their own cabin. (There were about two hundred families in Whitingham in 1801.) By spring they were in their new sixteen-foot-square home, complete with bunk beds, stick chimney, and fireplace. Until the harvest they had to live on wild turkeys, pigeons, partridges, berries, nuts, rabbits, deer, and bear, as well as use up any provisions, such as flour and corn, that they might have brought with them from Hopkinton.

On June 1, after John and the older boys had "sugared off" the maple trees and planted the corn, Nabby gave birth to her ninth child and fourth son. John and Nabby named him Brigham, after the surname of Nabby's maternal grandparents. Because Nabby continued to suffer from spells of coughing and was so weak that she could not properly care for him, "Briggie," as he was called, was bottle-fed by his thirteen-year-old sister, Fanny. "No one could pacify him but sister Fanny," one of the family declared. It is said that he became so attached to Fanny, who was "gentle and deft-handed," that she had to carry him on her hip even while she milked the cow.

The family's lot was a hard one, and Nabby, though weak, was proud to be making her contribution. She continued to sew, churn, read to her children, and visit with neighbors. One wonders how the children could have escaped the tuberculosis from which she suffered, since it was highly contagious. As we shall see, little Nabby, her mother's namesake, did not escape. The eldest daughter, Nancy, perhaps because of her own heavy workload at home, left to marry when she was sixteen. Fanny left shortly thereafter for the same purpose. Rhoda did not join the family until 1809, six years after the older girls left; in the intervening years, much of the housework, as well as the care of Nabby, had to be done by John and the boys.

In the meantime, John Young was discovering that Whitingham did not really have good agricultural potential. There were few level acres fit for cultivation, and most of the land was stony. The winters were also long and hard on Nabby. After three years the Youngs decided to make another move, this time west of the Alleghenies to Sherburne, Chenango County, in central New York. The family moved there in the spring of 1804.

More primitive than Whitingham, Sherburne was rich in wild berries, nuts, and wild animals, large and small. During that first year John and the boys (John Jr. was now thirteen, Joseph seven) were able to clear and plant enough corn to hold them through the next winter. Meanwhile, work proceeded on a log cabin, and a baby girl, Louisa, was born shortly after their arrival. Three years later the eleventh and last child of John and Nabby was born, a son whom they named after Lorenzo Dow, the great exhorter who had made an indelible impression on the family at a revival in nearby Smyrna. The excitement of the new birth was subdued by the family's grief over the death of little Nabby of consumption, no doubt acquired from her mother. Apparently the same year the family moved a short distance away to "Dark Hollow," some three or four miles from Sherburne.

John and the boys once more cleared land of trees and brush; plowed, planted, and cultivated; trapped and hunted wild game; and made furniture for their home. By now Brigham was eight and could help with many tasks, both inside and out. John is always described in contemporary sources as a "worker." During that period farmers cut hay and grain with a hand scythe. Lorenzo remembered his father as "the best mower in the section where he lived." Even after John was fifty, one young man declared, "Uncle John Young is the best mower in this town." The family endured many privations and hardships, but Nabby stood loyally by her husband, and encouraged her sons to hire out to clear and work the land of others for such income as they could earn. The girls apparently worked with straw, making baskets and hats.

Through it all, Nabby conducted a school in the evenings and on Sunday, teaching the younger children, as she had taught the older ones before, to read, write, and do sums. Brigham later said that he received eleven days of formal schooling. All the rest came from his mother.

After an absence of eight years, daughter Rhoda, now nineteen, returned to join the family. Joseph, who was now twelve, said that "it seemed as though an Angel had visited our house, and to add to our happiness had come to abide with us." Rhoda remained four years, after which she married John P. Greene, a Methodist preacher, who lived in Aurelius, six miles from the upper end of Cayuga Lake. Perhaps at the insistence of Rhoda, who wanted to be helpful in looking after Nabby and the younger children, the Youngs took the remainder of their family there.

About the time of the move, John Jr. married, and a year later Susannah also took the step, so five children remained with John and Nabby: Joseph, Phinehas, Brigham, Louisa, and Lorenzo. Brigham, who later in life reminisced publicly about the family, reported that the boys baked bread, milked the cows, and made butter. He spoke of fixing breakfast for the family, carrying his mother from the bed to the table and then to a chair in front of the fireplace, and then going out to work for the day. Upon his return he would prepare supper, carry his mother once more to the table, and after the meal back to her chair, and then tidy up things for the family's evening together at home.

It is, of course, misleading to simply report Nabby's worsening condition. There were no tranquilizing drugs, no sedatives. Tuberculosis was painful, and the slow disintegration of tissues, especially of the lungs, and the pain this produced, must have tormented not only Nabby but her husband and children as well.

That she continued to function as a wife and mother, despite her inability to work and despite her wracking cough, increasingly emaciated frame, and bodily pain, suggests the magnitude of her courage. In a very real sense, she was heroic. Witnessing her struggle, the children also developed compassion, a quality they retained throughout their lives. Moreover, in a very direct way, the experience with his mother prepared Brigham for a similar problem. His first wife, Miriam Works, also contracted the dreaded disease after bearing two children, and he found himself caring for the children, preparing meals, and carrying Miriam to and from her chair at the fireplace, just as he had done with his mother. Miriam died in 1832.

In a very real way Nabby and John prepared Brigham and his brothers and sisters to receive positively the "restoration of Bible religion," as one of the children called it, which was Mormonism. His parents, Brigham said, "were some of the most strict religionists that lived upon the earth." They did not permit playing cards in their home, and they would not let the children say "darn it" or "the devil." "When I was young," he explained, "I was kept within very strict bounds, and was not allowed to walk more than half-an-hour on Sunday for exercise. . . . I had not a chance to dance when I was young, and never heard the enchanting tones of the violin, until I was eleven years of age; and then I thought I was on the highway to hell, if I suffered myself to linger and listen to it."

Brigham described his father as "very circumspect, exemplary and religious," never demanding of his children behavior he himself did not display. He never heard his father swear, "not so much as a darn it or curse it or the devil." Although the children remembered Nabby as tempering the sternness of her husband, she was just as fervent in her beliefs, not tolerating in her children "the least act that was wrong according to her traditions." Said Brigham:

"My mother, while she lived, taught her children all the time to honour the name of the Father and the Son, and to reverence the holy Book. She said, Read it, observe its precepts, and apply them to your lives as far as you can; do everything that is good; do nothing that is evil; and if you see any persons in distress, administer to their wants; never suffer anger to arise in your bosoms. . . . Never did my mother or my father countenance any of the children in anything to wrong their neighbour or fellow-being, even if they were injured by them. If they have injured me, says my father, let me return good for evil, and leave it in the hand of the Lord: he will bless me for doing right and curse them for doing wrong."

The Youngs had been in Aurelius for two years when Nabby finally lost her extended and painful battle against consumption. She had long since relinquished her share of household burdens, but her death, on June 11, 1815, at age fifty, brought about a significant disruption of the family. John took leave of the farm and its many improvements and with three of his sons (Joseph, eighteen; Phinehas, sixteen; and Brigham, fourteen) moved thirty-five miles west to the "Sugar Hill" district of Steuben County, near Tyrone, on the Tioga River. Louisa and Lorenzo were left with Rhoda and John Greene in Aurelius. When John came home one day with a new bride, the widow Hannah Brown, and her several children, Nabby's boys soon left. Joseph and Brigham went to live with their sister, Susannah Little, and Phinehas got married.

Nevertheless, the influence of Nabby continued strong. The family lived close together, they kept up their church affiliations, and they held frequent get-togethers. Early in 1830 family members were introduced to the Book of Mormon. Within two years, all ten of the living children, their spouses, and their father, John, became Latter-day Saints. They remained loyal to its principles and practices throughout the rest of their lives. "God bless my mother," said Brigham in a sermon delivered after he became president of the Church. "No better woman ever lived in the world than she was."

SOURCES

Although no Abigail Howe Young papers are known to be in existence, several of her children left information about her. This includes letters of Fanny Murray;

personal histories of Joseph, Phinehas, Brigham, and Lorenzo Young; and other documents and papers, all in the LDS Church Archives in Salt Lake City. Genealogical and historical material is from the Susa Young Gates Collection, Utah State Historical Society Library, Salt Lake City.

Books that mention Abigail and John include Richard F. Palmer and Karl D. Butler, *Brigham Young: The New York Years* (Provo, Utah: Brigham Young University Press, 1982); S. Dilworth Young, *"Here Is Brigham": Brigham Young, the Years to 1844* (Salt Lake City: Bookcraft, 1964), esp. pp. 13–49; Eugene England, "Young Brigham," in *Brother Brigham* (Salt Lake City: Bookcraft, 1980), pp. 1–33; and Leonard J. Arrington, *Brigham Young: American Moses* (New York: Alfred Knopf, 1985), esp. pp. 7–30.

Valuable information is found in Gene A. Sessions, "John Young: Soldier of the Revolution," in *Latter-day Patriots: Nine Mormon Families and Their Revolutionary War Heritage* (Salt Lake City: Deseret Book, 1975), pp. 20–41; S. Dilworth Young, *Young Brigham Young* (Salt Lake City: Deseret Book, 1962); Susa Young Gates, "Mother of the Latter-day Prophets: Abigail Howe Young," *Juvenile Instructor* 59 (January 1924): 6; Susa Young Gates, "Notes on the Young and Howe Families," *Utah Genealogical and Historical Magazine* 11 (January 1920): 182–83; Rebecca Cornwall and Richard F. Palmer, "The Religious and Family Background of Brigham Young," in *Brigham Young University Studies* 18 (Spring 1978): 286–310; Leonard J. Arrington and JoAnn Jolley, "The Faithful Young Family: The Parents, Brothers, and Sisters of Brigham," *Ensign* 10 (August 1980): 52–57; and Ronald K. Esplin, "The Emergence of Brigham Young and the Twelve to Mormon Leadership, 1830–1841" (Ph.D. diss., Brigham Young University, 1981), esp. chapter 1.

Many biographies of Brigham Young contain some information about his mother. The most useful is Susa Young Gates and Leah D. Widtsoe, *The Life Story of Brigham Young* (New York: Macmillan, 1930).

AGNES TAYLOR TAYLOR

Here rests a pattern of the female life
The woman, friend, the mother and the wife.
A woman form'd by nature, more than art,
With smiling ease to gain upon the heart
A friend as true as guardian angels are,
Kindness her law, humanity her care.
A mother, sweetly tender, justly dear,
Oh, never to be nam'd without a tear. . . .
Love in her heart, compassion in her eye,
Her thoughts as humble, as her virtues high. . . .
Born to relieve the poor, the rich to please,
To live with honour, and to die in peace.
So full of hope, her wishes so resign'd,
Her life so blameless, so unstain'd her mind,
Heaven smil'd to see, and gave the gracious nod,
Nor longer would detain her from her God.[1]

Agnes Taylor, mother of John Taylor, third president of the Church, was born on August 22, 1787, the second daughter and fourth child of John Taylor and Agnes Whittington Taylor. Three additional sons and one daughter followed her. At the time of Agnes's birth, her parents lived in the small village of Pooley, Barton Parish, Westmorland County, in northwest England. Agnes later married a James Taylor, who became the father of President John Taylor, but it was coincidental that the last names

---

[1] A 1767 inscription by William Thomson in the chancel of the parish church in Brough, England, often visited by Agnes Taylor as a child.

Agnes Taylor Taylor

of her father and husband were the same; there was no blood relationship.

In 1787 England was ruled by King George III, the same sovereign who, a few years before, had lost the American colonies to the new nation, the United States of America. King George would continue to govern England for another thirty-three years after Agnes's birth. His successor was his son, George IV, who ruled until Agnes, at the age of forty-three, left England for Canada. They were years of rapid economic and religious change, but Agnes lived a traditional life, both as a child and as an adult.

Agnes's father was an exciseman for the British government, that is, a collector of internal revenue and an enforcer of tax regulations. Although he moved several times, he and his wife remained all their lives in Westmorland County. Agnes's mother was a descendant of the family made famous by Richard Whittington (better known as Dick Whittington), who, left without property when his father died intestate, apprenticed himself to a dealer in textile fabrics in London, made a fortune, and became an alderman, high sheriff, three times Lord Mayor of London, and member of Parliament. He made loans to Henry IV and Henry V, started a college, built an almshouse, and was knighted. Agnes's own grandfather, Christopher Taylor, who owned a gristmill at Kent and lived to be ninety-seven, took pleasure in repeating the many Whittington legends. Grandfather Taylor was a favorite of Agnes, who visited him often until she was middle-aged.

Westmorland County is in England's Lake District, just across the Irish Sea from the Isle of Man and northern Ireland. Bordered on the north by the Cumbrian Mountains, the highest mountains in England, and on the west by Morecambe Bay, an inlet of the Irish Sea, the county includes lovely Lake Windermere.

In many respects this area was idyllic. This is where William Wordsworth grew up, received his schooling, and wrote his lovely poems celebrating the beauties of nature. Also in the Lake District were the most popular of all climbable peaks, Helvellyn, Grasmere, and Rydal Mount, with settings and scenic views eloquently described by Wordsworth. Beyond the lakelands and mountains was the rocky south, with its "auld grey town" of Kendal and its several fine castles and houses. Toward the east was Westmorland's Vale of Eden, valley of the river Eden, where sheep and cattle grazed, granite and slate were quarried, and woolens were manufactured. Kendal had produced famous woolens since the fourteenth century.

At the time of Agnes's birth, there were probably not more than a dozen families in Pooley. All of them owned their homes and a few acres of land that had been purchased by their ancestors from the Earl of Sussex in 1680. Situated at the foot of the Cumbrian hills, near the Ullswater, Pooley got its name from the nearby pool or lake. There was plenty of water and wood. The farmhouses and cottages were of gray stone, roughcast and then whitewashed. Not far from the village was Dun Mallard Hill, named for the mallard ducks that spent most of their summers there. There was good fishing in the lake and a small fish market in the town.

The Taylors remained in Pooley until Agnes was two. They then moved to Brough, where they remained for six years. Brough, located a few miles southeast of Pooley, was a larger village, with about two hundred families. The outstanding architectural achievement was St. Michael's Church, named for the archangel in the book of Revelation who led the hosts of heaven in the battle against the forces of evil.

As with other girls in the area, Agnes would have had a variety of indoor and outdoor tasks at home. She would have taken her turn gathering the dead sticks that blew down in the nearby forest. She would have lit the fire on occasion, taken out the ashes, rubbed down the fender and fire irons, swept the floor, washed the hearthstone, set the table for meals, and carried in the milk. After each meal she would have washed the dishes, and perhaps she would have gone on errands for her parents. She would have taken walks in the countryside, strolling along the hedgerows and in the green fields, plucking yellow buttercups and bright daisies. She would have watched the ducks and geese, with their bright, white feathers, swimming in the pond, the mother hen shepherding her little chicks about the yard, the sheep nibbling the tender grass, the lambs leaping about, and the busy bees humming among the bushes and flowers.

The days in the English villages as she grew up were not dull. There was a weekly market day, where she would have enjoyed the excitement and noises, if not all the smells, at the market. On May Day each year the girls, dressed in white with appropriate trimmings, would sing and dance around the village maypole. On Easter, brightly colored eggs were rolled down the hillside to symbolize rolling the stone from Christ's tomb. In July the children carried their "bearing" (wooden crosses decorated with flowers and rushes or baskets of flowers) as they walked through the village singing a special hymn. On November 5, Guy Fawkes Day, a village bonfire was lit and a carnival atmosphere prevailed. Other days of celebration were Halloween, Christmas, and New Year's. Agnes would also have enjoyed the village folklore—the stories that had come down from the old Celtic tales. One of these surely told in the Westmorland village in which the Taylors lived was "Babes in the Wood," which told of a little boy and girl who wandered off into the woods and became lost. They were not found, and eventually they lay down to die. Only the redbreasted robin knew where they were, and, in reverence for them, scattered strawberry leaves over their little bodies. It was a sad tale, and its continued retelling was no doubt intended to warn little children against wandering away from home into the forest. It also helped them to learn respect for and to identify with the birds and animals of the region.

When Agnes was nine her parents moved to Shap, a village west of Brough and south of Pooley. Here Agnes remained until she left home during her late teenage years. Anciently, Shap had been a large forest, and there was still forested land in the area when the Taylors lived there. About one hundred eighty families comprised the village. Here also the church was named for St. Michael—there were many St. Michael churches in England. Not only did John Milton feature Michael in *Paradise Lost* as prince of the celestial armies, but the whole nation celebrated his feast on September 29 as Michaelmas. It was a good day for hiring servants, for leasing an apartment, for paying a debt, for almost any important activity. This was the day when even poor families ate goose.

As Agnes moved into her teens, the various village celebrations became more meaningful. There was an annual well-dressing, when the villagers, grateful for their good water, decorated their well and offered a prayer of thanksgiving. The decorations often depicted a religious theme and were executed by pressing flowers and petals into clay. Sometimes on May Day, and in other villages at

Easter, there was a Morris dance, in which the villagers dressed in costumes, often resembling characters in the Robin Hood legend, and participated in a folk dance.

Occasionally a village would be visited by mummers (traveling actors or minstrels who wore masks or fantastic disguises), who came on festive occasions to provide entertainment in song, dance, and plays in which the story and characters were taken from sacred history or the legends of the saints. These were often performed on horse-drawn carriages or stages that moved from one village to the next. The performances, which were both serious and comical, were sponsored by the town government. Some were performed in pantomime.

The villages also held athletic contests, pancake races, rabbit pie scrambles, rugby and cricket matches, marble contests, and cheese-rolling competitions. Often, on a date important to the village such as the date of its founding, the construction of its cathedral, or the death of a prominent citizen, there might be a celebration in which the mayor or other local leader, costumed and wearing a huge garland of flowers, led a pilgrimage to the church for music, an oration, the presentation of awards, and other festivities. Hot cross buns would be provided for everyone—a special treat to the poor who often could only afford black bread.

Unfortunately, we have no direct evidence of the schooling received by Agnes. Considering that both of her parents were educated and that she attracted a husband who was also well-educated, it is fair to assume that she attended the village grammar school, played hopscotch on the playground, participated in the Christmas plays, and learned character-building poems and songs. Since the schools were close by, she would have walked to school in the morning, home for a midday dinner, and back to school in the afternoon.

The one thing we can be sure about is that Agnes learned to sew, spin, and weave. By the time a girl was thirteen, she almost always had learned to prepare wool and work with a spinning

wheel by drawing out, twisting, and winding the fibers. Agnes
would have darned and knitted socks and mittens as well as cut out
and sewed clothes; learned embroidery, tatting, and needlepoint;
made buttonholes; and in other ways helped to clothe the family.
A local rhyme, first published shortly before Agnes was born, testifies to the pride of villagers in the proficiency of their girls:

> She knows how to sing and knit
> And she knows how to carry t'kit
> While she drives her kye [cow] to t'pasture.

There is evidence that Agnes's parents were active in the local
Church of England. All of the children were duly christened shortly
after birth, their marriages were performed in the church, and
members of the family are buried in the parish graveyard. The
family would have been visited regularly by the Episcopal parish
priest. Agnes would have attended Sunday School, participated in
family Bible readings, and been taught to pray. Some doctrines
would not have appealed to her: that God was incomprehensible,
incorporeal, and inscrutable; that unbaptized infants were con-
demned to hell; that men and women were creations of God but
not children of God; and that the human spirit or soul did not exist
prior to conception or birth. And it would have been difficult for
her, as for other young people, to believe in the natural or innate
sinfulness of people because of the fall of Adam and Eve. Yet she
believed devoutly in the teachings of Jesus, and she was brought
up to be a moral and happy person.

After they reached the age of sixteen, most girls in English
villages who were not required at home because of the illness of a
parent went to work as domestics at a manor house in the region.
There is no direct evidence that this was done by Agnes, but it
would be surprising if it were not the case. All of the indirect
evidence points to that happening. After the church, manor houses
were dominant features of the landscape. A country gentleman who
owned a manor, in most instances a descendant of a knight who

acquired the land in years gone by in return for military service, was the squire—the justice of the peace, judge, philanthropist, patron of the arts, leading political figure, and principal employer. Employed in his house or castle, Agnes would have helped with the housework, the meals, the sewing, and other chores. She would also have had free time to visit in town—Kendal or Penrith—and would have gone with a fellow employee or friend to the seasonal fairs. She would also have gained experience in dealing with local artisans—blacksmiths, cobblers, watchmakers, butchers, saddlers, and tailors. She might go to a shop to get a half dozen eggs, a yard of cloth, or a shoe that had been repaired. She might also pick up the latest gossip. And, of course, she might meet a local swain. Perhaps in this way she met James Taylor. They were married when she was eighteen and he twenty-two.

James and his parents lived on an estate known as Craig Gate, Ackenthwaite, Westmorland, a short distance southwest of Kendal, the county seat. James's ancestors had lived there for several generations, but James was the third son of his father, and under the English laws of primogeniture the estate went to the oldest son. Thus, James and his other brothers and sisters had to fend for themselves. Nevertheless, he acquired a good English education, including some proficiency in Latin and Greek and the higher branches of mathematics. He started out as an apprentice to a carpenter, but eventually an uncle on his mother's side bequeathed to him a small estate in the Westmorland village of Hale, and he ended up as a farmer.

James and Agnes were married in Kirkoswald, some twenty-five miles down the Eden River from Agnes's parents' home in Brough. We can be sure that the marriage ceremony was filled with Christian texts and admonitions and performed before the altar with appropriate ritual and vestments. A poem of admonition said to have been commonly used at the time is the following:

> In wedlock bands,
> All ye who join with hands,

Your hearts unite:
So shall our tuneful tongues combine
To land the nuptial rite.

After the ceremony, which occurred on December 23, 1805, Agnes and James made their first home in Ackenthwaite.

From the time of their marriage in 1805 until their migration to Canada in 1830, Agnes and James had ten children, eight sons and two daughters. The oldest son, Edward, died in his early twenties; two other sons, William and George, died during their first year; and their last two sons, George and Edward, died in boyhood. (They did not hesitate to name later sons after earlier ones who had died.) So Agnes and James ended up with a family of five—three boys and two girls. Given the state of health and medicine at the time, this heavy mortality rate was not unusual. The first five children were born in the parish of Heversham, near Ackenthwaite. The second of these children was Agnes and James's most famous child—John Taylor, who would succeed Brigham Young as president of The Church of Jesus Christ of Latter-day Saints. He was born November 1, 1808, at Bridge End farm in Stainton, near Milnthorpe, a small seaport on the Bay of Morecambe near Ackenthwaite. The last five children were born near Hale, where the Taylor family settled on an estate James inherited from an uncle.

Because of his education and the status of his family, James Taylor received a government appointment collecting customs duties, which led to his moving from place to place. The family lived at Milnthorpe for a time, then moved to Liverpool, and finally settled in 1819 on the estate at Hale, about one mile from Beetham. The place of the estate is known today as Hale Green, but the contemporary term for it was Hale Grange, meaning an outlying farmhouse or group of buildings belonging to a manor where crops and tithes in kind were stored.

We can only surmise at Agnes's experiences as a young mother in Milnthorpe, Liverpool, and Hale. She was a good housekeeper,

had a contagious sense of humor, and maintained high standards
for her husband and family. There was unity in the family, and family
members enjoyed their life in the home. In addition to household
tasks, she and James sent their children to school, associated with
their local parish, made sure the children were taught the cate-
chism and prayers of the church, and in other ways sought to prepare their children for life. John, the future prophet, said that after
their move to Hale when he was eleven, he went to school at
Beetham. "I well remember some of my boyish freaks [pranks,
whimsies] as I wended my way with satchell to school," he wrote
in his early history. At Hale, he said, "I got mixed up with plough-
ing, sowing, reaping, haymaking, &c, . . . and have indelibly
impressed on my mind some of my first mishaps in horsemanship
in the shape of sundry curious evolutions between the horses'
backs and terra firma."

John was apprenticed to a cooper—one who makes wooden
casks or tubs—in Liverpool when he was fourteen. When the business failed after a year, the youth returned to Hale and remained
with his family until they arranged for him to go to Penrith to learn
the business of a turner—one who fashions or shapes wooden
objects on a lathe.

Something happened while John was in Penrith that would
have a far-reaching effect on his family. A year after he went there,
he heard the Methodist doctrine taught and was converted. "It
seemed to me more of a matter of fact, personal thing, than the
Church of England," he wrote. He prayed frequently, studied the
Bible, and read works on Christian theology.

The next year, while still apprenticed as a turner, he became a
Methodist exhorter or local preacher. His first appointment was at
a small village seven miles from Penrith, probably Temple Sowerby.
A man from the Penrith church accompanied John as he walked to
the village. After they had gone about a mile, John later wrote, "a
peculiar influence overpowered me and I stood still and remarked
to the brother who was with me: 'I have a strong impression on my

mind that I have to go to America to preach the Gospel.'" At that time, he knew nothing about America except what he had learned in geography class in school. However, this impression remained with him: "I could not shake it off. . . . I had some work to do which I did not then understand." He repeated this experience to Agnes and James, and they accepted it as a legitimate whispering of the Spirit.

When John was twenty and had mastered the art of turner, he returned to Hale and went into business for himself under the auspices of his father. Shortly thereafter, in 1830, because of John's wish to go to America, Agnes, now forty-three, and James, forty-seven, with the four younger children, emigrated to Upper Canada (present-day Ontario). They left John behind to dispose of some unsold property and to settle the affairs of the estate. Two years later John joined them in Canada and the family was once more united, this time in the New World.

The Taylors settled on a farm near York, the capital of Upper Canada. (It was incorporated as Toronto in 1834.) During the years after 1815, several thousand English, Scottish, and Irish settlers had gone there, among whom were the Taylors, and formed the basis for the strong British-oriented culture of that region in the early years of the nineteenth century.

Once more, however, the welfare of Agnes and James and their family would be affected by an action of their son. John, who established a turner shop adjoining his home, had continued to preach Methodism in Canada, but he was becoming increasingly dissatisfied with the doctrines of the church. "I often wondered," he wrote, "why the Christian religion was so changed from its primitive simplicity, and became convinced, before I dared acknowledge it, that we ought to have Apostles, Prophets, Pastors, Teachers and Evangelists—inspired men—as in former days." He found other persons who entertained similar views, mostly local preachers of the same church, and they met together several times a week to study the scriptures and pray. He continued to preach, but, to use his words, he was more interested in teaching "the leading doctrines of the Christian religion, rather than the peculiar dogmas of Methodism." He married Leonora Cannon, an immigrant from the Isle of Man and Liverpool, in 1833.

One day in 1836, Elder Parley P. Pratt, one of the finest of the early Latter-day Saint evangelists, arrived in Toronto, as York was now called, and was introduced to John. John's response, as given in his 1838 history, was as follows: "I wrote down eight of the first sermons that he preached, and compared them with the scriptures. I also investigated the evidence concerning the Book of Mormon and read the Doctrine and Covenants. I made a regular business of it for three weeks and followed Br. Parley from place to place. At length being perfectly satisfied of the truth of Mormonism, I was baptized by him. . . . [and] my wife was also baptized at the same time. I have never doubted any principle of Mormonism since."

John was soon ordained an elder and began preaching the glad tidings of the restoration of the gospel to his parents; they were baptized by John in May 1836. Their enthusiastic reception of the gospel paved the way for the conversion of their daughters Elizabeth and Agnes and of their youngest living son, William.

John served as the Church's presiding high priest in Canada for the next two years. In July 1838 he was called by revelation to be one of the Council of the Twelve Apostles, and he and Leonora prepared to join the main body of the Saints, then gathering in Missouri. Agnes and James, John's parents, prepared to move also. The Taylors set out for Missouri in the fall of 1838, arriving there as mobs were driving the Saints from that state. They fled to the Mississippi River and found temporary refuge in Quincy, Illinois, then in Warsaw.

John received a call to serve a mission in the British Isles, leaving in the summer of 1839. While he was gone, Leonora and the children found refuge in an abandoned army barracks in Montrose, Iowa, across the Mississippi River from Nauvoo (formerly Commerce), Illinois, the new headquarters of the Church. Agnes and James moved on to a wilderness area thirty miles north of Nauvoo, to a place called Oquawka, the county seat of Henderson County. They would remain there until the winter of 1845–46, when they joined the Nauvoo Saints in preparation for the migration west.

When John returned from his mission in 1841, he settled his family in Nauvoo. His mother, Agnes, occasionally visited the family there. Elder Wilford Woodruff mentioned in his diary that a group of Saints helped him celebrate his (Wilford's) birthday on March 1, 1842, and among the guests were John Taylor, his wife Leonora, and his mother, Agnes. Agnes was apparently not in Nauvoo long enough to have been active in the Female Relief Society.

One episode at Oquawka has special interest. In 1842 an attempt was made on the life of Governor Lilburn W. Boggs of Missouri. Enemies of the Church in Missouri determined to extradite Joseph Smith to the state to stand trial for that and other crimes of which he was accused. Certain that he would not receive a fair trial in Missouri, which had earlier expelled the Saints, the Prophet sought to avoid arrest. He had also received word that some persons were determined to return him to Missouri, dead or alive, and, indeed, in September 1842 his home was searched. He managed to elude the kidnapping party, which had come without legal documents permitting an arrest. On October 7, 1842, the Prophet's diary, as kept by Willard Richards, states: "From the situation and appearance of things abroad, I concluded to leave home for a short season, until there should be some change in the proceedings of my enemies. Accordingly, at twenty minutes after eight o'clock in the evening, I started away in company with Brothers John Taylor, Wilson Law, and John D. Parker, and traveled through the night and part of the next day; and, after a tedious journey, arrived at Father James Taylor's [feeling] well and in good spirits."

The Prophet remained with Agnes and James for two weeks, went back to Nauvoo to be with his family for one apprehensive

night, then returned to the Taylors for still another week. He obviously enjoyed Agnes's twinkling eyes and respectful and helpful
attitude. We can be sure that he liked her potato pie and roast lamb
smothered with her special Cumbrian sauce.

Agnes often expressed her pleasure at this three-week visit of
the Prophet. As one of her friends wrote at the time of her death:
"She highly appreciated the confidence which he [Joseph Smith]
reposed in the integrity of her partner and herself in selecting their
residence as a place of retreat at a time when he was menaced by
great danger. His friendship and the teachings which she received
from him during those days were among the most pleasing recollections of her subsequent life."

When it became clear that the Saints would have to leave
Illinois, as they had left Missouri, Agnes and James moved to
Nauvoo in the winter of 1845–46 and prepared for the journey
west. They crossed Iowa in early 1846, and stayed at Winter
Quarters, Nebraska, until the spring of 1847, leaving there on
June 19, 1847. Agnes, fifty-nine, and James, sixty-three, traveled in
a group of fifty Saints under the leadership of their son, William
Taylor, now twenty-three. With them also on the trip were their
daughters Elizabeth and Agnes (with her three children), their
daughter-in-law Lovina (wife of William), and, of course, John and
Leonora. One month out on the trip, on the North Platte, Elizabeth
was married to George Boyes in a ceremony presumably performed
by John. The party arrived in the Salt Lake Valley in September
1847.

Agnes and James lived until 1849 in a section of the Old Fort,
which had been finished by the advance group of pioneers. Then,
with the assistance of John, they were able to move into a log cabin
in the Salt Lake Fourteenth Ward, west of Main Street and south of
North Temple Street. John was in the same ward, as were Elder
Parley Pratt, who had converted John, and Elder Wilford Woodruff,
always a good friend. John Murdock, a close friend of the Prophet

Joseph Smith, was the first bishop, followed in 1851 by Abraham Hoagland.

Agnes died on November 15, 1868, at age eighty-one. She left five children—John, Elizabeth, Agnes, and William in Utah, and James in Canada. Her husband, James, to whom Agnes had been married almost sixty-three years, died eighteen months later, on May 27, 1870, at age eighty-seven.

One of those who knew Agnes best was George Q. Cannon, an apostle at the time of her death and a brother of Leonora Cannon Taylor, the wife John had married in 1833 in Canada. George, whose parents were from the Isle of Man and Liverpool, had much in common with Agnes and James. Upon her death, he wrote:

"[Agnes] was always of a buoyant, hopeful and cheerful turn of mind, and deeply religious withal. She took great delight in her religion, and until last fall, when she was prostrated by a severe sickness, her presence was rarely missed at meetings, no matter how stormy the weather might be. Until she had that sickness she was remarkable for her sprightliness, energy and strict attention to business, and the weight of years sat as lightly upon her as upon many who were not half her age. . . . During her sickness she maintained her cheerfulness and equanimity. Death had no terrors for her, and his approach could not disturb her happiness. She knew in whom she had trusted: He had never forsaken her, and in her last hours He sustained and comforted her. She fell asleep calmly and without a struggle, and her face, in death, wore a peaceful and happy smile."

SOURCES

Although we have not been able to find a single word written by Agnes Taylor, and although there is very little information specifically about her in existing manuscripts and publications, we believe that we have been able to put together a credible biographical sketch by careful study of mission histories, biographies of her son John, histories of the villages in which she lived, and sources in the LDS Church Family History Library in Salt Lake City.

Taylor family group sheets are in the Family History Library, and clipped items about Agnes indexed under her name are in the Journal History of the Church in the Church Historical Department. An obituary was published in the *Deseret News Weekly*, November 25, 1868. There is a "History of John Taylor by Himself," in the Manuscript History of the Church, Book G, pp. 265–75, Church Archives.

One mention of Agnes is found in a footnote in B. H. Roberts, ed., *History of the Church* 3 (Salt Lake City: Church of Jesus Christ of Latter-day Saints, 1946): 154. Other information in this six-volume set was helpful.

Book-length and shorter biographies of John Taylor that mention Agnes include B. H. Roberts, *The Life of John Taylor* (Salt Lake City: George Q. Cannon and Sons, 1892); Samuel W. Taylor, *The Kingdom or Nothing: The Life of John Taylor, Militant Mormon* (New York: Macmillan, 1976); Francis M. Gibbons, *John Taylor: Mormon Philosopher, Prophet of God* (Salt Lake City: Deseret Book, 1985); Richard L. Jensen, "The John Taylor Family," *Ensign* 10 (February 1980): 50–56; Nellie T. Taylor, "John Taylor, His Ancestors and Descendants," *Utah Genealogical and Historical Magazine* 21 (April 1930): 48–52; Andrew Jenson, "Taylor, John," in *Latter-day Saints' Biographical Encyclopedia,* 4 vols. (Salt Lake City, 1899–1936), 1:14–19; G. St. John Stott, "John Taylor's Religious Preparation," *Dialogue: A Journal of Mormon Thought* 19 (Spring 1986): 123–28; Preston Nibley, "John Taylor," in *The Presidents of the Church* (Salt Lake City: Deseret Book, 1971), pp. 69–98; and Paul T. Smith, "John Taylor," in Leonard Arrington, ed., *The Presidents of the Church* (Salt Lake City: Deseret Book, 1986), pp. 75–114.

Three valuable histories are Joseph Nicolson and Richard Burn, *The History . . . of the Counties of Westmorland and Cumberland,* 2 vols. (London, 1777); Thomas Rose, *Westmorland, Cumberland, Durham and Northumberland* (London, 1835); and John Hadfield, ed., *The Shell Book of English Villages* (London: Michael Joseph, 1980).

BULAH THOMPSON
WOODRUFF AND
AZUBAH HART
WOODRUFF

O God, console the heart of my stepmother, Azubah,
who has watched my wants, my youth, and my life.
And when my mother, Bulah, rises from the grave, let
the union of my father be like a three-fold cord not easily broken. True friendship is always eternal. —*Wilford
Woodruff*

Connecticut was one of the oldest English colonies in
America. Facing the Atlantic Ocean, or to be more precise
the Atlantic Inlet of Long Island Sound, the first permanent
settlement took place in 1635 and 1636, when settlers from the
Massachusetts Bay colony founded the three river towns of
Hartford, Windsor, and Wethersfield. In 1639 these communities
adopted the first American constitution based on the consent of the
governed. Shortly thereafter, in 1640, the Puritan settlers founded
Farmington (Farming Town) as a site for expanded agricultural
production. The soil was rich, there was a vast open valley with
hundreds of acres of clear meadowland, and the luxuriant vegeta-
tion gave promise of abundant crops. The river's waters would also

power the gristmills and sawmills needed for industrial and agricultural self-sufficiency.

Connecticut residents were solid supporters of the war for independence; General George Washington passed through the region several times, stored war material there, and felt it a secure place to lodge British prisoners of war. While there was no enemy action in the central Connecticut villages around Farmington, the French army commanded by the Comte de Rochambeau traveled through the region on its way from Providence, Rhode Island, to New York City, and, after the battle of Yorktown, returned through the region in 1782.

After the war, when a new constitution for the United States of America was proposed, Connecticut was the fifth state to ratify it and was one of the original thirteen states of the Union.

Because of its Puritan founding and the strong Puritan influence on its life and thought, Connecticut has been called the Land of Steady Habits. Its strict laws enforcing observance of the Sabbath also led to its being referred to as the Blue Law State. Another nickname is the Nutmeg State, so-called because peddlers in the state always carried supplies of nutmeg seeds brought back by merchants and sailors from the Spice Islands in the East Indies. Connecticut kitchens were well saturated with the pleasant aroma, and Connecticut cuisine featured nutmeg powder in custards, puddings, pies, and even in some meats and vegetables.

A true descendant of the Connecticut Puritans was Bulah Thompson, whose ancestors were in Farmington as early as 1640. The only child of Lot and Anna Hart Thompson of Farmington, Bulah was born on April 22, 1782, just two months after Lord Cornwallis surrendered at Yorktown, an event that led to British recognition of United States independence and the evacuation of British land and naval forces.

Bulah's life experiences inevitably began in the kitchen of the family's home north of Farmington in a place later incorporated as Avon. She would have spent most of her first year in a rocking

*The First Church of Christ, Congregational, in
Farmington, where Bulah probably worshiped*

cradle while her mother tended to various household tasks. The first family exercise in the morning was reading the Bible, followed by prayer. A fire burned in the fireplace nearly all day, keeping a soup pot perpetually hot. An oven in the brick wall of the fireplace was often full of baked goods. Herbs and corn hung from the ceiling, and there were hanging baskets with drying fruit. The kitchen was the gathering place for visiting relatives and friends. The kitchen was Bulah's first home.

Since Bulah was an only child, her mother would have taken her with her as she worked in the garden in the summer. Bulah was no doubt nearby as her mother fed the chickens, milked the cow, and did other tasks around the yard.

Bulah's earliest experiences away from home—aside from visiting grandparents, uncles, and aunts, many of whom were in the Farmington area—were in the community church (Congregational). Preparations began Saturday evening with the weekly bath—in a cedar tub filled with water heated on the hearth. The Sabbath started at sundown on Saturday, and since cleanliness is next to godliness, the bath was almost a religious ritual. Church services on Sunday usually started at nine in the morning and lasted until dusk. No lights were allowed in most churches because of the danger of fire, nor were there stoves or chimneys, so during the wintertime worshippers took foot warmers, pillows, and blankets to keep warm. In deepest winter, bread sometimes froze at the sacrament table, and the parson wore an overcoat, earmuffs, and a muffler when he gave his sermon. He kept a flask of warm water under his coat to insure warm water for christening. Bulah was christened the first Sunday after her birth.

The Farmington church had a steeple with a bell that served as a kind of town crier, ringing out as the congregation assembled for worship service, and also three times each day—at seven in the morning, noon, and at nine o'clock in the evening as a signal for curfew. When there was a death in the community, the bell rang out three times for a man and twice for a woman, and then the number of years the deceased person had lived. Such emphasis was given to Sabbath observance that residents did not work, play, or travel on that day except to go to and from the meetinghouse.

Bulah's life as a girl was a mixture of work, play, and school. The work included helping her mother in the kitchen, chores in the yard, and helping with the important tasks of carding wool, spinning, weaving, and sewing. The play would have included picking apples, gathering chestnuts, picking cranberries, spotting birds, and romping with lambs and calves.

Farmington had good schools for the time. Since Connecticut had an official religion (Congregationalism), religion and morality were prominent in the daily routine. Students were expected to read the Bible every day, and the teacher was required to close the daily class with prayer. They would have used Noah Webster's first blue-backed speller, Timothy Dwight's *Geography Made Easy*, and an anthology of patriotic readings. Good handwriting was emphasized.

At the age of nineteen Bulah fell in love with twenty-three-year-old Aphek Woodruff, who was also a native of Farmington (Avon). They were married on November 25, 1801.

The Woodruff family was also in Farmington on the date of founding in 1640. Aphek was named for a fortified bastion in ancient Judea mentioned in the books of Joshua, Samuel, and Kings. He began a flour milling business when he was eighteen, ran a gristmill and a sawmill, and also operated a farm. He was generous with his customers and did not accumulate wealth, but he was a religious person and was loyal to the best traditions of the Puritans.

The responsibility of a wife in those days was to follow the will of her husband, and this was no problem for Bulah, who was brought up to be polite and agreeable. She was also thrifty and industrious. Although Aphek was priest in the family and led out in the prayers and Bible reading, he spent most of his time at the mill, and so the moral nature of the family devolved upon Bulah.

During the seven years after their marriage, Bulah gave birth to three children: Azmon, born in 1802; Ozem Thompson (Thompson), born in 1804; and Wilford (the future prophet), born in 1807. There were, of course, no hospitals or maternity homes at the time, and no anesthesia, so in most early farmhouses the children were born in a room just off the kitchen fireplace called the "borning room," usually with knowledgeable neighbor women in attendance. One might bring herbs from her field and garden to relieve the discomfort. The women would offer prayers and emotional support, and one of them might hold the mother in her lap as she sat on the low "midwife's stool." Thus, while childbirth was a long and dangerous travail, there was plenty of help and empathy. Often one of the women brought refreshments so all, including the father, could celebrate the glorious event.

Tragedy came to the Woodruff home on June 11, 1808, when Bulah died of spotted fever at the age of twenty-six. Accompanied by pain, nausea, vomiting, skin spots, delirium, and eventual systemic collapse, the disease had reached epidemic proportions during this time in the Farmington River Valley. At the time of Bulah's death, Wilford—the future prophet—was only fifteen months old.

On Bulah's tombstone in the church graveyard in Avon the following verse was inscribed:

> A pleasing form, a generous gentle heart
> A good companion, just without art.
> Just in her dealings, faithful to her friends,
> Beloved through life, lamented in the end.

Following Bulah's death, the evidence suggests that the children were cared for by relatives, probably maternal, while Aphek was at work.

Seventeen months after Bulah's death, Aphek married Azubah Hart, a first cousin of Bulah, and possibly the person who was most involved in looking after the children and the house of Aphek. They were married on November 9, 1809, in Avon. Azubah, who was now the stepmother of Azmon, Thompson, and Wilford, and the only mother Wilford would remember, was born in Avon on July 31, 1792. At the time of her marriage, she was seventeen and Aphek was thirty-one.

An intelligent, industrious, and religious woman, Azubah served well as a second wife and mother. She and Aphek had six children of their own: Philo (1811), who died in 1827 at age sixteen; Asahel Hart (1814), who died in 1838 at age twenty-four; Franklin (1816), who died two and a half months after birth; Newton (1818), who drowned at the age of two; Julius (1821), who died young but no definite date is known; and Eunice (1820), who died in 1853 at age thirty-three. Of this second family, only Eunice lived to be an associate of Azmon, Thompson, and Wilford in their middle ages. Azmon lived to the age of eighty-six; Thompson to age eighty-nine; and Wilford to age ninety-one.

The lot of a farmer and miller in those days was not easy. He was responsible for the acres he tilled—for his grains, his root crops, his flax and hops, and his orchard. He bred, milked, and pastured his cows. He found grazing for the sheep, sheared them in late spring or early summer, and kept them in warm sheds in winter. He cared for the swine, oxen, and horses. He cut and stacked the hay; plowed the fields; and cultivated, fertilized, and harvested the crops. In October he picked apples, ran the cider press, and helped his wife make apple butter. In November he butchered. In December he banked up the north sides of houses and barns with cornstalks, hay, leaves, and sawdust so they would withstand the winter. He also readied sleds and sleigh bells. (The bells were as necessary, especially when driving the otherwise noiseless sleigh at night, as horns on automobiles.) In January and February, when he could not work in the fields, he built and repaired fences; split fence rails; kept his harness in order; husked, threshed, flailed, and winnowed grain; repaired the house, shed, and barns; shoveled and plowed snow on paths and roads; and cut firewood endlessly. All of this was in addition to running his grist-mill, sawmill, fulling mill, and wool carder.

With the encouragement of Azubah, and sometimes under her supervision, the Woodruff boys helped their father with his many tasks. For example, Wilford recalled that his chore at age six was to feed the cows and the bull, and that he and his brothers used to fish in the stream that fed his father's mill, and also did hunting and trapping. He remembered his father's incessant labor: "Most of the time he labored eighteen hours a day."

Azubah's work was equally demanding. A caring wife and mother, she fed and clothed her family and cared for their social, educational, and religious needs. She doctored and nursed them; she supervised the children's play, both indoors and out; she churned butter, made soap and candles, and assisted with the butchering.

New England wives were expected to furnish the family with woolen clothing. To keep warm during the long winter season, both adults and children wore long woolen underwear, which was full of the tickling and scratching impurities of homespun wool.

But, the wearers boasted, "If you fall out of a tree and catch your long underwear on a limb, you are saved."

By remaining close to the house, Azubah was at the communications center of her husband's various activities and had some responsibility for passing on information and directions to workers, pacifying creditors, and helping friends and neighbors. She probably helped her husband keep his mill books straight. She also participated with neighboring women in huskings and quiltings, picking berries and spinning; they benefited from her sharing their work just as she benefited from them sharing hers.

One year during the children's growing up would prove to be memorable because of a strange meteorological event. The year 1816, when Wilford was eight, was the year without a summer. Snow fell in July and August, ruining crops and causing famine. Many places in New England saw ice and snow during every month of the entire year. In Farmington, at the July 4 celebration, men were seen pitching quoits in the middle of the day with their thick woolen overcoats on. Only half enough corn ripened that year to furnish seed for the next crop. Many persons, believing that New England was becoming frigid, headed south and west.

Azubah's responsibilities for caring for Wilford, Bulah's youngest child, were particularly important. Wilford seemed to be accident prone. When he was three he fell into a kettle of boiling water and almost died; he did not recover fully for nine months. Another time he toppled from the top of the barn to the floor and landed on his face. One Saturday evening, while playing with his brothers Azmon and Thompson, he made a misstep and fell to the bottom of the stairs, breaking one of his arms. By the time he left home at the age of twenty, he had broken his leg in a fall from a carriage, had been kicked in the stomach by an ox, had been buried alive when a hay wagon overturned on top of him, and had narrowly escaped when a horse bolted down a hill while pulling a wagon he was in. Other incidents include these: He was caught in a blizzard but was saved by a neighbor; he fell fifteen feet from a tree limb and landed flat on his back; he nearly drowned in thirty feet of water; he split open the instep of his left foot while chopping wood with an ax; and he was bitten by a dog that had rabies. Finally, when he was seventeen, a bad-tempered horse he was riding threw him on a rocky hill, breaking both ankles and one leg in two places. Because he survived so many accidents and injuries he believed that the Lord was protecting him for some important future calling.

Azubah and Aphek saw that the children attended the nearest school, two miles from their home in Avon, and also supervised their religious education. Wilford remembered a Baptist revival in 1815, when he was eight. Aphek invited the preachers into his home, and Wilford attended meetings, prayed, and, as he expressed it, tried to feel religious, but could not. When he was fourteen the Presbyterians had a strong revival, and again he attended meetings, went to Sunday School and prayer meetings, and tried to get religion but couldn't. This didn't bother him, however, for Azubah taught him and his brothers and sister that "the Church of Christ was in the wilderness, that there had been a falling away from pure and undefiled religion before God, and that a great change was at hand."

Wilford left home when he was twenty. For three years he worked at his Aunt Helen's flour mill. He read the Bible during his free time and prayed frequently. He and his brother Azmon then bought a farm near Richland, New York. While they were out in the fields one day, two Mormon missionaries came to the house and talked to Azmon's wife. Without waiting to eat supper, Wilford left to attend their meeting at the schoolhouse. Because of what he had been taught as a child—that the church of Christ was not on earth at the time but would one day be restored, and that what he had read in the Bible supported the doctrines that church would espouse—Wilford knew instantly that what the missionaries said was true. He was baptized on a cold, wintry day in December 1833. The snow was three feet deep and the water was mixed with ice

and snow, but he said he didn't feel the cold. His brother Azmon
was baptized at the same time.

As with his Puritan ancestors, once Wilford had been persuaded, he was totally converted. A valiant Latter-day Saint, he
moved to Kirtland, Ohio, where the headquarters of the Church
was located. In 1834 he joined the little army that marched from
Kirtland to Missouri to assist the Saints who had been driven out
of their Jackson County homes. He was ordained an elder and later
a seventy, and served as a proselyting missionary in Tennessee and
Kentucky. Back in Kirtland from 1836 to 1837, he married Phebe
Carter, received his patriarchal blessing from Joseph Smith Sr., and
was sent on a proselyting mission to the Fox Islands in Maine.
While on that mission he went to the home of his family in
Farmington (Avon), Connecticut, and saw his parents for the first
time in seven years. "It was a happy meeting," he wrote. This was
in July 1837. A year later, in connection with another mission, he
was back in Connecticut, and on July 1, 1838, he baptized his
father, mother, and sister. Wilford's diary entry for that day tells of
the drama of that important event in his family's history:

"I began to cry unto God for my father and his household and
the Lord showed me in a night vision that a great victory was nigh.
But the devil fell upon the whole household with great wrath and
temptations. Some of the time one was ready to fall back and reject
the gospel and then again another. His power rested upon me at
the same time as if to devour me at once. But after being confined
to my bed for several hours under his grasp, in the name of Jesus
Christ I with my friends burst the powers of darkness. I went and
stood before the people and declared the gospel of Jesus Christ, and
shout O Heavens, and rejoice O earth for the victory the Lord hath
given us. For after preaching the gospel to the people, I immediately assembled upon the bank of Farmington River where there
was much water and led six of my friends into the waters of baptism. Five of them were my relatives, viz. my Father, my Mother,
and my only Sister Eunice, Aunt Anna Cossett, and Cousin Seth

Woodruff and the other was Mr. Dwight Webster, a Methodist class
leader who was boarding with my father's family. I organized the
small number of nine persons . . . into a branch of the Church, . . .
and administered unto them the Sacrament. It was truly a day of
joy to my soul. . . .

"Many eyes were turned to behold this scene and deep solem-
nity veiled their faces while I took my Father by the hand. My
Father did I say?? Yes, HE Covenanted to walk with God and for
the remission of his sins I baptized him. Feeling the victory won
my Mother followed his steps and by obedience was sealed a Saint,
a member of the kingdom. Eunice my sister my only sister was
ready. Her noble soul by Ephraim's spirit inspired, her garb of pride
had rent and broke the gentiles' chain. Fearless of the world's
despising she freely received the watery bed her Master to imitate
while her firm example should say Celestial glory is my boast, the
garb of the Saints, my pride. . . .

"Thus ended this scene of wonder shall I say?? Yes and, of
mercy too, for heaven countenance'd the deed for it was God's command, an ordinance of the gospel. To be permitted to stand in one's
own native land and the gospel of JESUS CHRIST to declare in the
last dispensation and while [proclaiming] the word through the
power of the priesthood to his kindred, his townsman, to behold
the pride of the great, the rich, the learned, by the spirit of God
humbled at his feet. Then to experience the living reality of a
Father, a Mother, an only Sister meekly with other kindred receiving the ordinances of the house of God at the hand of their Son and
brother is to me at least a scene of interest."

The next day he wrote in his diary:

"After evening prayers with the family, Father retired to rest
and I spent a season in conversation with Mother and we felt sen-
sibly the weight of the powers of temptation that try the souls of
men. But out of them all the Lord delivers his Saints. I also spent a
short time with Sister Eunice before retiring. We mingled our sym-
pathys, tears, and prayers together before a Throne of Grace. Truly

how strong is the Cord of Consanguinity and of the Blood of Christ united in binding the hearts of Saints together. And how blessings brighten as they take their flight. This was the last night I spent beneath my fathers roof. May the Lord protect thy household and bring thee safe to Zion."

A month later, after he returned to the Fox Islands, Wilford received a communication that he had been called by revelation to be an apostle.

According to his diary, Wilford received letters two or three times a year from Azubah indicating his parents' continued faithfulness in the Church—"the New Covenant," as she called it. He was ordained an apostle in 1839, and undertook a mission with the Twelve to Great Britain from 1839 to 1841. While he was there, he wrote that on July 2, 1840, his mother, Bulah, appeared to him in a dream. She "clasped me in her arms and kissed me three times and said the Lord Almighty bless thee forever and ever." Two years later, he was able to arrange for her baptism by proxy.

Subsequent to his return to Nauvoo, Wilford served as business manager of *The Times and Seasons,* a Church magazine published in Nauvoo, and went on a proselyting mission to the Eastern States. During a visit to his parents in September 1843, he explained to them the principle of the gathering. He wrote: "They seem to understand it pretty well. Mother says if we follow the good spirit of the Blessed Jesus we will do well." In July 1844, on his way to Great Britain to serve as president of the European Mission, he once more visited his parents. He wrote in his diary: "O God . . . console the heart of her [Azubah] who has watched my wants, my youth, my life, and when my mother [Bulah] rises from the grave, let the union of my father be like a three-fold cord not easily broken. . . . What I say unto one I say unto all. Watch, for thoughts dwell deep, but words pass away."

Having raised the question with them earlier, Wilford wrote to his parents from England in December 1845 telling them he would be returning to America in January and that he expected them to go with him to Nauvoo. As he expressed it in his diary, he could then "redeem [his] father and mother from Babylon." He arrived at his father's house in March 1846, and on March 23, he, his wife Phebe, their children, and Aphek and Azubah left Farmington. They traveled by wagon to New Britain, Connecticut; by steamboat to New York City; by railroad to Philadelphia; by stagecoach to Brownsville, Pennsylvania; and by steamer to Pittsburgh, then via the Ohio River to the Mississippi, and up the Mississippi to Nauvoo. As they steamed up the Mississippi, Azubah busied herself writing letters to friends and relatives she had left behind in Connecticut. Wilford and Aphek "diverted ourselves by looking at objects through my spy glass as we passed along."

Nauvoo, when they arrived in April 1846, was in turmoil. Thousands of Saints had already crossed the river and traveled through Iowa on their way to Winter Quarters in eastern Nebraska, where they would be spending the winter. Others were still in Nauvoo hurriedly getting ready to make the same trek. A few were determined to remain behind, refusing to follow the leadership of Brigham Young and the Twelve Apostles. Unfortunately, some of the latter got to Wilford's sister Eunice and her husband, Dwight Webster, and they "worked on" Aphek and Azubah, trying to persuade them not to go west. Wilford's parents, particularly Azubah it seems, were affected. Bitterly, Wilford wrote: "I called the family together and freed my mind upon the subject."

The parents did go with Wilford to the public dedication of the Nauvoo Temple on May 1. However, in June, Wilford wrote that Azubah "handed me a lengthy epistle of complaint written in a book of thirty pages, against several persons, their treatment of her, &c." He went on to comment: "It was like a tempest in a teapot, a bubble not worthy of notice. The more I have provided for her of late the more she has complained. She has manifested much of a spirit of fault finding and watching for iniquity since she came to Nauvoo."

Wilford finally persuaded Aphek to go with him to Winter

Quarters that spring, while Azubah remained behind with her daughter. In May 1846 the little company of which Wilford had charge, consisting of his wife and children, his father, and a few other members of the family, left Nauvoo. They had three baggage wagons, one family carriage, six yoke of oxen, six cows, four calves, one yearling, and a pair of mules. His father was aged and had no grown sons other than Wilford to assist him, so the weight and responsibility fell upon the son.

There now began the tedious journey across Iowa. On the first day out their wagon mired down in the mud; the wagon tongue and several chains were broken in the effort to extricate it. On May 27, Wilford wrote, his father fell to the ground while trying to climb into the wagon, and both wheels of the wagon, which was loaded with twenty-five hundred pounds, ran over his legs. It was miraculous that no bones were broken.

At Farmington, Iowa, they bought four barrels of flour. On Sunday, June 7, they came to a long swale or swamp that covered a distance of one and one-half miles. Wilford got his carriage across by dark, but in the center of the swamp the wheels of his baggage wagons sank almost to the hubs. He worked most of the night in mud and water nearly knee deep to free the wagon. Finally on June 15 they reached Mount Pisgah and, after a brief rest, drove on to Winter Quarters. Azubah joined them there in late fall.

We do not have much information on the family's experiences in Winter Quarters except a reference in Wilford's diary to a special meeting on February 5, 1847, when the Saints held a religious service, then a feast, and ended with a dance. Wilford wrote: "It was truly an interesting sight to see the old men and women, some nearly a hundred years old, go forth and dance together in fulfillment of the ancient prophets. The Quorum of the Twelve spent the afternoon and evening with them. Father and Mother Woodruff was among the number."

Wilford was one of the company appointed by Brigham Young to make the pioneer journey to the Great Basin during the summer of 1847. Wilford, indeed, first set foot in the Salt Lake Valley on July 24 and called it a "Land of Promise, held in reserve by the hand of God as a resting place for the Saints."

In the Salt Lake Valley Wilford waited anxiously for news from his family in Nebraska. Finally, on August 29, he received three letters from his wife Phebe with discouraging news. His father, Aphek, now sixty-nine, was on his way west in the fourth hundred of the John Taylor–Parley P. Pratt train, due to arrive in Salt Lake on September 25, 1847. His mother, however, had listened to her daughter Eunice and had gone back to Iowa to live with the Websters. Wilford wrote: "Some persons who I have tried to do good and save, are filled with folly and the poison of asps are under their tongue and are tatling, lying and destroying themselves and using every exertion to destroy the peace of my family. . . . They are foolish and do not choose things which are right and righteous." It must have hurt Wilford very much that his mother would not follow him and his father to be with the Saints.

In the years that followed, Azubah wrote to her husband and to Wilford. But she was not destined to live long in Iowa. She died on March 20, 1851, still away from her husband and still outside the pale of the Church. Wilford regretted for the rest of his life that she had not chosen to leave "Babylon." Aphek, however, lived until May 29, 1861, when he died at age eighty-two. He was buried in the Salt Lake City Cemetery.

SOURCES

Although we have found no surviving papers of Bulah Thompson Woodruff or Azubah Hart Woodruff, we believe we have been able to piece together a believable and trustworthy account of their lives from histories of the areas where they lived and from the diaries and letters of their son and stepson, Wilford. One of the Church's most avid record keepers, Wilford Woodruff made diary entries for almost every day from 1834 to 1898. With the assistance of Ronald K. Esplin and Marilyn Rish Parks, we have been able to locate and study the many entries that mention his mother and stepmother. The diary is in the LDS Church Archives in Salt Lake City. A typescript was published in eight volumes in 1983 by Signature Books of Salt Lake City. Also in the Church Archives are three letters from Wilford to his parents: one from Tennessee, dated May 9, 1836; another from Tennessee, dated August 25, 1836; and the third from Nauvoo to his father, dated May 16, 1843. In the excerpts we have used, we have regularized the spelling and punctuation in most instances.

Local and regional histories that have been particularly helpful include two books by Eric Sloane: *American Yesterday* (New York: Wilfred Funk, 1956), and *The Seasons of America's Past* (New York: Wilfred Funk, 1958); David M. Roth, *Connecticut: A Bicentennial History* (New York: W. W. Norton, 1979), Christopher P Bickford, *Farmington in Connecticut* (Canaan, New Hampshire: Phoenix Publishing, 1982); Jarvis Means Morse, *A Neglected Period of Connecticut's History, 1818–1850* (New Haven: Yale University Press, 1933); Catherine Fennelly, *Life in an Old New England Country Village* (New York: Thomas Y. Crowell Co., 1969).

Book-length biographies of Wilford Woodruff that mention his parentage are Matthias F. Cowley, *Wilford Woodruff: History of His Life and Labors* (Salt Lake City: Deseret News, 1909) and Thomas G. Alexander, *Things in Heaven and Earth—The Life and Times of Wilford Woodruff, a Mormon Prophet* (Salt Lake City: Signature Books, 1991). Biographical essays include Andrew Jenson, "Woodruff, Wilford," in *Latter-day Saint Biographical Encyclopedia*, 4 vols. (Salt Lake City, 1899–1936), 1:20–26; Preston Nibley, "Wilford Woodruff," in *The Presidents of the Church* (Salt Lake City: Deseret Book, 1971), pp. 101–35; and Dean C. Jessee, "Wilford Woodruff," in Leonard J. Arrington, ed., *The Presidents of the Church* (Salt Lake City: Deseret Book, 1986), pp. 117–43.

On the role of the wife and mother in early America, we have profited from reading Laurel Thatcher Ulrich, *Good Wives: Image and Reality in the Lives of Women in Northern New England, 1650–1750* (New York: Alfred A. Knopf, 1982), and Page Smith, *Daughters of the Promised Land: Women in American History* (Boston: Little, Brown and Company, 1970).

ROSETTA LEONORA PETTIBONE SNOW

A more kind, indulgent, and affectionate parent than her [my mother] no man ever had. She was good, and virtuous, benevolent, and charitable to all—true and faithful in the New and Everlasting Covenant. I am comforted in the thought that her spirit rests in peace in the presence of her Great Father. Oh that my daughters may live out their probation with no more blots upon the page of their history than angels see upon that of their grandmother whose head lies low, yet honorable in the grave. *—Lorenzo Snow*

When Connecticut was chartered by the British Crown in the seventeenth century, it was granted a strip of land about seventy miles wide extending westward all the way to the Pacific Ocean. After the British surrender and the decision to form a United States of America, Connecticut, in 1786, ceded to the nation all its claims to western lands except a tract of four million acres extending about 120 miles along the southern shore of Lake Erie, west of Pennsylvania. Connecticut insisted upon reserving this land to sell or give to citizens who had been burned out by or had otherwise suffered inordinately from the predations of the British army and navy. This land was referred to as the New Connecticut or Connecticut's Western Reserve.

A semiofficial agency, the Connecticut Land Company, bought

most of the land in 1795, and the next year one of its directors, Moses Cleaveland, surveyed and established the first permanent settlement in the region, Cleveland. With the completion of the survey in 1798, the Land Company partitioned the region in a way to equalize the holdings and distribute them all at once. This meant the settlements would be widely scattered. Small groups—families or members of church congregations—fought their way through the wilderness to an assigned area and then would chop out a hole in the forest, erect cabins, plant a few acres of corn or wheat, and struggle to stay alive. Connecticut abandoned jurisdiction over the region in 1800, and the land was incorporated into Ohio Territory.

Among the first persons to buy land in the Western Reserve was Jacob Blair, a Revolutionary War veteran from Blandford, Hampden County, Massachusetts. In 1799 he purchased three hundred acres in a township thirty miles southeast of Cleveland called Mantua, after the village of the Roman poet Virgil. He later sold the land and returned to Massachusetts, but in 1804 he returned to Mantua, bought another three hundred acres, built a log cabin, and made some improvements. He returned to Massachusetts to pick up his family and in the spring of 1806 returned to Mantua and settled on his land.

Living in Tyringham, Massachusetts, not far from Blandford, was Oliver Snow, brother of Blair's wife, Charlotte. A native of Becket, Massachusetts, he had married twenty-one-year-old Rosetta Pettibone on May 6, 1800. When Blair told the Snows about Mantua, they decided to make the month-long journey there in 1805. They could occupy Blair's cabin until he took his own family there in 1806. Thus the Snows were one of the earliest families to locate permanently at Mantua. They were soon joined by both Snow and Pettibone relatives.

Oliver Snow was descended from Puritan stock. He was well-educated and had been employed for several years as a schoolteacher in Massachusetts. Rosetta came from an even more distinguished family. Born Rosetta Leonora Pettibone on October 22,

1778, she was the oldest of the seven children of Captain Jacob
Pettibone and Rosetta Barber. Both parents were descendants of
"genuine Puritan stock"—that is, descendants of some of the original Pilgrims who landed in 1620 at Plymouth and inaugurated the
Massachusetts Bay Colony. Experiencing some frustrations over
limits placed on their freedoms in Massachusetts, and perhaps
desirous of richer land, these ancestors migrated to a lush northern Connecticut valley in Hartford County, along the Farmington
River. There, in the village of Simsbury, they had been farming and
raising their families for four generations by the time Rosetta was
born.

Rosetta's father, Jacob, was one of a hundred men from
Simsbury who volunteered just three weeks after the first blood of
the Revolution was shed at Lexington in April 1775. He was
twenty-six at the time. His father, Jacob Pettibone Sr., was a soldier
too, having served in the French and Indian War in the First
Regiment of Connecticut.

Patriotism evidently ran high in Simsbury. Lucius Barber wrote
in the *Memorial History of Hartford County:* "In the War of the
Revolution, few, if any, of the towns of the state [of Connecticut]
furnished a larger number of enlisted men than Simsbury. With
great unanimity the inhabitants of this town espoused the cause of
freedom, and rendered essential aid in the great struggle for independence."

Though the Farmington River Valley contained fertile farmland, production of crops (mostly tobacco and Indian corn) was
still backbreaking labor involving the entire family. Farming tools
were wrought by hand—literally manufactured—by the local
blacksmith or by Rosetta's father or grandfather. Axes, hoes, forks,
spades, ploughshares, and scythes would not be mass-produced for
many years to come. As the oldest child, Rosetta shouldered a lot of
responsibility at home and was constantly at her mother's side,
learning domestic skills that she would later teach her own
daughters. A major portion of her time was spent producing cloth

items: blankets and sheets, tablecloths and towels, bed curtains and window curtains, flannels for the family, and even carpets, when carpets came into vogue. Lucius Barber described a typical scene in Simsbury in the late eighteenth century:

"In the morning the lawn was white with 'pieces of linen' spread out to bleach, and the meadow covered with flax to rot. All these were the work of women. They made the bread, the butter, the cheese. They milked the cows, they cooked over an open fire, they washed and ironed, they scrubbed the doors and sanded them, they made soap and candles, they raked hay, they pulled flax, they dug potatoes. When they visited, they 'carried their work.' When they sat by the fireside to rest, they were knitting or patching the children's clothes or darning their stockings. Of an autumn evening they were paring apples and quartering them for the children to string and hang in the morning in festoons on the outside walls. All were busy—always busy!"

Simsbury supported schools for the community, and Rosetta probably received a respectable education, although no record indicates how long she attended. As early as 1703, a committee, appointed to carry out the community's educational goals, voted to obtain four "school dames" and a schoolmaster, and "to keep said school: to teach such of [Simsbury's] children as are sent to read, write, and to cypher, or to say the rules of arithmatick." To finance the schools, they sequestered the local copper mines and, before the copper was refined or wrought, a percentage of it was set aside to pay the teachers and maintain the school buildings.

After her marriage Rosetta was prepared, just as other Farmington girls including Bulah and Azubah Woodruff were prepared, to assume the responsibilities of the typical New England household. In addition to teaching school, Oliver ran a farm near Becket, and Rosetta had plenty of housework and yardwork to do. Their daughter Leonora was born in 1802, followed by Eliza in 1804.

We can only wonder at the decision of Oliver and Rosetta to

leave their comfortable home in Massachusetts and tackle the wilderness in New Connecticut. Perhaps their difficulties in Massachusetts were such that no hardship on the frontier seemed insupportable. Were they disappointed with the thin soil saturated with glacial boulders? Did Jacob Blair glow as he told them of the fat loams and salubrious climate of the Western Reserve? Did they suppose that, with a few years of hard work and sacrifice, they could become persons of property—landed gentry? At any rate, emboldened by their faith in the new country, their own Yankee ingenuity, and their capacity for endurance, the Snows decided to go across the mountains into the Ohio wilderness.

They were not alone. In addition to Oliver and Rosetta and their family, Jacob W. Pettibone, Rosetta's younger, unmarried brother, went with them. Franklin Snow, Oliver's brother, joined them in Mantua the next year. And, of course, Jacob Blair and his family joined them in 1806 and his brother John in 1807. So they would have some family and close friends nearby.

We cannot be sure whether Oliver and Rosetta traveled by oxcart or by horse-drawn wagon. They had, of course, their daughters Leonora, age three, and Eliza, not quite two. If they were able to afford a horse and covered wagon, they would have also taken a bed, a blanket chest, a churn, earthen pots and jars (crocks), a few dishes, the family gridirons, some quilts and featherbeds, and a trunkful of clothing, as well as the family Bible and *Webster's Spelling Book*. Oliver, with a long walking stick in his hand and a floppy felt hat on his head, would walk beside the horse; Rosetta and the girls would probably sit in the wagon.

They arrived in Mantua in the fall and temporarily occupied the one-room log cabin left there the year before by Jacob Blair. The cabin, which had a leather-hinged door and greased paper at the windows to let light in but keep the weather out, must have been crowded at times, since the Snow family was joined by the family of Oliver's brother Franklin and by Rosetta's brother Jacob.

Oliver and Franklin settled on land that Samuel Barrows had

selected in 1798, made some improvements on it in 1799, and abandoned it in 1800. While the family stayed temporarily in Jacob Blair's cabin, Oliver, with the presumed help of Jacob Pettibone, built a log cabin in which he and his family lived for the next ten years.

Mantua was located along the Cuyahoga River, which wound its way south to what later became Akron and then flowed north into Lake Erie at Cleveland. First settled on a permanent basis in 1801, Mantua was in an area heavily wooded with oak, chestnut, beech, maple, black walnut, and hickory, providing abundant timber with which to build fences, homes, and outbuildings. By the time the Snows arrived, a water-driven sawmill and gristmill had been erected up the river at Burton.

Making a living during the first few years in Mantua was a stern and rugged adventure. The land was potentially rich, but a long period of sacrificial development lay ahead. Oliver and Franklin worked together to fell trees, dig out roots, and prepare the land for planting. By spring they had put in crops, built roads and bridges, dug a well, and erected a barn. Rosetta's task was to provide food for her own family, tend the children, make clothing, and keep the house as clean and livable as possible. Oliver helped her set out apple and peach trees.

The going was not easy. There were frosts every month in 1806, so very little of the corn matured; it was difficult to get even enough to save for seed for the next year. The 1807 growing season was equally disastrous. Life was hard, but Rosetta and Oliver bore it with resourcefulness and earned the respect of their neighbors. Eventually they prospered, and they remained in Mantua for thirty-two years, until 1837.

The family continued to grow. Two girls followed Leonora and Eliza: Percy Amanda, born in 1808, and Melissa, born in 1810. The first son, Lorenzo, was born in 1814. That same year the family, having outgrown the log cabin, built a substantial two-story frame home, the fourth dwelling house built in Mantua and the second that would be classed as a "good residence." There were four rooms on the main floor and two big bedrooms upstairs. Two additional sons were later born to Rosetta: Lucius in 1819 and Samuel in 1821, completing the family of three boys and four girls.

Rosetta and Oliver became influential citizens of Mantua. Three years after their arrival, Oliver was elected county commissioner, an office he held for two terms (1809 to 1815). He was also justice of the peace for several three-year terms, town councilman, and a member of the board that supervised the county fair in nearby Ravenna. During his involvement in these public affairs, Oliver employed his daughter Eliza as his secretary, a position she felt competent and proud to hold. She later wrote, "This experience proved of great benefit to myself and to others at different periods of my variegated life."

In the fall of 1808, under Oliver's supervision, the men built a log cabin for a schoolhouse; it also served as a church meetinghouse. Oliver taught there during the winter of 1809–10 and again in the winter of 1813–14. In the summer of 1819 a frame schoolhouse was built as an improvement on the old log cabin. This house was used also as a Baptist meetinghouse.

The skills Rosetta learned as a young girl in Connecticut seemed to serve her well as a mother. Eliza later wrote of her: "Whether my mother anticipated or originated the wise policy of Queen Victoria, concerning the training of girls, does not matter— at all events, my mother considered a practical knowledge of housekeeping the best, the most efficient foundation on which to build a magnificent structure of womanly accomplishments—that useful knowledge was the most reliable basis of independence."

Hence, Rosetta's daughters were trained early in cooking, housework, straw weaving, the making of bonnets, hats, and clothing, and various kinds of needlework. She took great pride in the fact that Eliza won first prize from the Committee on Manufactures at the Portage County Fair for the best manufactured leghorn (a hat made of smooth, plaited straw).

In addition to the homey skills, Rosetta and Oliver believed their daughters as well as their sons should receive a good education. Great importance was placed on their studies. Above all, Rosetta taught the children that useful labor, physical and mental, was honorable, and that idleness and waste of time were not only disgraceful but also sinful.

Young Lorenzo and his sister Eliza shared a love of literature, a curiosity about history, and the patriotism of their grandfathers, both of whom had been soldiers in the Revolutionary War. Many an hour they sat at the knee of their Grandfather Snow listening with quickened pulse to the tales of soldiering and battles. Eliza wrote of one particularly harrowing experience: "My Grandfather (Pettibone) when fighting for the freedom of our country was taken prisoner by the British troops, and confined in a dreary cell, and so scantily fed that when his fellow-prisoner by his side died from exhaustion, he reported him to the jailor as sick in bed, in order to obtain the amount of food for both—keeping him covered in their blankets as long as he dared to remain with a decaying body."

Lorenzo was evidently enthralled by such stories, for at the age of twenty-one he announced his plans for a military career. Although Eliza was alarmed at the possibility her brother's life would end prematurely on the battlefield, she agreed to sew his first, and most important, military uniform—his so-called "freedom suit." Although it was "beautiful—magnificent," Lorenzo's martial dreams were cut short by his desire to obtain a college education at nearby Oberlin College.

In 1809 a group of kindred souls from Mantua and such nearby villages as Aurora, Hiram, and Nelson formed a Baptist church. Oliver and Rosetta were among those who were baptized that year in the Cuyahoga River, near the location of the log chapel. The Snows actively supported the congregation; Oliver was an ordained deacon, and, indeed, had held Baptist meetings in their home before the meetinghouse was built. However, he and Rosetta

Rosetta Snow's daughter Eliza and son Lorenzo

were open-minded. They were not, Eliza recalled, "of the rigid, iron-bedstead order." They freely invited preachers of any faith or religious persuasion into their home to share meals and religious conversation. Thus, the Snow children had ample opportunity to form acquaintances with persons of all religious persuasions. One of these visitors was thirty-three-year-old Sidney Rigdon, a "reformed" Baptist preacher in nearby Kirtland and Mentor, Ohio, who was employed in 1826 as preacher for the Mantua congregation. This was an important event, because Mr. Rigdon was then in the process of changing from orthodox Baptist to Campbellite Baptist.

A leading religious figure in the American West in the early years of the nineteenth century was Alexander Campbell, an Irish immigrant of 1809 and a notable orator in frontier pulpits, who believed the fragmentation of sects weakened the cause of Christ's kingdom. He proposed to unite the divergent sects by concentrating on the simple faith and practice of the early New Testament church. They would adopt the name of Disciples of Christ or Christian, as followers of Jesus were first called at Antioch. Campbell preached this doctrine widely and effectively throughout the Western Reserve and won many converts. When Sidney Rigdon organized his church in Mantua on Campbellite principles in 1827, the Snows and most of the other Baptists in the region were quite willing to follow, and thus became Campbellite Christians.

Sidney Rigdon was the most brilliant of Campbell's converts. Thirty-seven years old in 1830, he was a powerful preacher. He differed with Campbell on two issues: He believed the second coming of Christ was imminent, as the early Christians believed, and he believed in the communal life practiced by the first Christians, as recorded in Acts of the Apostles: "All that believed were together, and had all things common; and sold their possessions and goods, and parted them to all men, as every man had need." (Acts 2:44–45.)

A number of Rigdon's believers decided to found a Christian Family at Kirtland, a town first established by Turhand Kirtland, a field representative for the Connecticut Land Company. Among the converts in Kirtland was a twenty-three-year-old religiously inclined young man, Parley P. Pratt (the same person who, as a converted Latter-day Saint elder, preached to Agnes Taylor and Mary Fielding in upper Canada). He became an ardent evangelist and went off to New York in 1830 to carry the Christian message he had learned from Sidney Rigdon. There he came upon a copy of the Book of Mormon, read it, and was so impressed that he interrupted his mission to go to Palmyra to see Joseph Smith. The Prophet was in Pennsylvania, but Parley stayed up all night talking with the Prophet's brother Hyrum. What he heard delighted him; here was what he was looking for—the ancient gospel restored, complete with the proper authority. He was baptized, ordained an elder, and continued his mission, this time as an advocate of the restored gospel. He went back to Ohio to win over the Campbellites to this newer revelation. Sidney Rigdon listened attentively, read the book, prayed earnestly, and announced that it had been revealed to him that the book was authentic, and he was ready for baptism. He then went to New York, met Joseph Smith face to face, accepted his leadership, and was soon designated as the Prophet's first counselor.

Late in December the Saints in New York were commanded by revelation to gather in Ohio, and indeed, for the next seven years the Western Reserve was the home of the Saints. It proved to be both a sacred place and a place that seemed to generate evil.

During the last of January 1831, Elder Rigdon drove Joseph Smith in a sleigh from New York to the Reserve. Most of his followers there were now prepared to accept Joseph as their prophet, and his personal appearance generated an atmosphere of rejoicing and spiritual bliss. There were miraculous healings, the exercise of heavenly gifts, and the thrill of associating with a modern-day prophet.

About this time, in February 1831, Rosetta Snow heard a knock at the door. She could not imagine who it could be; there were few visitors to their home during the winter. As she opened the door, a twenty-six-year-old man with sandy hair stood before her. It was Joseph Smith! After inviting him in to warm himself in front of the fire, she called her husband, Oliver, and their seven children down to meet this new prophet whom the family had first heard of a few months earlier.

Rosetta's twenty-six-year-old daughter, Eliza Roxcy, was especially fascinated. "I scrutinized his face as closely as I could without attracting his attention," she later wrote, "and decided that his was an honest face."

Prayerful investigation of Joseph's message and of the Christian gospel he preached during the next few weeks led Rosetta and her oldest daughter, Leonora, to be baptized. Rosetta was fifty-two, Leonora twenty-nine. They were followed within the next five years by Oliver, their daughter Eliza, and their son Lorenzo. Unknown to them at the time was that their commitment to the new faith would mean suffering, persecutions, being uprooted and moved numerous times, and being severely tested spiritually and emotionally. Rosetta would not live to see her beloved Eliza and Lorenzo rise to

positions of influence and leadership in the new religious community. Lorenzo would ultimately carry the family name to the very
helm of the Church, serving as fifth prophet, seer, and revelator.

Kirtland was located on a hill above the beautiful Chagrin
River Valley, some twenty-five miles north of Mantua. Converts to
the new Church of Christ, as it was then called, began to swarm
there. In discontinuing the "Family" that Elder Rigdon had set up
earlier, the Prophet introduced the Lord's plan for a well-ordered
community by practicing the law of consecration and the order of
stewardships. Rosetta's son Lorenzo would later establish a cooperative community in northern Utah under similar principles.

The Prophet also announced that he had received a revelation
that they should erect a holy building, a temple, on the crown of
the high bluff overlooking the valley of the east branch of the
Chagrin. The construction of this enduring mansion to God and
monument to Zion was to be a common enterprise, financed by
tithes and donated labor. Joseph Smith himself would serve as fore-
man in the quarry. The women would forward the work by knitting, sewing, and spinning clothes for the laborers. The Snows and
dozens of others would contribute of their means to help build it
during the years 1833 to 1836. All the materials except the glass
and hardware were taken from the forests of walnut, white oak, and
cherry and from the quarries in the vicinity of Kirtland.

After three years of labor, the temple was ready for dedication
on March 27, 1836. Impressive indeed were the dedicatory
ceremonies, attended by more than a thousand converts. Oliver
and Rosetta were probably there, although we have no direct evidence to be sure. There was an outpouring of spiritual gifts; people
spoke in tongues, some saw glorious visions, and there were visitations by angels. Joseph Smith himself was transported into the
Divine Presence and was visited by such ancient prophets as
Moses, Elias, and Elijah. The ceremony lasted just two days, but
the Saints lived in spiritual ecstasy for many weeks thereafter. (The
temple, owned today by the Reorganized Church of Jesus Christ of

Latter Day Saints, still stands serene and dignified among the trees
on the bluff south of the Chagrin River.)

Rosetta and Oliver continued to reside on their farm until
spring of 1837. By that time all of their family except their third
daughter, Amanda (who had previously married and moved away),
had joined the Church. Thirty-three-year-old Eliza, having joined
the Church in 1835, and being a woman of talent, was invited to
Church headquarters to teach "a select school for young ladies."
Lorenzo went to Oberlin in 1836. Oliver and Rosetta then sold
their farm early in 1837 and moved to Kirtland with their family,
which consisted of their two teenage sons, Lucius and Samuel, and
their daughter Leonora, and her two daughters. Although they
would remain in Kirtland less than a year, Rosetta and Oliver shel-
tered the Prophet for a period after one of his escapes from a mob.

When the tensions in Kirtland in 1838 made life difficult and
dangerous, Church leaders and their faithful followers, many hundreds of them, went to the new gathering place at Adam-ondi-
Ahman, near Far West, Missouri, more than one thousand miles to
the west. There the Snows purchased a double log house.

Despite their firm resolves and high hopes, however, the Saints
had to move again less than a year later. Old-time Missourians
resented the newcomers and their restored gospel of Christ. Fearful
of civil war, the governor ordered the Mormons to clear out, on
pain of extermination. Early in 1839, the Snows, along with several
thousand other Saints, moved to Quincy, Illinois, where the people
were more sympathetic and hospitable. They later moved north
and west to the new city of Nauvoo, which Joseph Smith, Sidney
Rigdon, and others established as the new gathering place for the
Saints. Something of Rosetta's state of health during these perilous
times is suggested by Eliza's mention of the move from Adam-ondi-
Ahman, when Rosetta's daughters sat by her all night so she could
sleep and not be stepped on by other people in the same cabin.

With their settlement in Nauvoo, the Snow family was once
again united after numerous separations. Except for Melissa, who

had died in Mantua, and Amanda, who stayed with her husband in Mantua, Rosetta and Oliver were together, albeit briefly, with their children. Lorenzo, who was baptized in 1836, was back in Nauvoo, having served a mission to the Eastern States (but he was soon to be called on another mission, this time to England).

Rosetta found many friends. She joined the Female Relief Society at their meeting on April 28, 1842, in the Nauvoo Lodge Room. Joseph Smith was present on this occasion and stated, "I now turn the key to you in the name of God, and this Society shall rejoice, and knowledge and intelligence shall flow down from this time—this is the beginning of better days to this Society." Rosetta's daughter Eliza served as secretary of this first Relief Society.

The spring of 1842, however, was a time of great turmoil for the Snow family. John C. Bennett, a counselor to Joseph Smith and mayor of the city, lost his faith and began delivering a series of anti-Mormon lectures. He also published a history of Mormonism that purported to be an exposé of its secret practices. Oliver Snow, who was inclined to be critical of people in authority, decided to leave. He bought a home in Walnut Grove, Knox County, Illinois, some seventy-five miles east of Nauvoo, and moved his family there. Rosetta did not want to go, but eventually she acquiesced and went with him. Eliza reflected in her journal her sorrow that her parents "did not in their trials draw out from the springs of consolation which the gospel presents, that support which was their privilege, and which would have enabled them to rejoice in the midst of tribulation and disappointment." Eliza, of course, remained with the Church in Nauvoo, teaching a school that included the Prophet's children. Lorenzo was on a proselyting mission in England.

The exodus to Utah completed the separation of the Snow family. Oliver died in October 1845, just four months before the Saints left Nauvoo. And on December 22, 1846, Eliza, having gone with the Saints to Winter Quarters, got word of her mother's death two months earlier on October 12. Rosetta was sixty-seven years old.

Rosetta's children proved loyal and helpful during her last days, and three of them went on to make substantial contributions to the latter-day kingdom. Leonora and her second husband, Isaac Morley, helped to colonize Manti, Utah; and after Isaac's death, Leonora was a much-respected mother-figure for the settlers of that area. Eliza, "Zion's Poetess," became general president of the Relief Society in 1867 and remained so until her death in 1888. Lorenzo, ordained an apostle in 1849, founded the progressive community of Brigham City, in northern Utah, and finally became President of the Church in 1898, serving until his death in 1901. Through such children, Rosetta lived on among the Latter-day Saints.

Perhaps the most fitting tribute to Rosetta was paid by Eliza in the journal entry she made after being told of her mother's death: "About the last of December I received the sad news of the death of my mother, in which, altho' accompanied with a feeling of heavy bereavement, I realized a sweet, soothing sensation in the thought that she was free from all earthly ills. She had lived a good age, and been a patient participator in the scenes of suffering through the persecutions of the Saints. Her mortal remains sleep in peace—her grave, and that of my father, whose death preceded hers less than a year, are side by side, in Walnut Grove, Knox Co., Illinois."

SOURCES

In the absence of any papers of Rosetta Snow, we have used existing papers of Lorenzo Snow, LDS Church Historical Archives, Salt Lake City; Journal and Notebook of Eliza R. Snow, Church Archives, Salt Lake City; Eliza R. Snow Journal, 1846–1849, Henry E. Huntington Library and Art Gallery, San Marino, California; and Eliza R. Snow, "Sketch of My Life," holograph, Bancroft Library, Berkeley, California. We have also made extensive use of Orrin Harmon, "Historical Facts Appertaining to the Township of Mantua," photographic copy of handwritten manuscript, 1866, in possession of Maureen Ursenbach Beecher. The original is in the Western Reserve Historical Society, Cleveland, Ohio. Harmon was the town clerk of Mantua, Ohio, in the early nineteenth century.

Biographies of Lorenzo Snow that have been helpful include Eliza R. Snow

Smith, *Biography and Family Record of Lorenzo Snow* (Salt Lake City: Deseret News Company, 1884); Thomas C. Romney, *The Life of Lorenzo Snow* (Salt Lake City: Sons of Utah Pioneers Memorial Foundation, 1955); Francis Gibbons, *Lorenzo Snow: Spiritual Giant, Prophet of God* (Salt Lake City: Deseret Book, 1982); and Clyde J. Williams, ed., *The Teachings of Lorenzo Snow* (Salt Lake City: Bookcraft, 1984). Shorter biographies include Preston Nibley, "Lorenzo Snow," in *The Presidents of the Church* (Salt Lake City: Deseret Book, 1971), pp. 137–76, and Heidi S. Swinton, "Lorenzo Snow," in Leonard J. Arrington, ed., *The Presidents of the Church* (Salt Lake City: Deseret Book, 1986), pp. 145–76.

Eliza R. Snow, An Immortal (Salt Lake City: Nicholas G. Morgan Sr. Foundation, 1957) is a collection of her writings, autobiography, and poems. Biographical essays, all by Maureen Ursenbach Beecher, include "Eliza: A Woman and a Sister," *New Era* 4 (October 1974): 10–16; "The Eliza Enigma: The Life and Legend of Eliza R. Snow," in *Charles Redd Monographs in Western History* 6 (1974–1975): 29–46; "Eliza R. Snow," in Claudia L. Bushman, ed., *Mormon Sisters: Women in Early Utah* (Cambridge, Massachusetts: Emmeline Press, 1976), pp. 25–41; "Eliza R. Snow's Nauvoo Journal," *Brigham Young University Studies* 15 (Summer 1975): 391–416; "Leonora, Eliza, and Lorenzo: An Affectionate Portrait of the Snow Family," *Ensign* 10 (June 1980): 64–69; and "Eliza and Her Sisters: Nineteenth Century Mormon Women," typescript in possession of the author, Salt Lake City.

The best history of the Western Reserve is Harlan Hatcher, *The Western Reserve: The Story of New Connecticut in Ohio* (Indianapolis, Indiana: The Bobbs-Merrill Company, 1949).

Local histories that mention the Snows and their environs include *History of Portage County, Ohio* (Chicago, 1885); Lucius I. Barber, "Simsbury," in *Memorial History of Hartford County, Connecticut* (Boston, 1886); *Rolls and Lists of Connecticut Men in the Revolution, 1775–1783* (Hartford: Connecticut Historical Society, 1901); *Rolls of Connecticut Men in the French and Indian War, 1755–1762* (Hartford: Connecticut Historical Society, 1903).

Genealogical sheets on the family are in the Family History Library, Salt Lake City. Also located in that library and in the Cache Family History Center, Logan, is VaLoie R. Hill, "Ancestors of Lorenzo Snow," photocopy of a typescript, 1973.

MARY FIELDING SMITH

O! my God, how I love and cherish true Motherhood!
Nothing beneath the celestial kingdom can surpass my
deathless love for the sweet, true, noble soul who gave
me birth. My own, own Mother. O! she was good! She
was true! She was indeed a Saint! A royal daughter of
God! To her I owe my very existence, as also my success in life, coupled with the favor and mercy of God.
—*Joseph F. Smith*

In 1793 John Fielding, forty-four-year-old resident of Halifax, Yorkshire, in northern England, received an invitation to become a tenant on one of his uncle's farms in Honidon (also spelled Honeydon), Bedfordshire, some fifty miles northeast of London. A Methodist minister, John had been married for three years to Rachel Ibbotson, also of Halifax, and their union had been blessed by two sons in addition to Sarah, child of John's first marriage. Rachel, who had first become converted to Methodism at age sixteen, was now twenty-five, and she and John had every expectation of remaining in Halifax the remainder of their days.

Upon receipt of the invitation, John, more out of family loyalty than of the desire to make a change, journeyed to Honidon and looked over his uncle's house and farm. He was not favorably impressed. As he began his return to Halifax, however, he opened his Bible, as he did at every opportunity, and noticed a passage that appeared so remarkably appropriate that he felt the Lord was telling him Honidon should be his future residence.

When John returned to Rachel, he honestly reported the unpromising nature of the Honidon situation, and this was seconded by the servant who accompanied him. There followed a long discussion, after which John decided once more to settle the matter by opening the Bible. His eyes settled on a passage similar to the one he had previously noted. He could no longer doubt that the Lord wanted him to move to Honidon. Rachel, herself a strong believer, nevertheless found the decision a trial.

About the middle of May 1794, they arrived in Honidon, a country village nine miles northeast of Bedford, a market town of about 6,000 inhabitants on the River Ouse. To use the words of one of their children, "They had exchanged a populous town for a lonely village; a large and commodious house for a small and inconvenient cottage, a circle of friends and relations for a place in which every face and character were to them alike unknown; and the immediate neighborhood of a Methodist chapel for a place four miles distant from one." Nevertheless, they decided the Lord was putting their Christian graces to the trial. They remembered the Lord's assurance that "As thy days, so shall thy strength be." (Deuteronomy 33:25.)

Although they expressed gratitude many times later for having made the move, because of the opportunity it offered for Christian service, their principal disappointment was in the uncle, James Dyson. They had every reason to expect from him kindness and forbearance; instead he was unreasonably harsh and severe. Only by the most diligent industry, economy, and frugality were they able to bring up their large family.

Rachel was unusually subject to divine impressions. When she was fourteen her mother died, and a few months later her father also. She was taken by an uncle, a medical doctor, to raise. Her life with her uncle's family was happy and carefree, and she took up such "worldly amusements" as playing cards, attending the theater, and wearing elegant dresses. One day when she was twenty-one, while she was taking a Sunday walk with a friend, she passed a woman on her way to a house of worship. Rachel immediately stopped and exclaimed, "Oh, how I wish I was like that woman!" She then turned around and followed the woman to the Methodist chapel. The preacher was a powerful persuader. "Convinced of sin," in accordance with the description for those converted to Methodism, Rachel began at that time, according to a daughter, "her journey to the kingdom of heaven."

Some time later, against her better judgment, Rachel allowed her friends to persuade her to attend a play. She was so distressed with the performance that she vowed she would never again go to the theater, and she kept that vow the rest of her life.

At the age of twenty-three Rachel married John, who at the time was already a Methodist preacher. Not long afterward, invited to spend a day with him in the country, she went to her room and prayed that she would never do anything that would give offense to God. Upon her return from the outing at the end of the day, she felt an assurance that her prayer had been answered. "The love of God was shed abroad in her heart," her daughter wrote, "and she could rejoice in His forgiving love, His Spirit bearing witness to her spirit that she was a child of God." She then repeated the lines of an appropriate hymn:

> My God is reconciled,
> His pardoning voice I hear;
> He owns me for his child,
> I can no longer fear;
> With confidence I now draw nigh,
> And, Father, Abba, Father, cry!

She was now as happy as she imagined she could ever be. Her cup ran over. Soon she had two sons, born in Halifax. Then came the move to Honidon—with its trials and vexations. There were also eight more children, four sons and four daughters. With John's daughter Sarah, that made a total of eleven, only two of whom died in infancy. The one in which we have particular interest was Mary, born in Honidon on July 21, 1801, John and Rachel's sixth child and second daughter.

Mary was inevitably influenced by her mother. Rachel was a good manager and provided well for her children and for her husband's parishioners. She also tried to cultivate their spirituality by indicating God's mercy, by administering a word of exhortation, and by taking her family, good weather or bad, to the Sunday Methodist services at St. Neot's, a four-mile walk. By taking a large share of the family responsibilities upon herself, Rachel left her husband more freedom to fulfill religious and pulpit engagements. "His temporal comfort and spiritual prosperity lay near her heart," wrote her daughter. Rachel was a real helpmeet for John.

Rachel was fond of reading, especially the Bible, which, to her, was as daily food. She also read works of Christian commentary, including the *Wesleyan Magazine*. She often introduced the subject of religion in groups in which she was present. She was particularly pleased that her oldest daughter, Ann, married a minister who effected a union of the local Church of England and the Methodist Church and served as curate of Colmworth Parish, the chapel of which was just a mile from her home in Honidon. Rachel died, apparently of a heart attack, in 1828, when she was sixty-one. Her husband, John, died eight years later, at age seventy-six. Rachel's last words, as befitted one who had lived forty years as a devout Christian, were: "Jesus is my Saviour. I cannot doubt. I have felt of late an unusual deadness to the world. Whenever I have seen anything that has for the moment given me pleasure, I have turned from it and said, 'O this will not do! My God, and my all; my God, and my all.'" At her funeral the following Sunday at St. Neot's Methodist Chapel, the Reverend James Golding used as his text, "Therefore be ye also ready: for in such an hour as ye think not the Son of Man cometh." (Matthew 24:44.)

The following is a list of children of Rachel and John (John's daughter Sarah is not included), the year of their birth, and the

considerable number of them whose lifelong profession was
Methodism:

1. John, 1791; a well-to-do farmer in Gravely, Bedfordshire,
   and an ardent Methodist.
2. James, 1793; pastor of the Methodist Church in Preston,
   Lancashire, England.
3. Thomas, 1795; active in the Church of England in
   Papworth, Bedfordshire.
4. Joseph, 1797; went to Canada in 1832. More of him later.
5. Ann, 1799; married T. R. Matthews, curate of the
   combined Church of England–Methodist Church of
   Colmworth, Bedfordshire.
6. Mary, 1801; went to Canada in 1834. More of her later.
7. Martha Ibbotson, 1803; married Peter Watson. Donated to
   early Mormon missionaries but remained unbaptized.
8. Benjamin, 1805; died as a baby.
9. Mercy Rachel, 1807; went to Canada in 1832. More of her
   later.
10. Josiah, 1809; died as a baby.

It was a religious family, and each of the members was strongly
influenced by the forceful and enthusiastic Methodist teachings of
Rachel and John. Mary, for example, as with her brothers and sisters, was brought up to be a trusting person, willing to "depend
upon the unseen hand of our Heavenly Father." Believing that suffering is a necessary part of life for the righteous, and that the
proper response to problems is not despair but hope, she accepted
the biblical promise that "all things work together for good to them
that love God." (Romans 8:28.)

Upon the death of Rachel, her son Joseph went to Gravely,
Bedfordshire, to work for his brother John. He was compassion-
ately looked after by his brother's wife, and active in the local
Methodist Church. But in 1832, as with many other young
Englishmen (including John Taylor), Joseph and his sister Mercy,

now twenty-four, decided to migrate to Canada. They located on a farm at Chesleton Settlement, a few miles from York, later Toronto. Joseph did well as a farmer and was a reasonably active Methodist, though an independent-minded one. Preoccupied with the Millennium, he became convinced that biblical doctrine in its completeness was not fully understood by the Christian denominations of the day. He lost confidence in the pastors he had heard, and prayed the Lord to "send us the Gospel in its fullness and power."

In 1834, Mary, now thirty-three and still unmarried, joined Joseph and Mercy in Canada. The three often attended meetings held by disenchanted Methodists in the York area. In this way they became acquainted with John and Leonora Taylor.

From the story of Agnes Taylor, mother of John Taylor, it will be recalled that when Parley P. Pratt went to York (now Toronto) in the spring of 1836, he carried with him an introduction to John Taylor, the semiofficial leader of the little group of Methodist seekers in the Toronto region. Finding no encouragement there, he was about to leave when he met Izabella Walton, a widow who had stopped by. Out of fairness, Mrs. Walton opened her home to the Mormon missionary, and it was there that John Taylor listened to Elder Pratt and, with increasing interest in his message, volunteered to take him out to the farming settlement where the Fieldings lived.

News of their coming preceded them, and when Mary and Mercy saw them approach, they ran to a neighboring house "lest we should give welcome or give countenance to 'Mormonism.'" Joseph Fielding said that he was sorry they had come, and the Methodist meetinghouse was closed to them. When Elder Pratt inquired why Joseph and his sisters opposed Mormonism, Joseph lamely replied that the name Mormonism had a contemptible sound, and anyway, "We do not want a new revelation or a new religion contrary to the Bible." Elder Pratt smiled and said that if Mr. Fielding would call his sisters home and provide supper for everyone, "I will agree to preach the old Bible gospel, and leave out

Two of Mary Fielding Smith's grandsons, David A. Smith and
Joseph Fielding Smith, visit Black Creek, near present-day
Toronto, Canada, where Mary was baptized in 1836.

all new revelations which are opposed to it." An honest man,
Joseph agreed; Elder Pratt reported that "the young ladies came
home, got us a good supper, and all went to the meeting." "The
house was crowded," he added; "I preached, and the people wished
to hear more. In a few days we baptized Brother Joseph Fielding
and his two amiable and intelligent sisters. . . . We organized a
branch of the Church, for the people there drank in truth as water,
and loved it as they loved life."

Joseph Fielding wrote: "I soon discovered that he [Elder Pratt]
had the Spirit and Power of God and such Wisdom as none but
God himself could have given to man, by which he could explain
those prophecies of which the preachers of the day were ignorant,
showing the great design and connection of the scriptures throughout. He also spoke of and introduced the Book of Mormon. . . . He
at the same time said that the angel made known the record of the
fallen people, the Nephites. . . . It was necessary that the Covenant

should be renewed before a pure Church could be built up, to have the ordinances, gifts, and blessings of the Church of Jesus Christ as established by Himself; also that the Day of the Lord was nigh at hand, that those prophecies which speak of that great and dreadful day, in which the wicked should be cut off and the earth purified by fire, to prepare it for the coming of Christ to reign thereon with his Wants, was nigh at hand, even that the present generation should not all pass away until all those things should be fulfilled. Elder Pratt laid before us the ordinances of the Gospel, which were very plain, being perfectly in accordance with the scripture, being still more clearly expressed in the Book of Mormon."

On May 21, 1836, Joseph, Mary, and Mercy Fielding were baptized in a stream called Black Creek on Joseph's property, and the following spring they joined the Saints in Kirtland, Ohio.

The arrival of Mary and Mercy in Kirtland created quite a stir. Still single, they were both pretty, personable, well educated, and imparted an enthusiasm for the gospel that was contagious. Their entrance came at a time of dissent and division that was eroding the morale of many of the Kirtland Saints. Joseph Fielding wrote in his diary, "I found the Saints were far from being all righteous. There was great contention among them." But all three Fieldings stood fast. As Mary later wrote in a letter to Mercy: "Notwithstanding all of our defects, this is the only Church of Christ."

Shortly after their arrival in Kirtland, Mercy married Robert Thompson, a former Yorkshireman and former Methodist who had also migrated to York, Canada, and who was also baptized in May 1836 by Elder Pratt. The Thompsons soon left on a yearlong mission to the Toronto region. About the same time Joseph Fielding responded to a call to serve as a proselyting missionary in Great Britain. He joined Heber C. Kimball, Orson Hyde, Willard Richards, and others, remaining there four years. During two of those years he served as president of the British Mission. He was, however, unable to realize his most fervent hope, that he could convert his brothers and sisters.

While Joseph was away, Mary became acquainted with Vilate Kimball, whose husband, Heber C. Kimball, was also in England on a mission. Mary accepted Sister Kimball's invitation to live with her and remained several months. Mary referred to Sister Kimball as "a Christian old friend." She was kind, gave friendly counsel, and treated Mary as she would her own sister. The two of them occasionally had dinner with Joseph Smith and other Church leaders, including their wives and other leading women. When some of the brethren disputed the Prophet's leadership, Mary stood firmly behind him. She was certain that he would "yet stand in his place and accomplish the work God has given him to do, however much many seek his removal."

Mary took employment in August 1837 as a live-in teacher and governess for the children of David and Fanny Dort, who, because of the death of their mother (the eldest daughter of Temperance Mack, Lucy Mack Smith's sister-in-law) in 1827, were now under the care of their father and new stepmother, Mary (Polly) Dort. Fanny's younger sister was Almira Covey. In this way, Mary inevitably became acquainted with the Smith family.

Mary's admiration and affection for the Smiths is revealed in her letter of July 8, 1837, to Mercy. (Mary's letters are beautifully written in a handwriting style reminiscent of fine lace—small so she could get as much as possible on a page. The letters are lively and filled with Mary's personal worries and reflections.) At a meeting in the Kirtland Temple on a Sunday in June, Mary reported, it was gratifying to see "the venerable Patriarch [Joseph Smith Sr.] with his two aged brothers [presumably John and Jesse] in the upper stand, and in the next, four of his sons with President [Sidney] Rigdon in their midst, all I believe faithful servants of the Living God. Joseph and Hyrum I know best and love much. While I looked at them all my heart was drawn out in earnest prayer to our Heavenly Father in their behalf, and also for the Prophetess, their aged mother, whose eyes are frequently bathed in tears when she looks at or speaks of them."

Mary reported that she and others believed that angels were present at the meeting: "a bright light shone across the house and rested upon the congregation." She felt confident that the Church would continue to enjoy God's blessings and that the kingdom of God would prosper. "The Lord knows what our intentions are and He will support us and give us grace and strength for the day if we continue to put our trust in Him and devote ourselves unreservedly to His service."

Shortly after arriving in Kirtland, Mary, thirty-six and still unmarried, went to Joseph Smith Sr. for a patriarchal blessing. That blessing said, in part: "Thy heart is now pure. If thou wilt keep the commandments of God, from this time, no blessing shall be withheld from thee—none shall be too great. Thou shalt have all the righteous desires of thy heart. The Lord is willing that thou shouldest have a companion in Life—a man after thy own heart—thy children shall be blest of the Lord."

Mary had passed up opportunities to marry while she was still in England. Indeed, among her papers in the Church Archives are two drafts of letters, presumably sent, declining offers of marriage. The key sentence in the first letter is: "I never intend, whether I am right or wrong, to be united to any person whose religious sentiments do not agree with my own." This was essential, she explained, because "marriage is a matter of the greatest importance next to the salvation of the Lord." The key sentence in the second letter is: "It is the strong impression made upon my mind by the advice of my dear departed parent [Rachel] never to enter into the important and responsible situation of stepmother." The reference is obviously to Rachel's relationship with her husband's daughter Sarah. Having seen that situation again in the fall of 1837 when she worked for Polly Dort, Mary remarked in a letter to Mercy, "I desire [that situation] as little as ever I did."

But a tragedy occurred that caused her to change that opinion. On September 27, 1837, Joseph and Hyrum Smith and other Church leaders departed for Missouri to supervise the expansion of the Church in Far West and other nearby communities, leaving their wives behind. For Hyrum, leaving must have been especially difficult, for his wife, Jerusha, was about to deliver their fifth child. Nevertheless, the trip, which would take several weeks, seemed to be imperative.

A few days after he arrived in Far West, Hyrum received a letter from his brother Samuel in Kirtland, dated October 13, informing him that Jerusha had just died after giving birth a few days earlier to a healthy daughter. "We have done all that we could to save Jerusha, but in vain," Samuel said. In a postscript, younger brother Don Carlos Smith wrote, "Tell Hyrum that I shall take as good care of his family as I can until he returns." Although he left immediately, Hyrum was not back in Kirtland until early December. His brother Joseph soon followed.

According to the Smith family, Joseph inquired of the Lord what should be done, and he was instructed that Hyrum should marry the English convert, Mary Fielding. On December 24, 1837, just three weeks after his sad return from Missouri, Hyrum married Mary in Kirtland. Hyrum said later, "It was not because I had less love or regard for Jerusha that I married so soon, but it was for the sake of my children." There were five children under the age of ten. As for Mary, she certainly would not have undertaken the task of becoming mother to Hyrum's children had she not believed it to be the express will of the Lord.

Events in Kirtland were making it urgent for the Saints to leave. Their leaders were being hounded by mobs and lawsuits; their economy was faltering; their political future was unpromising. Late in December Brigham Young was forced to flee, and Joseph Smith and other leaders left in January. By April 1838, most of the faithful had left Kirtland for Missouri.

Hyrum and Mary left Kirtland in early March of 1838. Their family included Lovina, ten; John, five; Hyrum, three; Jerusha, two; and Sarah, just a few months old. The household also included "Aunty" Hannah Grinnels, who tended to the children after

Mary Fielding Smith and her husband, Hyrum Smith

Jerusha's illness and death, and an old British soldier they had looked after, George Mills. Mary learned valuable lessons in managing things as they traveled. They arrived in Far West in late May after a trip that Hyrum described as characterized by "many privations and much fatigue."

Hyrum arranged for farming land and a temporary house in Far West. "I fondly hoped, and anticipated the pleasure of spending a season in peace," he said. But it was not to be. Cattle and horses were stolen; people were forced from their homes and farms; fields of wheat and granaries were set afire. Finally, Governor Lilburn W. Boggs, who wanted an end to "the Mormon problem," sent out the militia with orders to drive the Mormons from the state. When Joseph Smith, Sidney Rigdon, and three other officials approached the camp of the general of the state militia under a flag of truce to negotiate a surrender, the general arrested them. The next day, November 1, the militia picked up Hyrum and placed him under guard as well. Although a secret court of officers ordered the prisoners shot, the colonel in charge refused to carry it out, so they were ordered to jail. After much importuning, they were permitted a brief visit to their homes to get clothing. Ill and heavy with child,

Mary commended her husband to God, saying "if indeed there is no God I should never expect to see you again in this world."

After spending time in jail in Jackson County and in Richmond, Ray County, Missouri, Hyrum, Joseph, and the other prisoners were sent to Liberty Jail in Clay County on November 30. They would remain there four months. During some of the period they were chained together in the dungeon.

On November 13, 1838, just a few days after Hyrum had been forced from his home at gunpoint, Mary gave birth to a son. He was named Joseph F. (for Fielding) Smith, and one day he would become President of the Church. Mary wrote: "Shortly after his birth I took a severe cold, which brought on chills and fever: this, together with the anxiety of mind I had to endure, threatened to bring me to the gates of death. I was at least four months entirely unable to take any care either of myself or the child; but the Lord was merciful in so ordering things that my dear sister [Mercy] could be with me at the time. Her child [Mary Jane] was five months old when mine was born; so she had strength given her to nurse them both, so as to have them do well and grow fast."

Latter-day Saint leaders, particularly Brigham Young, determined that the members had no alternative but to leave Missouri, and so, family by family, they walked or rode across the border into Illinois and set up a temporary camp at Quincy. Hyrum pleaded for Mary to bring little Joseph F. to visit him at the jail before they left (Liberty Jail was forty miles from Far West). Early in February, despite Mary's sickness, she and Mercy traveled on a bed on a wagon, possibly driven by Joseph and Hyrum's brother Don Carlos, to the jail. Their joy at seeing Hyrum was blunted by the fearful forebodings, but at least they spent a night. When the women left, they reported "the creeking hinges of the door closed on the noblest men on earth."

Later in February the women were transported on a bed in a wagon to Quincy. Mary gradually recovered, and the family in her charge, including little Joseph F., got along fine. On April 15

Missouri state officials, chagrined that they had no case against the prisoners, allowed them to escape. Within a week Hyrum was back with his family, this time in Quincy. The next month Mary and Hyrum and their children, along with several thousand other Saints, moved to Commerce (renamed Nauvoo), a town on the Mississippi River on the western border of Illinois.

Mary's years in Nauvoo were full of challenges. Hyrum was elected to the first city council, later served as vice-mayor, was assistant president of the Church, and was patriarch to the Church after the death of his father, Joseph Smith Sr., in 1840. He was nearly always at the side of his younger brother, Joseph the Prophet. So Mary inevitably had a public life that made her domestic life with her stepchildren even more difficult than it might have been if she could have given them her full attention. She also handled many of Hyrum's business transactions. She was always positive, always full of faith and hope, but her frustrations occasionally came out, as when she signed an 1842 letter to Hyrum, who was on a tour of Church branches in the Northeast, "Your faithful Companion and Friend but unhappy StepMother, M. Smith." She apparently felt that her best efforts were not always appreciated. Her challenges may not have been insurmountable, but she appreciated occasional reassurances.

On May 14, 1841, Mary was delivered of a daughter, Martha Ann. The joy occasioned by that birth, however, was shortly blunted by the death of Hyrum Jr. He was seven. Other deaths occurring during the fall of 1841 were those of Don Carlos Smith, brother of Hyrum, and Robert B. Thompson, husband of Mercy. Each was intelligent and skilled in writing, as well as especially helpful to Mary and her children.

A greater cause of anxiety was the continued difficulties of the Saints with their neighbors in Illinois. Hyrum was almost as vulnerable as his brother Joseph. There were threats; there were burnings and shootings. The mob-militia, as it was called, was vindictive and vicious. Mary called on the sick, attended meetings, and inaugurated the Sisters Penny Subscription to buy nails and glass for the Nauvoo Temple, but the general atmosphere was increasingly turbulent. Finally, on June 27, 1844, Joseph and Hyrum Smith were assassinated while being held in jail at Carthage, Illinois.

When Mary learned the news of her husband's death, according to Martha Ann, "she fell back against the bureau. The news flew like wildfire through the house. The crying and agony that went through that house and the anguish and sorrow that were felt can be easier felt than described."

The bodies were returned from Carthage, and Mary summoned her reserves of physical and spiritual strength to maintain a reverent composure in front of the children. An observer wrote:

"She [Mary] trembled at every step, and nearly fell, but reached her husband's body, kneeled down by him, clasped her arm around his head, turned his pale face upon her heaving bosom, and then a gushing, plaintive wail burst from her lips! 'Oh! Hyrum, Hyrum! Have they shot you, my dear Hyrum—are you dead? Oh, speak to me, my dear husband. I cannot think you are dead, my dear Hyrum.' She drew him closer to her bosom, kissed his pale lips and face, put her hands on his brow and brushed back his hair. Her grief seemed to consume her, and she lost all power of utterance.

"Her three daughters, and two young children clung, some around her neck, and some to her body, falling prostrate upon the corpse, and shrieking in the wildness of their wordless grief."

It was inevitable, of course, that the Saints should leave Illinois, as they had left New York and Ohio and Missouri. Mary was reluctant to leave, though she knew she would have to. Mary, Mercy, and their brother Joseph Fielding were among the last to leave, in the fall of 1846. By now, little Joseph F. was eight years old and Martha Ann five. Lovina was now married and had her own protector. John was fourteen, Jerusha eleven, and Sarah ten. Martha Ann described their leave-taking:

"We left our home just as it was, our furniture, and the fruit trees hanging full of rosy cheeked peaches. We bid good-bye to the loved home that reminded us of our beloved father everywhere we turned.

"I was five years old when we started from Nauvoo. We crossed over the Mississippi in the skiff in the dusk of the evening. We bid goodbye to our dear old feeble grandmother [Lucy Mack Smith]. I can never forget the bitter tears she shed when she bid us goodbye. . . . She knew it would be the last time she would see her son's family."

Mary's caravan was comprised of nine wagons, six of them belonging to her, one to Mercy Thompson, and two to Joseph Fielding. Mary's group totaled eighteen people; in Mercy's group was Mercy's little daughter Mary Jane; and in Joseph's group were nine people. In addition to their teams, they had twenty-one loose cattle and forty-three sheep. They finally arrived at Winter Quarters on October 21, 1846. They had now joined the main body of the Church. They would remain there until the spring of 1848—a stopover of about eighteen months.

In the fall of 1847, Mary decided to go to St. Joseph, Missouri, 160 miles away, to get food and clothing. She took with her Joseph F., Martha Ann, and her brother Joseph. They traveled in two wagons with two yokes of oxen on each. Joseph F., then nine, served as teamster. On their way back, as Joseph F. later recounted, they camped one evening on an open prairie on the Missouri River bottoms, by the side of a small spring creek. There they turned out their oxen to feed. The next morning they could not find their best yoke of oxen. Joseph F. and Joseph Fielding searched through the tall grass all morning, but they were not to be found. As Joseph F. returned to camp about noon, he saw his mother kneeling in prayer. He approached closely enough to hear her plead with the Lord not to leave them in a helpless condition, without a way of getting back. When she arose, she was smiling. In a few minutes her brother Joseph returned declaring, "Well, Mary, the cattle are gone!" Mary replied, "Never mind. Your breakfast has been waiting for hours. While you and Joseph are eating, I'll just walk out and see if I can find the cattle." "No chance," insisted Joseph. "We've been all over this country and they are not to be found. They've been driven off by someone, and it is useless for you to hunt for them." Paying no attention to him, Mary followed a little stream toward the river until she was almost on the bank, then beckoned to her brother and her son. "I outran my uncle and came first to the spot where my mother stood," said Joseph F. "There I saw our ox team fastened to a clump of willows growing in the bottom of a deep gulch which had been washed out of the sandy bank of the river by the little spring creek, perfectly concealed from view." Then he added, "We were soon on our way rejoicing."

It was natural perhaps that Mary and her children and stepchildren, Mercy and her children, and her brother Joseph Fielding and his group should make the trek to the Salt Lake Valley with President Heber C. Kimball's company in 1848. Mary had stayed with the Kimballs when Mercy was in Canada and her brother was in England, and President Kimball had committed himself to look after her, as of a wife, after the death of Hyrum. He was always kind and helpful. Mercy and Mary Jane had already gone west, traveling in Parley P. Pratt's company in the fall of 1847.

It was not easy for Mary and her brother to put together an outfit. Eleven of Mary's thirteen horses died in Winter Quarters, making it necessary to use wild steers, cows, and half-grown oxen to pull the wagons. The Indians had stolen most of her cattle. She had to have food enough to last several months, clothing, and firearms, powder, and lead. Her group, consisting of nine people, was assigned to the Third Ten of Captain Peter Lott, a venerable man who had enjoyed the esteem of both Joseph Smith and Brigham Young. Captain Lott would not leave without her, though she continued to delay him. Until the last moment there was real question as to whether she should go on or go back.

When Mary and her group finally reached Captain Lott's rendezvous point, he looked over her outfit and shook his head. It was folly for her to start under such conditions. She would not make it without considerable help, making her a burden on the whole company. After her valiant efforts to put together her outfit, Mary was hurt but determined. With only a moment's thought, she told the captain she would beat him to the valley—and without asking any help from him.

Mary had many resources—Heber C. Kimball, for example, and Howard Egan, and others. She had helped many people in months and years past; now they were prepared to help her. She and Joseph and the children joined the main company at the Elk Horn and headed west. They had four wagons (two of their own and two hired) and a big "ambulance," as they called it—a light wagon; each wagon was drawn by two yokes of oxen except for one that was drawn by two yokes of cows. They also had two additional cows and some sheep that had to be driven along in the rear. Captain Lott thought she should not come without reserve oxen; she was "traveling thin."

All went well until they reached a point midway between the Platte and the Sweetwater rivers. One of Mary's best oxen lay down, as if poisoned, and seemed to be stiffening in the throes of death. Captain Lott busied himself to help her out, but she wanted no help. She went to her wagon, came back with a bottle of consecrated oil, and asked her brother Joseph and James Lawson to administer to the fallen ox. After the prayer of healing was uttered, the moribund ox stirred, gathered its huge hind legs under it, stood, and started off as if nothing had happened. They hadn't gone far when another ox, "Old Bully," lay down under the same circumstances. Once more the holy ordinance was performed and the results were the same. The brave, fatherless family did well.

When they finally reached the edge of the Salt Lake Valley, on September 22, 1848, Mary, who by now was ahead of the captain, was elated—and thankful. She had brought Hyrum's and her own children to the Promised Valley. John, the oldest, turned sixteen the

day of their arrival. The next day they rolled down to the Old Fort
to spend their first winter in the new land.

Mary secured a lot at Second West and Second North streets.
Nearby were the lots of Joseph Fielding, Mercy Thompson, and
James Lawson. Wanting a farm, Mary rode out to Mill Creek, about
six miles southeast of the settlement, and found a place at the base
of a hill with cool water gushing forth to form a pool. She bought
the spring and forty acres of land. But they spent their first winter
in their wagons near the Old Fort. The next spring she started construction of a two-room adobe house, which was completed in
1850. Located then at what was later named 27th South and
Highland Drive, the cottage is now part of the Pioneer Village
located near This Is the Place Monument.

Mary's years were full of trials, but she did well. Her livestock
multiplied, her land produced abundantly, and she was respected
and admired by her neighbors and the members of the Salt Lake
Sixteenth Ward. One incident told by her son Joseph F. is worth
mentioning as an illustration of her determined faithfulness:

"One spring when we opened our potato pits she had her boys
get a load of the best potatoes, and she took them to the tithing
office; potatoes were scarce that season. I was a little boy at the time
[possibly eleven or twelve], and drove the team. When we drove
up to the steps of the tithing office ready to unload the potatoes,
one of the clerks came out and said to my mother: 'Widow Smith,
it's a shame that you should have to pay tithing.' He chided my
mother . . . [and] called her anything but wise and prudent. . . . My
mother turned upon him and said, 'William [Thompson], you
ought to be ashamed of yourself. Would you deny me a blessing?
If I did not pay my tithing I should expect the Lord to withhold his
blessings from me; I pay my tithing, not only because it is a law of
God but because I expect a blessing by doing it.'"

Mary still had the assistance of Hannah Grinnels in raising her
children and stepchildren, managing the household, and running
the farm. Her home was a place of industry, with a spinning wheel,

a carding rack, and a weaving frame. Martha Ann, along with her stepsisters, learned to spin and weave and to cut out and sew cloth for dresses, bedsheets, jeans, and men's clothing. Mary had horses, oxen, cows, sheep, pigs, and chickens to look after; land to be plowed, harrowed, leveled, and furrowed; crops to be planted, irrigated, weeded, and harvested; animals to be butchered and meat to be cured; vegetables and fruit to be picked or dug and stored; soap and butter to be made; ditches to be dug and bridges to be built. She also attended general conferences and ward fast and sacrament meetings, and, above all, visited her sister Mercy and brother Joseph.

After four years in the valley, her hair showing streaks of gray and lines beginning to form around her mouth and in her forehead, Mary caught cold while attending a public function and drove by the home of President Heber C. Kimball to rest and receive a blessing. But she did not recover. After two months of debilitating illness, probably pneumonia, she died on September 21, 1852. She was fifty-one.

At the time of her death Joseph F. was almost fourteen; Martha Ann was eleven. Of Hyrum's children by Jerusha, Lovina, of course, had married and had remained in the Midwest; John was nineteen, Jerusha fifteen, and Sarah fourteen. In the years after Mary's death, George A. Smith, a cousin of Hyrum's, an apostle, and later Church Historian and member of the First Presidency, took the family under his wing and supervised their upbringing with fondness and dedication. Joseph F. was ordained an apostle in 1866, served as a counselor in the First Presidencies of John Taylor, Wilford Woodruff, and Lorenzo Snow, and became President of the Church in 1901, serving until his death in 1918. Martha Ann married William J. Harris in 1857, lived most of her life in Provo, and had eleven children. She died in 1923 at age eighty-two. John married in 1853 when he was twenty, became the sixth Presiding Patriarch of the Church when his grandfather died in 1854, and served until his death in 1911. Jerusha married William Pierce in 1854 and lived until 1912; Sarah married Charles Griffin, also in 1854, and died in 1876 at age thirty-nine.

As for Mary's brother and sister in the Valley, Joseph located on a farm at Mill Creek not far from Mary's, became a member of the Legislative Council, raised a large family, and died in 1863 at age sixty-six. Late in her life Mercy visited relatives in Canada and also in England. She died in 1893 at age eighty-six.

SOURCES

There is a splendid collection of letters to and from Mary Fielding Smith in the LDS Church Archives, Salt Lake City. These cover primarily the period 1833 to 1848 and are particularly informative on the Church in the late 1830s and early 1840s. Some of these have been published in Kenneth M. Godfrey, Audrey M. Godfrey, and Jill Mulvay Derr, *Women's Voices: An Untold History of the Latter-day Saints, 1830–1900* (Salt Lake City: Deseret Book, 1982), pp. 58–68.

Early printed sources include Ann Fielding Matthews, "Memoir of Mrs. Rachel Fielding of Honidon, Bedfordshire," *Wesleyan: The Methodist Magazine,* August 1830, pp. 514–22; Edward W. Tullidge, *The Women of Mormondom* (New York, 1877), esp. pp. 224–25, 249–58, 344–49; and [Joseph F. Smith], "A Noble Woman's Experience," in *Heroines of "Mormondom"* (Salt Lake City: Juvenile Instructor Office, 1884), pp. 9–37.

The basic biography is Don C. Corbett, *Mary Fielding Smith: Daughter of Britain* (Salt Lake City: Deseret Book, 1966). Biographical sketches include Andrew Jenson, "Smith, Mary Fielding," in *Latter-day Saints' Biographical Encyclopedia,* 4 vols. (Salt Lake City: Andrew Jenson Historical Company, 1901–1936), 2:710–11; Susa Young Gates, "Mothers in Israel: Mary Fielding Smith, Wife of the Patriarch Hyrum Smith," *Relief Society Magazine* 3 (March 1916): 123–48; Ben E. Rich, "A Mother's Influence [contains a June 1839 letter of Mary to her brother Joseph]," in Ben E. Rich, *Scrap Book of Mormon Literature,* 2 vols. (Chicago: Ben E. Rich, 1913), 2:535–39; Gracia Denning, "The Role of Women in the Kirtland Era," given at Joseph Smith Sr. Family Reunion, Kirtland, Ohio, August 1977.

A particularly thoughtful discussion of Mary Fielding Smith as a role model in Mormon literature is Lavina Fielding Anderson, "Mary Fielding Smith: Her Ox Goes Marching On," in Maren M. Mouritsen, ed., *Blueprints for Living: Perspectives for Latter-day Saint Women, Volume Two* (Provo, Utah: Brigham Young University Press, 1980), pp. 2–13.

Biographies of Joseph F. Smith that contain references to his mother are Joseph Fielding Smith, *Life of Joseph F. Smith* (Salt Lake City: Deseret News Press, 1938); Francis M. Gibbons, *Joseph F. Smith: Patriarch and Preacher, Prophet of God* (Salt Lake City: Deseret Book, 1984); Scott Kenney, "Joseph F. Smith," in Leonard J. Arrington, ed., *The Presidents of the Church* (Salt Lake City: Deseret Book, 1986), pp. 179–209; and Preston Nibley, "Joseph F. Smith," in *The Presidents of the Church* (Salt Lake City: Deseret Book, 1971), pp. 179–215. Material relating to Mary Fielding as the wife of Hyrum is in Pearson H. Corbett, *Hyrum Smith, Patriarch* (Salt Lake City: Deseret Book, 1963).

We are particularly grateful to Ronald K. Esplin for the opportunity of perusing his unpublished manuscript, " 'Called to Endure': The Letters of Mary Fielding and Hyrum Smith." We are also grateful to the Fielding family for the typewritten "Diary of Joseph Fielding," which covers the years 1832 to 1859.

In the contemporary quotations, we have regularized the spelling and punctuation in some instances.

Rachel Ridgeway Ivins Grant

My mother was both father and mother to me, as father died when I was but nine days old. So near to the Lord would she get in her prayers that they were a wonderful inspiration to me from childhood to manhood. When she died, the Pacific Coast manager of the New York Life Insurance Company, who once boarded at our home, wrote me: "If the God of nature ever did stamp peace, nobility, and serenity upon any human countenance, He did upon the face of dear 'Aunt Rachel.'" "To know 'Aunt Rachel,'" as mother was affectionately called, "was to love her," is an expression I have heard times without number. I do not recall ever seeing her angry, or hearing her speak an unkind word. Mother was indeed a lovable character, always looking for the good in others, and never for their failings. She was truly a noble woman, a true Latter-day Saint.
—*Heber J. Grant*

In the fall of 1837, Jedediah M. Grant and two companion Mormon missionaries began a series of sermons in Hornerstown, an agricultural settlement near Trenton in central New Jersey. Twenty-three-year-old Elder Grant was a popular preacher and a good student of the Bible. He had read widely, was clever with words, and delighted his listeners with his humorous and quick-witted repartee. Those who heard his first sermon came back

110

Rachel Ridgeway Ivins Grant

and brought their friends. Among those who enjoyed his lectures were members of the Ivins family. One of them, eighteen-year-old Rachel Ridgeway (sometimes spelled Ridgway) Ivins, who was an active Baptist, did not at first take the Mormons seriously, concluding that "they were some of the false prophets that the Bible speaks of." She took advantage of an opportunity to visit relatives in Philadelphia and thus avoided them. But her older sister, Anna Lowrie Ivins, and some cousins attended the meeting and in a short time were baptized.

When Rachel returned home, she found Anna "filled with the spirit of the Gospel. . . . She urged me to attend the meetings with her." Wrote Rachel: "I went to the meeting on Saturday, but when she asked me to go on Sunday I did not know whether I ought to break the Sabbath day by going to hear them or not, but through

her persuasion and that of a schoolmate, who had come some distance on purpose to hear them, I finally went, but upon returning
home I went to my room, knelt down, and asked the Lord to forgive me for thus breaking the Sabbath day."

She attended more meetings, read the Book of Mormon, Parley P.
Pratt's *Voice of Warning,* and other literature, and was soon convinced that they were true. She wrote:

"A new light seemed to break in upon me, the scriptures were
plainer in my mind, and the light of the everlasting Gospel began
to illuminate my soul. While thus investigating, a little child died
whose mother had joined the Latter-day Saints. The Baptist minister preached about it, regretting that its parents had neglected to
have it baptized and thereby it was lost and could not have salvation. Afterwards Elder [Orson] Hyde preached the funeral sermon
and portrayed the glories of our Father's kingdom and the saved
condition of the little innocent ones who died before they came to
the years of accountability—'For of such is the kingdom of
heaven.'

"The contrast was very great. I was steadily being drawn into
the Gospel net. One day while attending the Baptist prayer meeting our pastor admonished me for the course I was taking and said
if I did not stop going to the 'Mormon' meetings I could not hold
my seat in the Baptist church, and they would be obliged to dis-
fellowship me for they could not fellowship anyone who would
listen to such false doctrine. This seemed to settle the question
with me. One wanted to hold me against my convictions, and the
other was free salvation without money and without price. I soon
handed my name [to the Mormons] for baptism and rendered willing obedience to the first four requirements of the Gospel of Jesus
Christ as revealed through the Prophet Joseph. . . . And, oh, what
joy filled my being!"

The mother of the man who would serve as prophet and president of the Church longer than any other person in the twentieth
century had joined the Church.

Rachel Ivins was born March 7, 1821, in Hornerstown, the sixth of eight children born to Caleb Ivins Jr. and Edith Ridgeway Ivins. Her father was a merchant and a descendant of Dutch and English immigrants who had come to America as early as 1680. Both his paternal and his maternal ancestors were Quakers, the religion of many residents in central and southern New Jersey. Rachel's mother, of English ancestry, was described as "a lovely, spirited woman, liked by all."

When Rachel was four, her father was incapacitated by a sunstroke; after two years of being cared for as if he were a little child, he died. Four years later, when Rachel was ten, her mother died. Now orphans, Rachel and her brothers and sisters went to live with their grandfather, Caleb Ivins Sr. He was a compassionate Quaker who was called "the good Samaritan." Owner of a store, distillery, gristmill, and sawmill, he had a large country home that looked out on a beautiful orchard of chestnut, hickory, and walnut trees. With servants doing most of the chores, the children enjoyed a life of relative ease.

After two years, Rachel left Hornerstown to live with her cousins Joshua and Theodosia Wright in Trenton, New Jersey. This was a different kind of home. Theodosia ran a strict household. As a descendant wrote: "No speck of dust was ever allowed to enter the sacred precincts of her home." Rachel's tasks included caring for the bedroom, the silver, and the glassware. She learned to cook, dry fruit, cure meats, make cheese and butter and soap, and, of course, do needlework.

Rachel lived a life of rigid discipline and hard work. Her brothers and sisters, who continued to live with their grandfather, extended their sympathy, and Grandfather Ivins said he would welcome her back at any time. But strangely enough, Rachel said she preferred her new structured life and appreciated being forced to learn so many practical skills. Later she would look back and declare, "I could see the hand of the Lord in this very clearly after coming to Utah and having to assume such practical responsibilities."

Observing her excellent training and her cheerful attitude, her uncle, Richard Ridgeway, a widower, asked her to be his housekeeper. During this time she became more independent and earned a reputation as a thrifty and spotless housekeeper and a memorable cook.

As she grew up, the silent worship of the Quakers did not satisfy all of Rachel's needs. Music was not included in their worship services, and she longed to hear the beautiful hymns that her mother had taught her and the other children. "The spirit often moved me to burst out in songs of praise," she recalled, "and it was with difficulty that I could refrain from doing so." When she was younger, after a day's work at the Wrights' she would go to a nearby grove of trees and sit and sew for her dolls, singing contentedly to herself and her dolls.

When she was sixteen, with the consent of her relatives, Rachel joined the Baptist Church, which offered greater latitude of expression of opinion. She especially enjoyed the singing and the prayers, but she didn't like the often-loud sermons any more than the non-sermons of the Friends. She described herself as "religiously inclined but not of the long-faced variety. I thought religion ought to make people happier and that was the kind of religion I was looking for." When she was eighteen she was introduced to Mormonism. It offered the things she had found lacking in the other churches, and she was baptized. Not long after her conversion, the Prophet Joseph Smith visited the Hornerstown branch, and she enjoyed his friendly, open manner and his thoughtful and impassioned sermons. She thought him a handsome, noble-looking person, fully deserving of the title Prophet. She wrote, "The light of the Gospel was shed abroad in our hearts. The Bible I could understand as never before—its truths were made plain to me, and the plan of salvation lay clear before me. . . . I could sing all the day long, and rejoice in the glorious promises of the Gospel."

The elders, of course, preached the spirit of gathering, and when they proposed that she join the Saints in Nauvoo, she responded eagerly. Some of her cousins were going there, and she decided to accompany them.

Rachel was twenty-one when she arrived in Nauvoo in the spring of 1842. She lived there for two years. Her first year there was a happy one, for the Saints were enjoying comparative peace and prosperity. She became better acquainted with the Prophet, and she was especially pleased with the doctrine of salvation for the dead because it offered the hope that she and her brothers and sisters and her dead parents could all be united together "in happy family union in the eternity to come."

Feeling at home with the Nauvoo Saints, and always with a cheerful disposition, she made many friends. One of them, Emmeline B. Harris (later Wells), wrote of Rachel: "She was dressed in silk with a handsome lace collar, or fichu, and an elegant shawl over her shoulders, and a long white lace veil thrown back over her simple straw bonnet. She carried an elaborate feather fan. . . . One could easily discern the subdued Quaker pride in her method of using it, for Sister Rachel had the air, the tone, the mannerisms of the Quakers."

Rachel was active in the social life of Nauvoo. Many times she went to the home of the Prophet Joseph for dinners, parties, and receptions. She wrote of him: "He was a fine noble looking man. Always so neat. When he was preaching you could feel the influence and power. He was not at home very much. There were so few that he could trust or put confidence in. His life was so often sought that he had to be hid up. After he had been in hiding and had come out he was always so jolly and happy. He was different in that respect from Brother Hyrum [Smith], who was more sedate, more serious."

Years later, in a letter to one of her granddaughters, Rachel related how one Sunday the Prophet Joseph came to her cousins' home. Rachel's seventeen-year-old cousin was playing the piano. The Prophet surprised Rachel by asking her to sing "In the

Gloaming." It was not a church hymn. "Why, Brother Joseph, it's Sunday!" Rachel exclaimed. The Prophet put on a knowing smile and replied, "The better the day, the better the deed." Clearly, the gospel should work to expand spirits, not confine them.

Rachel's second year in Nauvoo was not so peaceful. There was much persecution and turmoil, and her life was threatened by malaria. Still, her faith did not waver. She was administered to many times and always felt better. Not all the Ivinses were as consistently loyal. When the doctrine of plural marriage was circulated in 1843–44, Rachel's cousin Charles joined a group that called Joseph a fallen prophet and advocated establishment of a new organization dedicated to the early gospel taught by Joseph. When the group published a disloyal paper called the *Nauvoo Expositor,* the authorities destroyed its presses. In the ensuing uproar, Joseph and his brother Hyrum were arrested, taken to Carthage, the county seat, and charged with riot and treason. On June 27, 1844, a mob of two hundred men with blackened faces broke into the jail and killed the two leaders.

As with the thousands of other loyal Latter-day Saints, Rachel was stunned and outraged. Her mental and emotional distress was heightened by malarial fever. Nevertheless, she was among the thousands who attended the meeting at which the Twelve Apostles were sustained to provide leadership for the Church. She recalled: "After the Prophet's death, when Sidney Rigdon came to Nauvoo and spoke, he thought it was his right and privilege to be president of the Church. Brigham Young jumped right up on the seat and spoke. If you had had your eyes shut you would have thought it was the Prophet Joseph. In fact, he looked like him—his very countenance seemed to change—and he spoke like him." Clearly, in her mind, Brigham Young was the divinely approved successor to Joseph Smith.

Rachel did not remain in Nauvoo, nor did she accompany the Saints in their exodus from Nauvoo to Winter Quarters. Deprived of the Prophet she had admired so much, disaffected from the dissident cousins with whom she lived, and weak from malaria, she felt desolate and alone. She decided to return to her family in New Jersey.

Rachel made her home with first one sister, then another, helping to care for her nieces and nephews. But she did not lose contact with the Church. She attended meetings and listened to visiting authorities and missionaries. Her sister Anna, who also remained faithful to the Church, had married her second cousin Israel Ivins in 1844 and now lived in Toms River, New Jersey. Israel was a staunch believer as well, and, indeed, was one of the first missionaries to preach in southern New Jersey. Rachel told Anna and Israel that if they ever migrated to the new gathering place in the Great Basin, she would accompany them. She welcomed the opportunity when it came in 1853.

In preparation for the journey, Rachel bought calico, bleach, linsey-woolsey, thread, needles, bedding, pillowcases, sheets, and other goods she wouldn't be likely to find in Utah. But, she later said, she gave away most of the items to people she thought had greater need than she did.

The 3,000-mile trip west took four months. The group was well-outfitted, traveling with two well-stocked wagons, two yoke of oxen, and a cow. With the milk from the cow, Rachel mixed cornmeal sprinkled with dried fruit and topped by milk—a nutritious if monotonous diet.

In addition to Israel and Anna Ivins, Rachel's companions also included the couple's eight-year-old daughter, Caroline (Caddie) Ivins, and their eight-month-old son, Anthony (Tony) W. Ivins (who would be a close companion to Rachel's future son and eventually an apostle in the Church). Rachel read, knitted, helped care for Tony, and told stories to Caddie. The trip was good for her health; a persistent cough that had troubled her for years disappeared. They arrived in the Salt Lake Valley around the middle of August.

Once in the Valley, they were met by Jedediah Grant, Rachel's first missionary, who had been one of the First Presidents of the Seventy since 1845. He had visited the branch in Hornerstown several times since 1839 and, indeed, had performed the marriage for Anna and Israel. He took the Ivinses to his home on Main Street, where they continued as his guests until Anna and Israel were able to arrange for their own home.

During the next two years Rachel received a number of marriage proposals, but her final choice was to become a plural wife of her host and benefactor, Elder Grant. They were married on November 29, 1855. At the time Rachel was thirty-four and Jedediah thirty-nine.

Rachel did her share of the work and more in the extended Grant household, and she enjoyed it. She helped to prepare meals, make and wash clothes, nurse sick children and adults, work in the garden, care for the livestock, and keep the house clean and in good repair. In a letter to one member of the household, Jedediah wrote: "And tell Rachel not to work so hard!"

Jedediah, who was born at Windsor, Broome County, New York, on February 21, 1816, was baptized a member of the Church in 1833, when he was seventeen. He was a member of Zion's Camp, that little army of two hundred men and ten women that traveled from northern Ohio to western Missouri in 1834 to assist the Saints expelled from Jackson County. A member of the First Quorum of Seventy in the Church, he performed his first preaching mission in 1835 and visited New York, New Jersey, Virginia, and North Carolina in 1836–37, and also in 1839–40. He met members of the Ivins family for the first time in 1839. Orson F. Whitney, after interviewing many who had known Elder Grant personally, described Jedediah as one of the Church's most able missionaries:

"Though not an educated man, he was wonderfully bright and intelligent, a natural logician, with a thorough knowledge of the scriptures, a ready and forceful delivery, and a most original and effective way of presenting and driving home an argument. Shrewd and quick-witted, he saw in a moment the weakness of an opponent's

Jedediah Grant

position, and like lightning attacked and demolished it. His style—for all that he was practical—was poetic, full of fire and replete with imagery. Withal, though of sound judgment, prudent and far-sighted, he was perfectly fearless, daring, dashing—just the man to please the chivalrous and fiery Southerners."

In 1843 and 1844 Jedediah presided over the Saints in Philadelphia. In the Salt Lake Valley he was the first mayor of Salt Lake City, a member of the legislature, and Speaker of the House, and in 1854 he was sustained as second counselor to Brigham Young in the First Presidency of the Church. He was also a top officer in the Nauvoo Legion, the territory's official militia. Because of this activity, he was gone from home much of the time.

Only twelve months and two days after her marriage, Rachel became a widow. Jedediah contracted typhoid, followed up by double pneumonia, in mid-November 1856, and he died on

Rachel and her only child, Heber Jeddy Grant

December 1, 1856, at age forty. Just nine days before his death, Rachel had given birth to Heber Jeddy, the future President of the Church. Because of Jedediah's death, she would henceforth have to provide for herself and son. She contemplated living with her sister and brother-in-law, Anna and Israel, but they were called to help colonize southern Utah in 1861, and that option was no longer open. Her relatives in New Jersey assured her financial security if she would return, but her commitment to the Church was too strong to leave the Promised Valley.

In an attempt to keep Jedediah's family together, his widows (including Rachel) agreed to marry George D. Grant, Jedediah's older brother. However, the experience was a very unfortunate one for Rachel and she obtained a divorce shortly thereafter. Her brief second marriage was an experience Rachel rarely spoke of the rest of her life, even to her closest friends and family members.

Taking the five hundred dollars she received when the Grant mansion was sold, Rachel purchased a small adobe house at 14 South Second East. For the first time in her life she was completely on her own. She decided to try supporting herself and her son by custom sewing. She was not able to earn much—and people often paid her with flour, potatoes, wood, butter, milk, or old clothes. She and Heber did not eat well; they seldom had sugar, butter, fresh fruit, or vegetables, all of which were scarce. The house was often cold for lack of wood. Heber remembered, as he grew older, working the pedal of the sewing machine to relieve his mother's tired feet. They often worked late into the night.

Struggle, however, did not preclude entertaining; there were frequent gatherings in her home. "They loved to come," Rachel declared, "and I loved to have them. . . . 'Sister Grant,' the boys would say, 'we have such good times here.'" In order to splurge when she entertained friends, she and Heber would restrict themselves to a diet of fried bread (warmed slices of bread in a greased frying pan). She had always been proud of her personal appearance, so she was careful to keep in good condition a best dress for very special occasions and a next-best dress for Sundays. "She could wear a dress longer than anyone I have seen and have it look fresh and nice," recalled a relative. "She always changed her dress in the afternoon and washed herself and combed her hair, and if at home put on a nice white apron. . . . It would not look soiled [for several days]." She often borrowed from several threadbare garments to produce something that looked new and usable.

Rachel's situation changed in the 1860s when gold was discovered in Idaho and Montana. Salt Lake City was the regional trading center, and enterprising persons arrived in the city to take advantage of new business opportunities. One day Daniel H. Wells, who replaced Jedediah as mayor of Salt Lake City and as counselor to Brigham Young, called to see Widow Grant. A non-Mormon friend was coming to Salt Lake City to open a business. "He will pay you forty dollars a month," Mayor Wells told her. "Will you allow him to board with you?" Knowing the sum was far more than she could earn sewing, Rachel agreed. The friend decided to marry in the meantime, so when he came he brought his bride and paid eighty dollars a month.

One day the boarder, Park Wood, invited a friend to dinner, Colonel Alex G. Haws, an officer of the New York Life Insurance Company. "Madam, I like your cooking, I like your face, and I am coming here tomorrow to board," he stated. When Rachel protested that she had no place to put him, Haws explained that he would pay to have a room fixed up. He gave her one hundred dollars. Haws boarded with Rachel for years and she enjoyed him immensely—his conversation, his friendliness, his generosity, his discretion, and presumably his monthly rent. The colonel was, in many ways, a second father to Heber.

Yet Rachel insisted upon a certain independence and distance. She refused to allow the colonel to take charge of Heber and pay the expenses of his education. Moreover, she refused her ward bishop's offer to repair the leaky roof of her home, telling Bishop Edwin D. Woolley that her son would one day build her a new home. Heber did build her a home, and Bishop Woolley, father of Olive Woolley Kimball, whose history is given later, dedicated it.

Rachel's attitude is revealed in one of her letters to her son during his mission in Japan: "I never felt humiliated at having to work and support myself and you, and I thanked my heavenly Father for giving me the strength and ability to do it. When talking to President Young I said if the Lord would give me health and strength, it was all I asked. He did, and now I am not under any obligations to anyone but to God. . . . Persons had said to me I was a fool for working as I did when your father killed himself [he died

Rachel Grant and her son Heber lived in this home in Salt Lake City.

of typhoid and pneumonia] working in the kingdom. I told them I did not wish to be supported by the church. I was too independent for that, and how well I feel about it now."

As well as insisting upon supporting herself and Heber, Rachel was also active in the Thirteenth Ward. She helped nurse the sick, made burial clothes for the dead, and for thirty-five years (1868–1903) served as president of the ward Relief Society, whose members made carpets for the Salt Lake Temple. Rachel served on a committee of female leaders to draft resolutions protective of Church interests, advocated woman suffrage, and spoke often at Relief Society and Retrenchment Society meetings and stake conferences. She emphasized that "faith without works is dead," that faith should always be coupled with good works.

Rachel was a supportive mother to her son. She encouraged him to play baseball and inspired him to do well in school; but, above all, she encouraged him to remain faithful and active in church and to respect the authorities of the Church. When Heber was a mere boy, Rachel predicted that he would one day be an apostle, and she wanted him to live worthy of it. She was probably the only person in the Thirteenth Ward who was not surprised when, at age twenty-six, he was called to be an apostle through revelation to President John Taylor. Rachel saw her son serve as an apostle during the last twenty-six years of her life. He also served as president of two overseas missions during her lifetime.

Satisfaction with her son, however, could not overcome a physical problem that became increasingly serious. In 1868, when Heber was about twelve, Rachel suffered an attack of quinsy (abscessed tonsils) that made her deaf. Although her health and longevity would carry her through her eighty-seventh year, she spent the last forty years of her life in almost total silence. The loss of hearing was accompanied by terrible head noises, "like a steam engine going night and day." She continued as president of the Relief Society, always attended church meetings, and sometimes was helped by special blessings. Although her deafness prevented her from hearing the music she loved, especially hymns, it did not stop her from singing. Her spirit of resignation is reflected in her statement, "I'm glad I can see. I feel blindness would be a great affliction." She made up for her loss of hearing by writing letters and reading hymns, magazines, and other "good thoughts and good books."

Rachel's last years were spent mostly with her grandchildren. She made one trip to New Jersey to visit the old homestead; she went with Heber to California, where they vacationed at Pacific Grove; and she enjoyed the many birthday celebrations held in her honor in Salt Lake City. Rachel carried herself like a queen and was treated like one. She reminded many people of Queen Victoria of England, who was only a year older.

When death came on January 27, 1909, at age eighty-seven, she was ready to go. "I have far more friends and loved ones on the other side than I have here," she said.

SOURCES

Among the Heber J. Grant Papers at the LDS Church Archives, Salt Lake City, are a number of biographical and autobiographical manuscripts and typescripts about and by Rachel R. Ivins Grant.

Published biographical sketches and appreciations include May Booth Talmage, "Coronets of Age: Rachel R. Grant," *Young Woman's Journal* 19 (April 1908): 182–85; Susa Young Gates, "A Tribute to Rachel Ivins Grant," *Young Woman's Journal* 21 (January 1910): 30; "Rachel Ridgeway Ivins Grant," *Improvement Era* 12 (June 1909): 585–99; Heber J. Grant, "My Tribute to Mother," *Improvement Era* 31 (May 1928): 541; Annie Wells Cannon, "Rachel Ivins Grant," *Improvement Era* 37 (November 1934): 643; Lucy Grant Cannon, "Recollections of Rachel Ivins Grant," *Relief Society Magazine* 25 (May 1938): 293–98; Mary Grant Judd, "Rachel Ridgway Ivins Grant," *Relief Society Magazine* 30 (April 1943): 229–31, 297, and (May 1943): 313–16.

By far the best sources for our purposes were the recent exemplary studies: Ronald W. Walker, "Rachel R. Grant: The Continuing Legacy of the Feminine Ideal," *Dialogue: A Journal of Mormon Thought* 15 (Autumn 1982): 105–21; Marlena C. Ahanin, "A Name and Place among the Saints: The Life of Rachel Ridgeway Ivins Grant," typescript (1976) in possession of the writers; and Ronald W. Walker, "Jedediah and Heber Grant," *Ensign* 9 (July 1979): 47–52.

Biographies of Rachel's husband and son contain material about her life and character. These include Gene A. Sessions, *Mormon Thunder: A Documentary History of Jedediah Morgan Grant* (Urbana: University of Illinois Press, 1982); Mary Grant Judd, *Jedediah M. Grant, Pioneer-Statesman* (Salt Lake City: Deseret News Press, 1959); Francis M. Gibbons, *Heber J. Grant: Man of Steel, Prophet of God* (Salt Lake City: Deseret Book Company, 1979); Andrew Jenson, "Grant, Jedediah M.," in *Latter-day Saints' Biographical Encyclopedia*, 4 vols. (Salt Lake City: Andrew Jenson Historical Company, 1901–1936), 1:57–58, 3:637; Ronald W. Walker, "Heber J. Grant," in Leonard J. Arrington, ed., *The Presidents of the Church* (Salt Lake City: Deseret Book, 1986), pp. 211–48; Preston Nibley, *The Presidents of the Church* (Salt Lake City: Deseret Book, 1971), pp. 217–62.

SARAH FARR SMITH

My mother was born in a Latter-day Saint home. . . .
She passed through the experiences of pioneer life in
such manner as to develop the best there is in a human
being. She began life with a strong physique and a
cheerful disposition. . . . Her training made her exceedingly frugal and economical so that when, as a young
girl, she married my father, . . . she began homemaking under the most favorable circumstances. . . .
Mother was and is one of the most industrious women
I ever knew. I well remember, when I was a child, how
she was the first one up in the morning and the last
one to bed at night. And during her experience of giving birth to eleven children and rearing eight of them
to man and womanhood not one of us was ever
neglected in any way. She was a strict disciplinarian,
and we always knew that when she told us to do anything she meant it. —*George Albert Smith*

Sarah Farr Smith had just finished cleaning the kitchen after
the family noontime meal when she heard a firm knock at the
back door of her home at 23 North West Temple in Salt Lake
City. Proceeding to the door, she was not particularly surprised to
see a poor but tidy-looking gentleman standing on her porch. She
didn't know the elderly man, but it was not uncommon for tran-
sients to come to her home from the nearby railroad station asking
for a meal. As Sarah often tired of serving food at all hours of the
day to whoever came by, her husband, John Henry, had purchased

"meal tickets" to give to those in need, which enabled them to eat a satisfying meal at a nearby restaurant.

There was something different about this particular man, and Sarah felt moved to invite him in to her kitchen table. As he was eating, the man suddenly asked where Sarah's young son George Albert was. She indicated that he was outside playing in the yard. He then asked her to call the youth into the house so he could see him. Again she felt compelled to comply, although she was hesitant to leave a stranger alone in the house. She found George Albert, who was about eight years old, playing at a nearby two-story build-ing north of their house, underneath a second-story balcony from which steps descended to the ground level. When she reentered her house with her young son at her side, the gentleman was gone. Sarah was searching through the house for him when she heard a loud crashing sound outside. She rushed out to see what had hap-pened and was astonished to discover that the balcony and stair-case under which her son had just been playing had collapsed, sending large beams and pieces of lumber crashing down onto playthings he had left behind just moments before.

Sarah was deeply moved and grateful for what she felt was divine intervention to save her son's life. Within a few years of this incident, it was made even more clear to her that her descendants had an important mission to fulfill in building the kingdom of God on earth. In 1881, at the age of thirty-one and just two weeks before the birth of her seventh child, she received her patriarchal blessing and was told that she and her husband would "raise up a posterity that shall be numerous and mighty and none shall excel them in Israel."

This must have been a humbling promise to a young mother who, by birth and by marriage, was associated with two of the most remarkable families in early Church history. The possibility that any of her children could measure up to their ancestors would be quite an accomplishment indeed.

Sarah Farr Smith's life began at the very time and place that one of the most remarkable colonization efforts in America had its beginnings. She was born October 30, 1849, just two years after her parents, Lorin Farr and Nancy Bailey Chase, entered the Salt Lake Valley in a covered wagon. She was the third of their eleven children, a family that included two sets of twins.

Sarah's mother, Nancy Chase, was born in Vermont in 1823, and at the age of four moved with her family to New York State, where they found the soil more suitable for farming. Several years later, when Nancy was fifteen, the family accepted the truth of the message of the restored gospel and were baptized. In 1839 the Chase family joined the main body of Saints in Nauvoo, Illinois, where they became well-acquainted with the Prophet Joseph Smith. During the terrible cholera plague of 1841, the Prophet healed eighteen-year-old Nancy of that serious illness, an experience that caused her to make a lifetime vow to "serve the Lord in every way possible."

In Nauvoo, Nancy became a charter member of the Female Relief Society, sang in choral groups for concerts and church activities, and studied history, language, and theology with such prominent leaders as Brigham Young, John Taylor, and Heber C. Kimball. She first saw her future husband, Lorin Farr, when they met at the well near their homes where both had gone to get fresh water for the evening.

Lorin Farr, also a convert, came from Vermont, where he was born in 1820. As a young boy, he witnessed the miraculous healing of his gravely ill mother by Elder Orson Pratt and his companion Elder Lyman Johnson, an event that eventually led to the baptism of Lorin and his parents. Their desire to join the rest of the Saints was strong, and Lorin's father sold his 2,000-acre farm for a fraction of its worth, left his prominent position as a county judge, and moved to Kirtland, Ohio. As a young man, Lorin lived for a period of time with the family of Joseph Smith and became one of the Prophet's closest associates. Lorin was serving a mission in the Eastern States when he learned of the Prophet's martyrdom in June

1844. The grief-stricken elder faithfully continued his labors, however, and did not return to Nauvoo until November 1844, the year
he met Nancy Chase. Lorin and Nancy were married New Year's
Day, 1845, in a ceremony performed by Brigham Young.

After their arrival in the Salt Lake Valley, Lorin and Nancy
immediately set about the task of building a new home. They were
assigned a fine lot northeast of the Temple Block, where they
planted fruit trees, berry bushes, and a garden. Lorin joined "snake
killing expeditions," in which several dozen men fanned out from
a given place and walked slowly toward the mountain, killing the
snakes and rodents in their path.

Their efforts at settling were expanded when the Salt Lake
Valley proved to be only a temporary stopping place for Nancy and
Lorin. Within a year of their arrival, they were called by President
Brigham Young to move north to the Weber Valley to oversee the
colonization of a new settlement, soon to be known as Ogden. In
January 1850 Lorin packed the scant belongings of the little
family—a plow on the side of the wagon, cooking utensils, a few
simple pieces of furniture, chickens in pens hanging on the back, a
cow trailing behind—and headed north, struggling over the snow-
covered trail. In the wagon, Nancy tucked her three small children
snugly next to her under blankets and buffalo robes: four-year-old
Enoch, one-and-a-half-year-old Julia, and two-month-old Sarah.

Although the Ogden settlement later proved a great success,
many were skeptical of the "farmability" of some areas of the
Weber Valley. Sarah's maternal grandfather, Ezra Chase, had arrived
there two years before Lorin and Nancy and, tongue-in-cheek,
assured them of three good crops: "The upper land would yield
good grain, but below, the land would produce one hundred bushel
of crickets to the acre and fifty bushels of mosquitoes." Lorin
agreed to colonize the upper district.

The Farrs lived briefly in what was known as Farr's Fort, three-
fourths of a mile west of Ogden Canyon. In 1853 they later moved
to the corner of Main and First Street (now Twenty-first and

Washington), where Sarah's father built a twenty-one-room adobe home. Larger than most other homes in the area, it was the envy of many because of its good wooden floors made of thick planks. As a toddler, Sarah played at her mother's knee while Nancy, with help from friendly Indian women who visited regularly, made rag rugs for each room. The home was simply furnished with tables and chairs made from home-cut lumber and doors hanging on leather hinges. The family ate from tin and pewter dishes and utensils. A typical evening meal for the family, which Sarah helped prepare when she was old enough, consisted of cornmeal mush and milk, homemade salt-rising bread, milk with plenty of cream, and old-fashioned hominy.

Bearskins and buffalo robes kept the children warm in their trundle beds on cold winter nights. When she was a little older, Sarah slept on a bed with a fresh straw mattress and sometimes cuddled under a tick made from carefully selected feathers. The pillows were stuffed mainly with goose feathers, although some of the more rugged pioneers found it difficult to sleep on anything so soft.

Open fireplaces furnished heat and a place for Sarah and her mother and sisters to cook the family meals. Matches for starting fires were made from dry, split pieces of pine dipped into melted sulphur. The family called them "lucifers."

Insects of all kinds were a constant plague for these early settlers, and Sarah no doubt was continually battling them. Flies, mosquitoes, and bedbugs were "almost as thick as the sands of the seashore," wrote her half-brother John Farr. A story circulated among the early settlers tells of a traveling salesman who, in seeking accommodations for the night, asked the landlady if there were any bedbugs in the house. She replied, "Not a single bug in the house." The next morning at breakfast he said, "Madam, you told the truth. You haven't a single bedbug. But you do have a thousand married ones, all with big families!"

One of the most disagreeable encounters Sarah had with insects was most likely the experience of accidentally stepping on "army worms" while she was working or playing outside bare-footed. These destructive pests have been described as being "green, horned, from four to six inches long and one-half inch thick." While driving cows to pasture or running errands for her mother, Sarah found it difficult to miss the worms, hard as she may have tried.

The family in which Sarah grew up would have to be considered both very unusual and highly successful. After his arrival in Ogden, because of the principle of plural marriage, Lorin Farr married additional wives. He fathered, in all, thirty six children.

As the second oldest child in such a large family (her older sister Julia died at the age of nine), Sarah shouldered a major responsibility in helping her mother with housework, cooking, sewing, and caring for the younger children. Her father became the first mayor of Ogden, a position he held for twenty-two years, and was also president of the Weber Stake for twenty years. Hence, the Farr home was a flurry of activity centered around the father's business, civic, and religious responsibilities. Sarah met and became well-acquainted with numerous important religious leaders, including President Brigham Young, as they came on visits and spent the night in the Farr home.

Sarah probably first attended school in her father's private neighborhood schoolhouse, which was located at 2039 Washington Boulevard. The twenty-by-thirty-foot building was used not only as a school but also for civic meetings and recreational activities until larger facilities were available. Interest in education was keen among the early settlers, although the facilities were not lavish. Sarah and her classmates, for example, walked on dirt floors in the school, sat on split log seats, and wrote their first ABCs with slate pencils. One Ogden schoolteacher in 1854 devised an effective and unique method of keeping order in her classroom. She kept a supply of small wooden blocks about an inch in diameter and required her pupils each to put one of these blocks in their mouths, to keep them from talking. The technique must have "inspired" good

behavior in Sarah Farr, for among her private papers at the
University of Utah Special Collections is a small card with a hand-
painted flower on the front and a handwritten message on the
back: "Reward of Merit—for not whispering in school. To Sarah
Farr from Harriet Canfield Brown, teacher."

Sarah grew up accustomed to the sight of Indian tents pitched
in the backyard of their home in Ogden. Friendly Indian women
came to the Farr home every fall, staying for three or four days and
asking for sugar, salt, and other foods and spices. They especially
liked brown sugar and nibbled constantly on the dried fruit Nancy
was happy to share with them. In return for the food they were
given, the women brought pine nuts and moccasins for the children and even made clothes for the girls' dolls. One particular
Indian woman, who was a favorite with Sarah and the other children, was known as Aunt Mary. She visited the Farr family periodically until she was in her nineties. After Nancy Farr's death in
1892, Aunt Mary brought a large handful of sego lilies each spring
to put on her grave.

On October 20, 1866, ten days before Sarah's seventeenth
birthday, she married John Henry Smith, eighteen-year-old son of
George A. Smith (cousin of the Prophet Joseph Smith) and Sarah
Ann Libby. It is not known exactly how Sarah and John Henry met,
but both of their fathers were very active in civic and religious
affairs, and the two men were undoubtedly well acquainted. John
Henry's father was a prominent colonizer of the West, the youngest
man ever ordained an apostle in the Church, and he eventually
served as counselor in the First Presidency of Brigham Young and
as Church Historian.

Sarah and John Henry became the parents of eleven children
over the next twenty-five years; the first eight babies were boys and
the last three girls. Sarah buried three sons who died in infancy:
John Henry Jr., Lorin Farr, and Charles Warren. The eight children
she raised to maturity were George Albert (whom John Henry
proudly named after the boy's paternal grandfather), Don Carlos,

Sarah Farr and John Henry Smith

Ezra Chase, Winslow Farr, Nathaniel Libby, Nancy Clarabell, Tirzah Priscilla (known as "Sib"), and Elsie Louise.

Sarah's upbringing proved to be excellent training for the life that lay ahead of her. The homemaking skills she learned at the side of her mother helped smooth her transition from daughter to mother. But even more importantly, Nancy Chase had set an admirable example for Sarah in how to live calmly and gracefully with a busy—and often absent—husband.

Sarah and John Henry Smith began their married life in humble circumstances, their first home being a log house with a mud roof in Provo, where John Henry worked as a telegraph operator. Although they had few worldly possessions, Sarah's cheerful disposition and frugal ways enabled the family to endure and accomplish much more through the years than they ever thought possible. She was quick to move herself and her children through the mountain of work that faced them each day, but slow to complain at the sometimes unfavorable circumstances surrounding her.

After a short stay in Provo, the family moved to Salt Lake City, where John Henry worked for the Central Pacific Railroad. In 1872 he was named assistant clerk to the territorial House of Representatives, an experience that sparked an interest in politics. He later served as a member of the Salt Lake City Council and as a representative in the Utah Legislature.

John Henry's devotion to the gospel sent him overseas twice to serve missions for the Church. On his first mission, to Great Britain at the age of twenty-five, he left Sarah with three small sons under the age of four. In 1882 he returned to Europe again, this time to preside over the European Mission, leaving Sarah with five children and expecting their sixth.

In the October general conference of 1880, John Henry, at the age of thirty-two, was called to be a member of the Council of Twelve Apostles. By this time he had broadened his experience by serving as bishop of the large and thriving Seventeenth Ward in Salt Lake City. Thirty years later he was called to be second counselor in the First Presidency of President Joseph F. Smith.

Although Sarah was completely supportive of her husband's enormous responsibilities in the Church and community, she retained her own individuality and could, at times, be somewhat headstrong. A favorite family story indicates some stubbornness: One evening John Henry was preparing to go to a church meeting and asked Sarah to pin his collar on after he had put on his shirt. When she began attaching the collar, he complained that she was sticking him with the pin in the back of his neck. She laughed this off with something like "Oh, I am not, don't be silly," and proceeded to put the collar on. Again John Henry winced and complained of being poked, and again Sarah insisted she was not hurting him. When John Henry returned from his meeting several hours later, still smarting, he removed his shirt to find tiny spots of blood on the back of the collar.

During her husband's missions and other long periods when he was away from home, Sarah, of necessity, had to take his place as head of the family, seeing to it that order was maintained in the home. She was a strict disciplinarian and did not accept lightly the responsibility of raising eight children. She taught her children much of what they learned about the gospel, tending to their prayers and making sure they attended Sunday School classes even when she was unable to go herself. In case of serious illness, she called in the elders to bless her children.

An accident in the family brought evidence that Sarah had succeeded in training her children to rely on faith and prayer in time of need. While reaching for something on the top shelf of her kitchen cupboard, she upset a teetering cupboard and it came crashing down on top of her. Young George Albert, hearing the noise, ran to her aid and found her unconscious on the floor. He was able to move the cupboard off his mother, but he couldn't revive her. Fearing that she was dead or dying, he prayed with all his might for the Lord to save her. In return, he pledged to devote his life to God's work. Sarah recovered, and George Albert never forgot his promise to the Lord.

Sarah took a great deal of pride in her home. An immaculate housekeeper who kept everything in good repair, she had a knack for mending things with whatever was handy. If she discovered an unwelcomed mouse in her cupboard, it would soon find its entrance covered with a piece of tin.

Sarah was a dedicated letter writer, whether she was corresponding with John Henry in the mission field, or inquiring as to the welfare of her loved ones at home when she herself was traveling. Her playful banter in these letters indicates that she was affectionate and had a charming sense of humor. She closed many of her letters to John Henry with such lines as "Your old sweetheart and young wife," or "Just consider yourself hugged and kissed."

In 1901, while visiting her sister and brother-in-law "Nine" (Diane) and Ben E. Rich, who was serving as a mission president in Tennessee, Sarah playfully teased her husband at home in Salt Lake City with this note: "I hope you don't think that I have found anybody down here that I am going to elope with. I think I had better keep the boat that has carried me through so far and satisfactorily. You don't need to think you can get rid of me so easy." (This note was written thirty-five years after their marriage and ten years after their last child was born.)

Sarah enjoyed traveling across the country, both on Church business with her husband and to see relatives in the mission field. She wrote a note to her son George Albert and his wife Lucy Woodruff while she was in Washington, D. C., with John Henry in 1906 and described an experience that must have given her much pleasure: "Emily Richards appointed me a delegate to the Woman's Suffrage Convention at Baltimore. Went to a birthday [celebration] to honor Miss [Susan B.] Anthony's birthday—she is 86 years old. Miss Alice Roosevelt is to be married tomorrow, it has taxed the White House to find room to store the presents."

As her children grew older, Sarah found a new measure of freedom to travel, but her later life also brought new trials that were increasingly hard to bear. Her health became a major challenge as she suffered from the effects of high blood pressure—a condition that caused her to suffer from headaches, dizziness, and anxiety. Early medical practices called for the doctors to bleed Sarah to relieve the pressure, which they did many times. This procedure did, in fact, help her feel better for two or three days at a time.

Another trial that worried Sarah daily was the health of her youngest child, Elsie, who suffered from epilepsy. Elsie had seizures virtually every day, and the family did its best to cope with them. When she felt a seizure coming on, Elsie would grab whatever she was close to, and sometimes that was a hot iron or pot on the stove, which caused numerous burns on her body. Sarah was convinced that the epilepsy resulted from Elsie's having been carried in the womb eleven months before she was born.

Sarah's love for her husband, family, and the Church were tested in other ways also. One year before his call to the apostle-ship, John Henry married another wife, Josephine Groesbeck, who was twenty-two. The relationship between Sarah and Josephine grew to be fond and affectionate. The two women were thoughtful of each other and treated each other's children as tenderly as their own. Josephine wrote a "Tribute to Aunt Sarah," which she read at a celebration honoring Sarah's seventieth birthday. Among the many lines of affection were these words:

> Nearly fifty years of married life
> We have journied together
> Aiding and helping each other along,
> Through fair and cloudy weather.
> Now you have reached three score and ten
> And I'm not far behind you.
> May peace and happiness ever attend
> As God, in love, designed for you.

Josephine was also a gifted musician and a woman of means—which brought some relief to the financial struggles that had troubled the Smith family.

On October 13, 1911, while Sarah was in Chicago with her sister "Belle" (Mrs. H. J.) Sears, John Henry died at Josephine's home of a hemorrhage of the lungs and a weak heart. Shocked and grief-stricken, Sarah rushed home. Before she arrived, Josephine had John Henry moved in his casket to Sarah's home. It was an emotional moment when the two women met and wept in each

John Henry Smith

other's arms. "Sarah," Josephine sobbed, "I have always loved you for sharing your wonderful husband with me."

Later, when the family was settling John Henry's estate and making financial arrangements to care for Sarah and the children, the more financially secure Josephine said to Sarah, "As long as I live, you and your children will be well-fed."

Sarah Farr Smith lived another nine years after the death of her husband, welcoming grandchildren into the family and taking pride in the accomplishments of her children. She had the distinction of having two sons serve as mission presidents, with Winslow in Chicago as president of the Northern States Mission and George Albert in Liverpool, England, presiding over the European Mission.

Both sons were holding these positions, in fact, when they received word of their mother's serious illness and impending death. George Albert was too far away to return home, but Winslow came quickly to her bedside at her home (then on Yale Avenue in Salt Lake City), where she had been unconscious for two days. He leaned over her bed and whispered softly, "Mother, this is Winslow. Do you know me?" She roused momentarily and answered, "Yes," which was the last word she uttered. She died February 4, 1921, at the age of seventy-one.

Among the speakers at Sarah's funeral was Elder Richard R. Lyman, who described her as "the power behind the throne of her great husband." He also added that John Henry was "no greater as a man than she was as a woman."

Perhaps one of the finest tributes honoring Sarah is part of a letter her oldest surviving son wrote to her on Mother's Day, 1912, from Ocean Park, California:

> My Darling Mother,
>
> This day is designated as one on which "Mother" is to be especially honored. In this sunny land I bow before my maker and thank him for you, who all my days has been all that that sweetest of names implies to me. No man ever had a better Mother, and today and in all days it is my desire to so live that you will be honored by what I do, and always be glad I am your son. You have had many trials in life but have borne your burden and taken your place like a queen among women.
>
> The Lord loves you, and know this my dear Mother, that he will over-rule every difficulty for your ultimate triumph and complete happiness. Your sorrows will pass away and standing by the side of your beloved husband you will gather your children around you (every one) and they with their children to the latest generation will call you blessed and love you.
>
> About Friday next I hope to be where I can see you again and you will see how fat I am growing.

Sarah Farr Smith

Praying the blessing of the Lord upon you. I am ever
Your affectionate son
Geo Albert Smith

SOURCES

Sarah's parentage and early life are described in R. Earl Pardoe, *Lorin Farr, Pioneer* (Provo, Utah: Brigham Young University Press, 1953), and John Farr, *My Yesterdays* (Salt Lake City: Granite Publishing Company, 1957).

Her life as a wife and mother is told in Merlo J. Pusey, *Builders of the Kingdom* (Provo, Utah: Brigham Young University Press, 1981). Additional information is found in "Papers of the George A. Smith Family," Special Collections, University of Utah, Salt Lake City, Utah; and Thomas C. Romney, *The Gospel in Action* (Salt Lake City: Deseret Sunday School Union, 1949), chapter 11, "Lorin Farr."

George Albert Smith's appraisal of his mother is given in his article "Mothers of Our Leaders, Sarah Farr Smith" in *Relief Society Magazine* 6 (June 1919): 313–15.

We conducted personal interviews in May 1986 with Dr. W. Whitney Smith, Logan, Utah, a grandson of Sarah Farr Smith; Robert Farr Smith, Salt Lake City, a grandson of Sarah Farr Smith; and Shauna Stewart Larsen, Champaign, Illinois, a great-granddaughter of Sarah Farr Smith.

We have also examined the family group sheets and pedigree charts in the Family History Library, Salt Lake City.

JEANETTE EVELINE EVANS McKAY

My Mother! God bless you!
For your purity of soul,
Your faith, your tenderness,
Your watchful care,
Your supreme patience,
Your companionship and trust,
Your loyalty to the right,
Your help and inspiration to father,
Your unselfish devotion to us children.
—*David O. McKay*

On a lovely April evening in 1883, David and Jeanette McKay gathered their four children around the fireplace of their white frame home in Huntsville, Utah. David had just returned from serving a two-year mission for The Church of Jesus Christ of Latter-day Saints in the highlands of Scotland, and nine-year-old David O., seven-year-old Thomas, and four-year-old Jeanette were eager to hear of their father's adventures in that far-off land. Two-year-old Annie sat on her father's knee and spent the evening getting acquainted with this gentle bearded man who had departed for Scotland ten days before she was born.

As David told the children about Scotland, describing the fields of heather, the music of bagpipes, the imposing castles, and the

Jeanette Eveline Evans McKay

thousands of sheep dotting the hillsides, one of his sons asked him if he had seen any miracles while on his mission. David's eyes immediately met those of his wife, Jeanette, and putting his arm around her and pulling her close, he replied, "Your mother is the greatest miracle I have ever seen on this earth."

Such fulsome praise was frequently expressed by David McKay and his children for their beautiful, dark-eyed Welsh wife and mother, Jeanette Eveline Evans McKay. As David toured the farm and home upon his return, he had good reason to believe his wife was able to work miracles.

David's mission call had come in 1881 at a most inconvenient time for the little family. Jeanette was expecting a baby right away, and her husband was reluctant to leave her home alone with the responsibilities of the children and the crops. They had just made their last payment on the farm, and their dream of enlarging their small home seemed now within reach.

Emotionally, David and Jeanette still felt the pangs of grief from the loss just one year earlier of their two oldest children. Margaret, age eleven, had died of rheumatic fever on March 28, 1880, and Ellena, age nine, died on April 1 of pneumonia. The two girls were buried in the same grave.

But when David's mission call arrived, young David O. observed what was the first and only open disagreement he saw his parents have. His father's reaction was "Of course I cannot go," to which Jeanette quickly replied, "Of course you will go! David O. and I will manage things quite nicely."

And manage they did. With the considerable help and support of friends and neighbors, Jeanette quickly set about supervising David O. and his younger brother, Thomas, in learning more about running the farm and helping with household chores. Priesthood quorums did the spring planting, and by summer an excellent crop of hay and grain was ready for harvest. But grain prices were low, so Jeanette decided to store her grain until spring. Because prices were good then, she realized a profit. Encouraged, she and her sons worked even harder the next season and were able to afford the addition to her house that Jeanette and David had planned before he left. Several new bedrooms were added, and the dining room and kitchen were enlarged. Jeanette took special pride in the new wide, straight stairway leading up to the boys' bedrooms. Many a winter night before the remodeling she had dressed warmly, gone outside, and climbed a ladder up the side of the house to tuck her children in bed and have evening prayers.

Jeanette's willingness to sacrifice by having her husband gone for this length of time surely reflected her own personal gratitude for the two humble missionaries who knocked on the door of her parents' home in 1850 in southern Wales and changed their lives so enormously.

Jeanette Eveline Evans was born August 28, 1850, the seventh of the eleven children of Margaret Powell and Thomas Evans. Margaret and Thomas were married in 1837 and made their home in a tiny cottage in Cefn Coed-y-Cymmer, near Merthyr Tydfil, Glamorganshire, Wales. Illustrative of their Welsh upbringing, it is said that before Thomas proposed to Margaret, in accordance with custom, he carved for her a wooden spoon which he presented to her as a token of his love. The intricate design on the spoon revealed just how much he cared. During the carving, he was said to be "spooning," a folk expression that came to be synonymous with courtship among Welsh peoples in the eighteenth and early nineteenth centuries.

In prehistoric times the British Isles were inhabited by the Cymric or Brythonic branch of the Celts. These accomplished people, successively pushed back by waves of Anglo-Saxons, Romans, Scandinavians, and Normans, ultimately remained the principal occupants of the western peninsula known as Cambria (Cymry), or Wales, an upland region dominated by the Cambrian Mountains, the highest and wildest in Britain. Numerous small streams and lakes dot the countryside, which has an almost theatrical grandeur. South Wales ultimately became a coal and iron mining center; it was at Merthyr Tydfil (named for the fifth-century princess martyr) near Cefn Coed that Richard Trevithick's steam locomotive was first tried on rails in 1804. Although conquered by the English in the thirteenth century, the Welsh retained much of their native language and culture, and Jeanette's family spoke Welsh in their home when she was growing up.

Because Merthyr Tydfil is in the very heart of the coal mining region of Wales, its lovely broad, low mountains and lush deep valleys were somewhat tempered in beauty by what Thomas Rees described in 1815, in *The Beauties of England and Wales,* as "the perpetual smoke and constant din of the forges." "At night, when the furnaces were opened," one visitor observed, "the sky looked as if a blazing volcano were erupting." Yet the misty bogs and grassy slopes surrounding these mining towns are among the most scenic areas of Wales.

Coal mining and metal processing had been the country's chief

industry since the Industrial Revolution began in Great Britain in
the 1700s, and it was in these mines that Jeanette's father, Thomas,
earned the family's income as an ironstone miner.

The house in which Jeanette and her ten siblings were born is
one of the many thousands of rowhouses that snaked through the
villages and across the hillsides. The house is certainly a humble
one by today's standards, but in those days even the poorest houses
were often comfortably furnished with a good sofa, table,
mahogany chest of drawers, knickknacks, porcelain figures, fire
irons, eight-day clocks, and painted jugs hanging from the rafters.
Religious prints or photographs of Queen Victoria and Prince
Albert were usually on the walls.

Jeanette surely accompanied her mother many times to the
Wednesday and Saturday markets, where over a hundred stalls
were occupied by traders selling everything from butter, cheese,
and bacon to drapery, shoes, and books. Village children of Cefn
Coed contributed to the market in their own small way by collecting bundles of bulrushes on the Cilsanws Mountain; the bulrushes
were later used as candle wicks.

Jeanette had pleasant memories of South Wales. Among other
things, she told her children that there was a stone shaped like a
chair just a little way up the stream from their cottage. She would
walk up the stream, take off her shoes, sit on the stone, and let her
feet dangle down in the water.

While Thomas spent long hours amid the hot furnaces of the
ironworks, Margaret did her best to provide pleasant and healthy
living conditions for her children. One author wrote concerning
Welsh women in the nineteenth century: "Women took great pride
in trying to keep their homes spotless, fighting a hard battle against
the squalor outside." Indeed, the 1849 Public Health Reports of the
Merthyr area paint a grim picture of the sanitary conditions the
Evans family contended with. The rapidly growing industrial
region had no sewage system and poor drainage, with little or
no access to fresh water, all of which dramatically affected the

incidence of sickness and death. Major epidemics of scarlet fever, typhoid, measles, and whooping cough raged through Merthyr, with the greatest toll among the young. The 1854 Public Health Report reads: "More than half of the funerals which took place are of children less than five years of age and more than one-fourth are infants under one year." The biggest killer was cholera, which claimed 824 lives in 1854 alone. The Evans family buried three children that year—a two-year-old daughter and infant twins, a boy and girl. Two years after this terrible experience, Thomas and Margaret decided they had more than one reason to pack up their belongings and seek a better life for their children.

A few months before Jeanette was born, her parents had heard the restored gospel, received a testimony of its truthfulness, and had been baptized in May 1850. A determined and active member, Thomas served as the president over the Merthyr Tydfil Conference of the Church. Family members later felt it was more than just coincidence that William and Ellen Oman McKay, parents of Jeanette's future husband, were baptized members of the Church the same year in Scotland. The Evanses of Wales and the McKays of Scotland were among the forty-three hundred European Saints who sold their property and immigrated to America in 1856.

Before they left, Margaret paid one last visit to the graves of five of her children. Then she and her husband journeyed to Liverpool, England, where they boarded the ship *Horizon* with their six remaining children: Ann, age sixteen; Thomas, fourteen; Evan, twelve; Howell, ten; Jeanette, six; and Elizabeth (Lizzie), an infant.

The family set sail May 25, 1856, and were among 856 Saints under the leadership of Edward Martin. All were eager to join the Saints in Utah. Ironically, about six hundred of this group later became members of the second handcart company to be caught in a terrible early storm on the prairie in late 1856, and some 145 of them perished. The Evans family, however, had decided not to travel all the way to Utah that year. They remained in Iowa for three years while Thomas accumulated provisions, equipment, and clothing. The McKay family also waited in Iowa. By 1859, Thomas and Margaret had obtained wagons, teams, and a milk cow and joined Philip Buzzard's Utah-bound company. They arrived in Salt Lake City August 24, four days ahead of young Jeanette's future in-laws, the McKays. Shortly thereafter both families moved to Ogden.

In spite of their surprisingly parallel travels, the Evans and McKay families never met until, shortly after the Evanses arrived in Ogden, fifteen-year-old David McKay saw the attractive nine-year-old Jeanette sitting on the tongue of her family's wagon. He later said he could not forget the large brown eyes under her pink sunbonnet. As Jeanette grew, she became one of the most attractive and popular young women in Ogden, and David's interest in her only increased.

Jeanette's family lived in a temporary log cabin before they moved into a comfortable four-room rock home—considered rather elaborate for this time. Jeanette helped considerably with the upkeep of the house and garden. She helped to gather fruits and vegetables to be bottled or dried and stored; learned how to make soap, butter, and tallow candles; and tended her sister, Lizzie.

Jeanette made friends easily, and many of her social experiences were combined with activities providing the necessities of life. Often she and her friends would gather together to make a quilt or rug, knit stockings, or peel peaches for drying. Dances were held nearly every Friday, and special holidays and these occasions were perfect opportunities for numerous young men to court Jeanette.

The early Latter-day Saint settlers in Ogden considered the proper education of their children second in importance only to the worshipping of God. They erected schools almost as quickly as they built homes. The first school in Ogden was established as early as 1849, just two years after the first company of pioneers arrived in the Salt Lake Valley. Jeanette was sent to the Second Ward School in Ogden, where she studied under two sisters, Harriet Canfield Brown and Rose Canfield, who were among the finest teachers in pioneer Utah. Harriet and Rose were from New York State and had graduated from an eastern academy. Harriet was converted to the Church in Council Bluffs, Iowa, in 1854 and migrated to Utah in 1856. She settled in Ogden in time to start the Second Ward School under Bishop Edward Bunker. Rose, her younger sister, arrived in Ogden later and assisted Harriet as a teacher in the school. Teachers in Ogden for more than thirty years, the Canfield sisters implanted a love for books and good education among the Evans children and hundreds of other pioneer youths. It was with the encouragement of the Canfield sisters that Jeanette started a lending library for friends and family members. She herself later became a fellow teacher for a short period of time, before her marriage to David McKay. (Harriet Brown was also a teacher of Sarah Farr.)

By the time he proposed, David had been courting Jeanette for many months and had finally earned enough money to pay for a small farm in Huntsville, in Ogden Valley east of Ogden. Even though Jeanette was not yet seventeen years old, he persuaded her parents to let him marry her. Their marriage was performed by Elder Wilford Woodruff of the Council of the Twelve on April 9, 1867, in the Endowment House in Salt Lake City.

They settled in a log cabin David had built in Huntsville. Jeanette was considered to be one of the prettiest girls in the region, and David wanted her to stay that way, so he refused to let her work in the fields. Later, when they could afford it, he also insisted on obtaining help for her in the house. He admired her beautiful hands and lovely, clear complexion. It is not accidental that the McKay boys acquired the reputation of being handsome and the McKay girls, strikingly beautiful.

As a new bride, Jeanette had to adjust to many things, including frequent visits of Indians to their farm. President Brigham Young had counseled the Church members to "feed them rather than fight with them," and Jeanette tried her best to be friendly and generous, but she was always somewhat nervous. On one occasion

David McKay

an Indian man decided that Jeanette would make a lovely bride for him. He came into the McKay cabin one morning while she was washing clothes and startled her with the announcement, "You be my squaw!" She grabbed a wet towel from the washtub, struck the surprised man in the face, and ran to the room where her husband was sleeping. As soon as the Indian realized Jeanette was not alone in the cabin, he hurried to his horse and disappeared.

Two daughters, Margaret and Ellena, were born to Jeanette and David while they were living in the log cabin. When the front part of their new frame house was completed, they moved into it. The new home was affectionately called "The Old Home." It was there that David Oman McKay was born on September 8, 1873. Seven more children followed: Thomas Evans, Jeanette Isabel, Ann

Jeanette Evans (second from the right) and her
fellow schoolmates in Ogden, Utah, 1867

Powell, Elizabeth Odette, William Monroe, Katherine Favourite, and Morgan Powell.

Motherhood was a role that fit Jeanette perfectly. Together with her husband she created an atmosphere in her home of tenderness, patience, and love. Daily prayer was held with the children, and gospel principles were taught by word and example. Surely the many hundreds of sermons President McKay would give later in his life can be traced to his own childhood experiences in "The Old Home," which he often referred to as "the dearest, sweetest spot on earth." He once described a nostalgic visit to the family home in 1938 in a letter to his brother Thomas, who was then serving as president of the Swiss-German Mission. He closed with these lines:

"It is only an old country home, but no palace was ever filled with truer love and devotion on the part of the parents, brothers, and sisters, than those which pervaded the hearts of the loved ones in that family circle. [When] I walked out of the front door, as the night-latch clicked, I thought it might have been the click of the

Jeanette Evans McKay's four daughters. From left: Jeanette M. Morrell,
Katherine M. Ricks, Ann M. Farr, and Elizabeth M. Hill

lid of a treasure chest that held the wealth of memories that no money could buy."

Jeanette and David made great financial sacrifices to ensure a good education for each of their children. They maintained a separate home on Madison Avenue in Ogden, where they lived during the winter so their children could attend school there. Then they returned to the farm for the summer months. With financial assistance from Grandmother Evans and by mortgaging their farm, they were able to send each of their eight surviving children to the university and all eight graduated with college degrees. Their children's educational accomplishments are impressive:

David O. attended the Weber Stake Academy (later Weber State College, then Weber State University) two years and graduated from the University of Utah as valedictorian of his class. He was principal of both the Huntsville School and the Weber Stake Academy.

Thomas E. graduated from the University of Utah and served on the faculty at the Utah State Agricultural College (now Utah State University).

Jeanette Isabel graduated from the University of Utah, was on the English faculty at Weber Stake Academy, and taught at both the Huntsville School and the Grant School in Ogden. She also did graduate work at the University of Chicago.

Ann attended the Weber Stake Academy and graduated with a two-year associate degree in business from the University of Utah. She worked as her father's secretary while he served in the Utah State Senate.

Elizabeth graduated from Utah State Agricultural College and served on the faculty there, teaching domestic science and serving as the first dean of women. She did graduate work at Columbia University in New York City.

William was on the faculty of Weber Stake Academy and then received a medical degree from the University of Chicago. He practiced medicine for many years in Ogden and became head of the Department of Health for the State of Utah.

Katherine received a degree in English from the University of Utah, taught English at the Weber Stake Academy, and did graduate work at the University of Chicago.

Morgan graduated from Utah State Agricultural College and became a county farm extension agent.

Seven of the children filled honorable missions for the Church, and Thomas and David O. also served as mission presidents.

Jeanette was involved with the Relief Society and Young Ladies Mutual Improvement Association in the Huntsville Ward, but most of her energy was spent rearing her family and supporting her husband as he served as bishop of both the Eden and Huntsville wards, as stake patriarch, and later as a member of the Weber Stake high council. He also served in the Utah Territorial Legislature, being elected a senator for three four-year terms.

Church leaders visiting the Huntsville area frequently stayed at the McKay home, since the town had no restaurant or hotel. The table in their large dining room was always extended to full length, and guest rooms were nearly always occupied, especially on

Jeanette Eveline Evans McKay

weekends. The McKay children met and ate dinner with members of the First Presidency, many other General Authorities, and general officers and members of the Church auxiliaries. At times when there were many guests for dinner, Jeanette had a special code, "FHB," which stood for "family hold-back." The children were encouraged to "hold-back" from taking too much food to be sure everyone at the table got enough.

The weight of her responsibilities eventually took a toll on Jeanette's health, and she experienced health problems at a relatively young age. She died at her home at the age of fifty-four on January 6, 1905, and was buried in Huntsville by her grieving family.

It would be difficult to find a woman who has been remembered as fondly and affectionately by her posterity as Jeanette McKay. Her son David O. spoke of her numerous times in sermons he gave during the many years he was an apostle and later as President of the Church. (He was ordained an apostle in 1906, became a member of the First Presidency in 1934, and served as President from 1951 until his death in 1970 at the age of ninety-six.) On one occasion he said of his mother:

"I cannot think of a womanly virtue that my mother did not possess. . . . To her children, and all others who knew her well, she was beautiful and dignified. Though high-spirited she was even-tempered and self-possessed. Her dark eyes immediately expressed any rising emotion which, however, she always held under perfect control.

"In the management of her household she was frugal yet surprisingly generous . . . in providing for the welfare and education of her children. . . . In tenderness, watchful care, loving patience, loyalty to home and to right, she seemed to me in boyhood, and she seems to me now after these years, to have been supreme. . . .

"During the intervening years [since her death] I have often wished that I had told her in my young manhood that my love for her and the realization of her love and of her confidence gave me power more than once during fiery youth to keep my name untarnished and my soul from clay."

President McKay and other members of the family visited Wales on several occasions to see the village and home where Jeanette Evans McKay was born. When President McKay was in London in 1958 to dedicate the London Temple, he expressed a desire to visit Wales, and he and his sister Jeanette McKay Morrell, accompanied by her daughter, Jeanette, were driven to the area by former British Mission President A. Hamer Reiser. President Reiser wrote the following account of part of their trip in his diary:

"'We're looking for Plas Helygen House, Clwyd Defagwr, Cefn

Coed y Cymmer near Merthyr Tydfil, South Wales, can you help us?'

"This was the question you will have to ask if you are ever in South Wales and want to see the birthplace of Jeanette Evans, mother of President David O. McKay.

"[Upon our arrival] we began making inquiry for the location. An older man, keeping a petrol station up the Cefn Road said: Clywd Defagwr is on the southwest hillside there near that new housing estate. So, we went to explore. Up a steep, narrow, rough and rutted hillside road, I drove in the direction of the old houses on the hillside.

"We came out by a group clinging to the road. There a second road led to a row of four or five terraced houses, each with its front yard enclosed by fence and gate.

"The President said, 'Let's inquire here.' We were at No. 69.

"Inside the fence came an old lady who looked friendly at me as I asked for directions.

"By this time President McKay had come into the yard. She turned to him and said:

"'Oh, I know you.'

"It was Ann Morgan, a spinster who had been born in the house 76 years ago.

"She assured President McKay that 'This is the place.' Then she showed President McKay and Mrs. Morrell into the small six-by-nine bedroom [in which their mother had been born] in which the bed completely occupied the narrow end of the room.

"They stood with arms around each other weeping their emotions at being in this beloved place."

In March 1961, three years after this visit, President McKay returned to Wales to break ground for a new Latter-day Saint chapel in Merthyr Tydfil and to unveil a commemorative plaque he was given permission to have placed at his mother's birthplace. The inscription reads:

Birthplace of
JEANETTE EVELINE EVANS
Born in Plas-Helygen,
69 Clywdyfagwyr
Merthyr Tydfil,
Glamorganshire, South Wales
Born August 28, 1850
Died January 6, 1905
At Huntsville, Utah
United States of America
Emigrated with her family
To America May 22, 1856
Married David McKay on
April 9, 1867 in Ogden, Utah
They were parents of ten
Children, of whom their
Eldest son and third child,
DAVID OMAN MCKAY
Became the Ninth President
Of the Church of Jesus Christ
Of Latter-day Saints on
April 9, 1951

The loving and jovial relationship between Jeanette and her children is illustrated in an anecdote President McKay told in the talk he gave just prior to his dedicatory prayer for the new chapel. "I went home one weekend when I was in college," he said. "Mother was sitting on my left where she always sat at dinner and I said, 'Mother, I have found that I am the only one of your children whom you have switched [whipped, as with a willow shoot].' She said, 'Yes David O., I made such a failure of you I didn't want to use the same method on the other children!'"

When Jeanette died in 1905, the *Salt Lake Tribune* said of her, "Few women in Weber County were more widely known or more universally loved than Mrs. David McKay, and the announcement of her death has caused a gloom of sorrow not only throughout Ogden City and Weber County, but over the entire state."

SOURCES

Biographies of David O. McKay and histories of his family that contain information about his mother include Francis M. Gibbons, *David O. McKay: Apostle to the World, Prophet of God* (Salt Lake City: Deseret Book Company, 1986); Jeanette Morrell, *Highlights in the Life of President David O. McKay* (Salt Lake City: Deseret Book, 1971); Llewelyn R. McKay, *Home Memories of President David O. McKay* (Salt Lake City: Deseret Book, 1956); Clare Middlemiss, *Cherished Experiences* (Salt Lake City: Deseret Book, 1955); and James B. Allen, "David O. McKay," in Leonard J. Arrington, ed., *The Presidents of the Church* (Salt Lake City: Deseret Book, 1986), pp. 275–313.

A special issue of the *Latter-day Saints' Millennial Star* (London) was issued in September 1963 to celebrate President McKay's ninetieth birthday; and there is an article by Jeanette M. Morrell, "Our Cover Picture," in *Instructor* (Salt Lake City) for July 1948. Also helpful was Gerry Avant, "Gospel Enhances Welsh Love of Family, Music, and Country," *Church News*, October 25, 1980.

Family group sheets for the McKay and Evans families are in the Family History Library, Salt Lake City. We have also conducted interviews in February and March 1986 with descendants of Jeanette Evans McKay: David Lawrence McKay, grandson; Lou Jean Blood, granddaughter; Jeanette Morrell, granddaughter; Elizabeth Shaw, granddaughter; and Genevieve Taylor, granddaughter.

Information about Merthyr Tydfil can be found in Afon Taf History Research Group, *Recollections of Merthyr's Past* (Risca, Newport, Gwent, Great Britain: The Starling Press, 1979), *and Merthyr Historian,* volume two, published by the Merthyr Tydfil Historical Society in 1978.

JULINA LAMBSON SMITH

I was trained at my mother's knee to love the Prophet
Joseph Smith and to love my Redeemer. . . . I used to
sit by [her] as a little child and listen to her stories
about the pioneers. . . . She used to teach me and put
in my hands, when I was old enough to read, things
that I could understand. She taught me to pray, . . . to
be true and faithful to my covenants and obligations,
to attend to my duties as a deacon and as a teacher . . .
and later as a priest. . . . I had a mother who saw to it
that I did read, and I loved to read. . . . I learned at a
very early day that God lives. —*Joseph Fielding Smith*

When Julina Lambson was born, on June 18, 1849, in
Salt Lake City, her father had been a member of the
Church for five years and her mother for twelve. Her
father, Alfred Boaz Lambson, was born in 1820 at Royalton,
Niagara County, New York. Reared in Michigan, he left with a
friend for St. Louis in 1843 to join a fur company going to Oregon.
They passed through Nauvoo, Illinois, to visit an uncle and to meet
Joseph Smith, the Latter-day Saint prophet. Alfred came down with
a serious illness (probably malaria) and was forced to remain there
while his friend went on to join the Oregon-bound company. Alfred
listened to the Prophet speak, was very much impressed with him,
and was, in fact, miraculously healed by him. Alfred then made a
study of the doctrines of the Church, was baptized in 1844, was
ordained a seventy, and undertook a proselyting mission the next

Julina Lambson Smith

month to Virginia. He was called back to Nauvoo after the murder of Joseph and Hyrum Smith.

In November 1845 Alfred married Melissa Jane Bigler, twenty-year-old daughter of a genteel West Virginia family who had joined the Church in 1837. The couple left Nauvoo with other Saints in the spring of 1846. They remained in Winter Quarters, Nebraska, for the winter of 1846–47, during which time Alfred served the Church as a mechanic and blacksmith. The first child of Alfred and Melissa, who was named after her mother, was born in Winter Quarters in November 1846. In 1847 the family made the trek across the plains to the Salt Lake Valley, with Alfred serving as chief mechanic, often working throughout the night to repair wagon tires and shoe oxen. Melissa was best remembered by the trekkers for her singing—around the campfire, in the evenings, in the groves at Sunday meeting, even in her wagon as the oxen trudged along.

After arriving in the Salt Lake Valley, Alfred immediately began to build a four-room house. It was the first house plastered in Salt Lake City, and he made all of the nails on his own anvil from wagon tires. It was in this house, located at First South and Second West streets, that Julina was born.

Julina's father was the leading blacksmith in the Salt Lake Valley during the early years. He forged out of wagon tires all the mill irons used in most of the early gristmills and sawmills in the area. He also forged the dies, punches, and other equipment used in the Deseret Mint, which made the first money in the valley.

In 1852, when Julina was three and her younger sister, Edna, was one, Alfred was called to serve as a proselyting missionary in the West Indies; he remained there for two years. He was home for two years, during which time a son, Alfred Jr., was born. Then he was assigned to go to Florence, Nebraska, to serve as a mechanic and blacksmith for the wagons being prepared to make the journey to Utah each summer. He remained there ten years.

Julina's mother, Melissa, was left behind in Salt Lake Valley with four small children to look after, apparently without any help from Alfred. Fortunately her sister Bathsheba, who had married George A. Smith, a member of the Council of the Twelve and a territorial officer, had a splendid home in Salt Lake City, just two blocks from that of Alfred and Melissa. Bathsheba enjoyed children and had two of her own, George A. Smith Jr. and Bathsheba Smith, who also enjoyed children. From the time she was seven, therefore—that is, when her father went to Florence—Julina lived at her Aunt Bathsheba's home, though she went home every day to see her mother. Young Bathsheba, five years older than Julina, was delighted to have a younger "sister" to play with. She had often taken Julina home with her when Julina's father was on his West Indies mission, so almost from the time she could walk and talk, Julina felt that she had two homes and two mothers. Cousin Bathsheba would make Julina dolls and would play with her.

In the summer of 1857, word came to Brigham Young, governor of the territory and President of the Church, that a federal army was advancing on Utah to "put down the Mormons." The valiant men of the territory organized to delay the army's invasion until negotiations could lead to a peaceful settlement. When that was worked out, the army was permitted to occupy a camp forty miles south and west of Salt Lake City. Brigham Young instructed the Saints in Salt Lake City to move to the south of the city in order to avoid any possible conflict with the troops marching through inhabited areas toward Camp Floyd, as the camp came to be called. The families were to prepare their homes for immediate burning in case the army indicated any intention of occupying Mormon land. "The people did not intend to give their homes and all they had labored so hard to get" to the enemy, wrote Julina, as she recalled the event. "They had been driven from Nauvoo and persecuted long enough. Rather than surrender all their property, they would destroy it themselves." The women packed trunks and boxes with things they could not take with them and left them in their houses. The young men drove the teams, and the older ones remained behind to face the enemy, should he determine to occupy their land. Julina recalled:

"My mother, with her four children, and her sister, Sarah Taylor and her six children, left in a big wagon such as the pioneers traveled in, with a neighbor boy to drive. I went with my mother, thinking the trip would be fun, for I was not old enough to realize the seriousness of it. [She was eight.] We went to Nephi [eighty miles south of Salt Lake City], where my mother's brother, Jacob G. Bigler, presided. He gave Aunt Sarah two rooms upstairs in his house and my mother occupied a room in a two-roomed house over the street. The other room was occupied by her cousin, Emeline Bigler Hess and her little family. We were not very comfortable. The town was new and the streets very dusty.

"When we left Salt Lake we expected Aunt Bathsheba to follow us, but she remained in Provo [forty miles south of Salt Lake City], and her son George took Aunt Susan on to Parowan [in southern Utah] where her folks lived. I was very much disappointed, and got homesick [for Aunt Bathsheba and Cousin Bathsheba], and spent most of my time crying. I wanted my cousin and aunt; I could not do without them. . . . Each day I got worse instead of better. Finally, my mother went to her brother Jacob and asked him if he could take me to Provo. I cried so much that she was getting alarmed. . . . So, on my ninth birthday, June 18th, Uncle Jacob hitched his team and I bid my dear mother 'good-by' and started with him towards Provo.

"I can remember that day better than any birthday I ever had. When we got to my aunt's home, she was standing at the table, and was dressed in a blue underdress [less formal than usual] of changeable linsey [a coarse fabric woven from linen warp and coarse wool filling], which she had woven herself. It was made in the style they called the Deseret Costume. This was a wrapper or one-piece dress fitted around the waist, with a full skirt and no belt. My Uncle George [George A. Smith] sat in a chair in the center of the room. I ran up to him, put my arms around his neck, and began to cry. He said, 'My girl, are you sorry so soon that you have come back to us.' Then I sobbed harder, for I thought he really believed his teasing words, and did not know that I was crying for happiness. He then drew me close to him and showed me I was welcome. My own dear cousin Bathsheba then brought a box filled with my doll things and other things that she had made for me, and I was happy."

They returned to Salt Lake City a month later. When they arrived, Julina recalled, they found the Smith house with the windows boarded up and the paths and gardens covered with weeds, which had grown up four feet high. "There was a great deal of work to do to make the place look like home," she wrote. She went over to her mother's home and found it in the same condition. She felt bad for her mother, her two sisters, and her little brother, since her father was still in Nebraska.

George A. Smith, with the cooperation of President Young, constructed a new home for the family on Brigham Street (now South Temple) just east of Main Street (about where the downtown Deseret Book store is now located). It would serve also as the office of the Church Historian, for George A. had been Church Historian

since 1854 (and continued to serve until 1871) and needed a large
room for an office and library.

In 1859 Julina's Aunt Susan (Susan West Smith, a plural wife
of George A. Smith and thus Bathsheba's "sister wife") had a baby
girl, Clarissa. Julina, who was living with her Aunt Bathsheba these
years, wrote, "The little tot added a great deal of joy to our home."
Julina was the "little nurse" for the child, and thus began her nursing career when she was ten.

Julina described her life in Aunt Bathsheba's home as follows:
"I used to get up at five in the morning and pull weeds, while Aunt
Bathsheba milked the cow. She did the outdoor work and the yard
work. Aunt Susan and Cousin Bathsheba did the housework and
tended the babies."

Sadness came to the family in 1860 when Julina's cousin
George A., by now eighteen, was killed by a group of Indians while
on a mission in northern Arizona with Jacob Hamblin. Young
George and his sister Bathsheba had been very close. Both were
good singers, and he played the accordion, flute, and drum for
their little home concerts. The news of his murder spread a gloom
through the household that lasted for many months. Julina said
that her cousin Bathsheba was so brokenhearted and lonely over
her brother's death that she decided to marry. Only sixteen years of
age, she married Clarence Merrill, a friend of George whom George
had approved of as a "special friend" for her. Clarence and
Bathsheba made their home with her mother, Julina's Aunt
Bathsheba, so Julina continued to enjoy association with them.
Their first baby, Annella, lived only a few days, but their second,
Leila, born when Julina was fourteen, was healthy, and Julina
helped look after her and played with her until the Merrills moved
to Fillmore in 1865.

Shortly after they moved, cousin Bathsheba became pregnant
and did not feel well. She asked her mother to allow Julina, who
was now sixteen, to come to help out with Leila and the household. Julina stayed in Fillmore for six months, during which time

little George Albert Merrill was born. Julina wrote, "I enjoyed myself with the young folks of Fillmore." She returned to Salt Lake City when she learned that her sister Melissa had married and her other sister, Edna, was ill. She managed to get a ride back with Brother and Sister Henry Lunt of Cedar City, who were driving to Salt Lake City for April conference in 1866. She arrived home on April 3, and just one month later, Julina was married to Joseph F. Smith, the twenty-seven-year-old son of Hyrum and Mary Fielding Smith and a nephew of the Prophet Joseph Smith.

Joseph F. Smith was born on November 13, 1838, at Far West, Missouri. As a boy of five he saw his father and his uncle, the Prophet Joseph, leave their home and beautiful city of Nauvoo, only to be murdered by a hostile mob on June 27, 1844. At the age of nine in 1848, he drove his mother's wagon as they made the three-and-one-half-month trek to the Salt Lake Valley. Upon his mother's death in 1852, he looked after his sister Martha Ann. General care of the two was under the supervision of George A. Smith, a cousin of Joseph's father and a member of the Council of the Twelve. Because of the closeness of Joseph F. Smith to George A. Smith, and because of Julina's closeness to George A. also, it was natural that the two young people should meet and have an interest in each other.

Joseph F. was called on a mission to Hawaii in 1854 and remained there almost four years. After his return, he married his cousin Levira. They had a few months of happiness together before he was called on a mission to Great Britain, where he remained for three years. Levira had health problems and went to California to live with her mother. Joseph brought her back to Salt Lake City upon his return from England, but when, after some months, he was called to undertake a mission to Hawaii, Levira went to live with her widowed aunt, Agnes Coolbrith Smith, in the Bay area. Agnes was not friendly to the Church or to Brigham Young, and she planted the seeds of doubt and discontent in the mind of Levira. When Joseph F. returned from his mission to Hawaii in

1865, Levira pled with him to remain in California, but he said he was duty-bound to return to Salt Lake City to give an account of his mission, and anyway, his home was there. Levira refused to go with him, so he returned home alone and boarded with his mother's sister, Mercy Fielding Thompson. Later, when Levira decided to return to Salt Lake City, Joseph F. fixed up their home and was delighted to receive her back.

It was at this stage that Brigham Young, who had been impressed that Joseph F. would become a future Church leader, advised him to marry another wife who could bear children and help look after Levira. (Levira was apparently unable to bear children.) By now a clerk for the legislature and assistant in George A. Smith's Church Historian's Office, Joseph proposed to Julina. Her account is as follows:

"He [Joseph F.] did not lose any time on my return [from Fillmore] in finding out whether or not I had found a companion for life. . . . President Young had advised him [to get a wife] and he had told him a number of times, so he thought he should obey. I have always thought that the President would have liked him to marry one of his [Brigham Young's] girls. And I know he could have had any girl he knew for the asking. He was a clerk in the Historian's Office and had a good opportunity to get acquainted with me, and see how handy I was with all kinds of work.

"When he asked me, my answer was, 'Ask my mother and Uncle George. I would not marry the best man living without his consent.' He gave his consent freely, but my mother knew how much he [Joseph] thought of his [first] wife Levira, and she said, 'Julina, Joseph has a wife whom he loves and he is not marrying you for love.' I answered, 'Mother, I love him and if I am good he will learn to love me. He is the only man I have ever seen that I could love as a husband.' [Her mother responded,] 'If that is the way you feel, all right.'"

Julina and Joseph F. Smith were married May 5, 1866. Julina commented that Levira was perfectly willing to have Joseph take

*President Joseph F. Smith and Julina on their fiftieth
wedding anniversary in 1916*

her for a wife because of Levira's semi-invalid condition. Levira told
her she was her choice for a plural wife for him. Julina remained
with Aunt Bathsheba for a week, while she was fixed up with
clothes and furnishings for a room in her new home.

Julina went to live with Levira and Joseph, and she reports that
they were happy. "Levira was very kind to me and I loved her. I did
all of the housework, washing, ironing, cooking, and took full
charge of the home and little Edward," an orphan Joseph F. had
brought back from England in 1863. Joseph was a home missionary and traveled from Brigham City in the north to St. George in
the south to speak to church congregations. While he was on one
of these speaking tours, Levira went back to California to live with
her mother and aunt, and they persuaded her to get a divorce. This
was granted in 1867. A month later, Joseph F. was sustained as an
apostle. A month after that, on August 14, her dear cousin
Bathsheba's birthday, Julina gave birth to her first child, Mercy
Josephine, who was lovingly referred to as Dodo.

In addition to raising a vegetable garden, canning, drying fruit,
tending a flock of chickens, looking after the cow and a span of
horses, and caring for her daughter, Julina was president of the
Sixteenth Ward Retrenchment Society (the early organization for
young women that later became the Young Women's Mutual
Improvement Association). She also worked in the Endowment
House, which served as a temporary facility for eternal endow-
ments and marriages until the Salt Lake Temple was completed, and
she became a member of the Relief Society general board. A second
daughter, Mary Sophronia ("Mamie") was born in 1869, and a
third, Donette, in 1872. Her greatest sorrow was the death of Mercy
Josephine ("our little chatterbox") in 1870 at the age of three.

Julina's diary, begun two and a half years after the birth of Dodo,
shows frequent attendance with her husband at performances at the
Salt Lake Theater; entertainment of relatives and friends, especially
George A. and Bathsheba Smith; occasional sleigh rides during the
winter; and two or three annual picnic excursions. Mostly, though,

she was at home tending her girls—nursing them through chicken-pox, whooping cough, diphtheria, and measles; making them clothes, rattles, and bed linens; serving them meals; and reading the scriptures to them. The diary shows lots of washing clothes, ironing, mending, scrubbing, dusting, and other housework. A listing of occasional purchases shows she bought shoes, calico, thread, flannel, linen, edging, a lamp chimney, shoelaces, cambric, delaine (high-grade worsted material), muslin, and clothespins. The diary also includes the words of some songs she obviously memorized and sang to her children: "Jesus Loves Me" and some play songs. She helped milk and feed the cow while Joseph F. was gone, tended the chickens, and took lessons on the organ. She listed the food she and her sister Edna took on a picnic for their children: bread, butter, radishes, beefsteak, mashed potatoes, green beans, gooseberry pie, and cake. On one occasion she sewed all day—"made twenty-eight diapers." She made a nightcap for her husband, some pillowcases, and a cap and neck handkerchief for a friend's deceased husband to be buried in.

In addition, Julina had several more children—eventually eleven, besides her adopted English child, Edward, and an adopted American daughter, Marjorie Virginia. Her first son was born in 1876. As the first son of the senior wife (Joseph F. had taken two other wives at the time), he was named Joseph Fielding Smith Jr. He would one day become President of the Church. All of Julina's children, except Mercy Josephine, lived to be married in the temple and bear children.

One spiritual experience that Julina appreciated was accompanying Joseph F. and the Brigham Young party to the dedication of the St. George Temple in the spring of 1877. This was the first temple completed in Utah. Young Joseph Fielding, who was just nine months old, was carried in Julina's and Joseph F.'s arms throughout the trip and the dedicatory services. "It was my first assignment in the Church," Joseph Fielding later reported. During the conference held in connection with these services, Joseph F. was called to preside over the European Mission of the Church.

Since Joseph F. by now had additional wives and had frequent need of a midwife (he eventually had forty-eight children, including five adopted sons and daughters), Julina decided to help out the family by getting professional training in obstetrics and nursing. She had already had many years of practical training, and was already the mother of four and adoptive mother of one. She completed her training in 1878. She then delivered hundreds of women, including herself and her sister wives. "It was always a joy for me to place a tiny one for the first time in its mother's arms," she wrote. A book in which she kept a record of these deliveries shows 1,025 babies delivered between 1875 and 1893 without the loss of a mother. She delivered many more, because the record ends years before she stopped practicing midwifery. She assisted in many operations—some in the Deseret Hospital and some in the LDS Hospital in Salt Lake City—and she placed many babies in good homes.

Joseph Fielding Smith, her oldest son, recalls his mother's faithfulness as a midwife. In the first years of her practice, she often hitched her horse and buggy and went to her cases alone in the darkest nights, long before there were any streetlights. She was known to drive as far as ten miles to wait upon a sister. Her usual charge was five dollars for each case, and this included all prenatal and postnatal calls to the home. She knelt in prayer before each delivery. When Joseph Fielding was old enough to help her, she recruited him to drive her to the homes of her patients. "I remember getting up in the middle of the night, taking the lantern to the dark barn, and hitching up the horse ('Old Meg') to the buggy," he said. "I would then drive my mother to the home of an expectant mother so she could serve as midwife and help with the new baby. I would sit in the buggy and wait. I wondered why babies were so often born in the middle of the night."

Young Joseph was helpful to his mother, often assisting in the kitchen, and sometimes cooking for his younger brothers and sisters when their mother was gone. He learned to bake bread and make mincemeat pie, and even how to piece quilts. He later acknowledged that his oldest sister, Mamie, was less impatient than he and served as "assistant mother" for years at a time to Julina's children. A daughter inherited the little brown leather satchel that Julina carried; it contained sterilized materials, a nursing apron, chloroform, and ergot, the latter used to prevent or check postpartum hemorrhage.

In the meantime, Joseph F. served as president of the European Mission in 1874–75. He was released after eighteen months of service when President George A. Smith died. Returning home, he helped look after Aunt Bathsheba as well as his own family, was given Church jurisdiction over Davis County, north of Salt Lake County, and worked in the Endowment House and at the Historian's Office. In 1877 he returned to England as president of the European Mission, but he was recalled to Salt Lake City upon the death of Brigham Young in August. He later became second counselor to President Young's successor, John Taylor.

In 1882 the Congress of the United States passed the Edmunds Act, which was designed to diminish the power and alter the practices of the Latter-day Saints. Among other things, the act provided for vigorous enforcement of antipolygamy laws. Many Church leaders subsequently went into hiding to avoid prosecution. President Taylor suggested to Joseph F. Smith that he should take Julina and go to Hawaii. They left Salt Lake City in January 1885 and remained in Hawaii until mid-1887, when they returned to Utah just in time for Joseph F. to be at President Taylor's side when the prophet died.

At the time they left for Hawaii, Julina had six children (Mamie, fifteen; Donette, twelve; Joseph Fielding, eight; David A., five; G. Carlos, three; and Julina Clarissa, almost one). She left Mamie, Donette, Joseph Fielding, David, and Carlos with Joseph F. Smith's plural wives in Utah and took with her Julina Clarissa (usually referred to as Ina). Although Julina's two years in Hawaii were filled with work, they were nevertheless interesting and exciting. She shared in the love that the Hawaiian people had for Joseph F. and for the missionaries.

Julina entered wholeheartedly into the spirit of the islands. She took lessons in Hawaiian, learned to say the blessing on the food in Hawaiian, attended native feasts, was active in the Lanikuli Relief Society, where only three of the forty women present were Caucasians, and went on excursions to scenic areas. She wrote regularly to her children and prayed that they would remain healthy. In Hawaii she gave birth to a son, Elias Wesley, delivering him herself. She also served as a midwife, delivering dozens of other mothers, both Caucasians and native Hawaiians. One day little Ina, two and a half years old, came in with her dress all wet. "She cannot let water alone," wrote Julina. Her mother must have scolded her, because Ina, just able to talk, replied, "Mamma, let me tell you something. If our baby [Elias Wesley, only two months old] gets in the water when he gets bigger he will have to be whipped." Ina's greatest joy came from having permission to eat poi with her fingers.

Julina managed the mission kitchen, which served some eighteen to twenty-five persons, mostly missionaries and wives and children; went on occasional horseback rides; swam in the ocean; did ironing, washing, and sewing; and managed to write an article on their experiences for the *Woman's Exponent*. She enjoyed gathering guavas, puanas, oranges, and limes.

After more than two years there, Julina returned to Utah, where she bore three more daughters in addition to adopting Marjorie Virginia. She continued her work as a midwife, served as a counselor to the general president of the Relief Society, Emmeline B. Wells, and continued to conduct herself with a quiet dignity and engaging geniality.

A special source of pleasure for Julina during these years was visiting with her mother, who lived until 1899, when she died at age seventy-four. (Julina's father died in 1905.) Concerning her mother, Julina stated: "From mother I learned that notwithstanding the trials and hardships of the journey to Utah, the Saints were united, and enjoyed each other's society. When the camp fires were built, after the day's travel, they would come together, pray, sing, and spend a social evening and the friendship that grew among them was sacred and lasting. The visits of those dear brothers and sisters with my mother I shall never forget. They continued up to the day of her death when those who were left came to pay a tribute of love to her."

The same year as the death of her mother, Julina's oldest son, Joseph Fielding, left to serve a two-year mission in England. She took pleasure in sending him cakes, cookies, and other special treats. As she had expected, he wrote home regularly—newsy, well-written letters. She always felt especially close to him; in fact, Joseph Fielding and his first wife, Louie, stayed after their marriage in a room in Julina's home at 333 West North Temple Street.

When Joseph F. became President of the Church in 1901, he and Julina and their unmarried children moved into the Beehive House, the official residence of the President. This two-story structure, faced with cement, was constructed in 1852 and served as the official residence of Brigham Young as governor and as President of the Church. Situated on the north side of Brigham Street (now South Temple Street) just east of the temple block, it was an imposing edifice with a tower surmounted with a gilded eagle. It had a magnificent drawing room for entertaining important visitors.

Once when Julina was having dinner with some of her family, Joseph Fielding began telling of some of the things he had done as a boy. He reported that he had made the bread, taken care of his brothers and sisters, planted the garden, and so on. Finally Julina looked at him and said, "Joseph, what did I do?" Somewhat taken aback, he muttered, "I guess you just puttered around!" Julina must have enjoyed that response. Her "puttering around" had brought up eleven children to be loyal citizens, worthy Latter-day Saints, and loving parents and grandparents.

In 1910 Joseph Fielding was ordained an apostle. During Julina's lifetime he wrote the most widely used book on Church history ever published (*Essentials in Church History,* 1922, which eventually went through twenty-four editions), and also *The Way to Perfection* (1931), a standard treatment on Church doctrine. He had already made significant strides toward becoming the Church's most reliable scripturist. Julina would have been very proud to have seen him sustained as President of the Church in 1970.

After Joseph F.'s death in 1918, Julina continued to work in the Relief Society, help her children and grandchildren, and assist in many Church and public causes. Seventeen years later she suffered a bad fall. She died on January 10, 1936, at age eighty-six. An editorial by Annie Wells Cannon in the *Relief Society Magazine* mentions Julina's frank, straightforward manner; her industry, frugality, and simplicity in dress; her graciousness and hospitality; her work in the Endowment House and the Salt Lake Temple; her management of the Beehive House as the official hostess of the President of the Church; and her determination to plant trees and flowers to beautify her home.

Julina had witnessed the change from the covered wagon to the airplane, from the tallow candle to incandescent light. She had known Presidents Brigham Young, John Taylor, Wilford Woodruff, Lorenzo Snow, Joseph F. Smith, and Heber J. Grant while they presided over the Church; and George Albert Smith, David O. McKay, and, of course, her sterling son, Joseph Fielding Smith, each of whom would serve as President of the Church after her death. Blessed is a virtuous woman, wrote the author of Proverbs, "for her price is far above rubies. . . . She looketh well to the ways of her household, and eateth not the bread of idleness. . . . Many daughters have done virtuously, but thou excellest them all." (Proverbs 31:27, 29.) That would have been a perfect description for Julina Lambson Smith.

SOURCES

There are four holograph diaries written by Julina in the LDS Church Archives in Salt Lake City. These cover the years 1870–1879, 1880, 1886, and 1886–1921. Excerpts from her 1886 diary are published in Kenneth M. Godfrey, Audrey M. Godfrey, and Jill Mulvay Derr, *Women's Voices: An Untold History of the Latter-day Saints, 1830–1900* (Salt Lake City: Deseret Book, 1982), pp. 343–57. The Joseph F. Smith Papers in the Church Archives also contain material about Julina. In 1927 she wrote a fourteen-page personal history, which is especially detailed about her life as a child and young bride. This is written in the personal record book of her grandmother Bathsheba Smith, the original of which is in the Church Archives. Bathsheba's history suggests that Julina went to live with her in 1855 and remained until her (Julina's) marriage in 1866. Finally, a "Record of accouchements [assists at birth] by Julina Smith, Accoucheuse," covering the dates 1875 to 1893, is in the library of the Utah State Historical Society, Salt Lake City.

Materials about Julina's mother and father include Nettie Davis Bradford, Donnette S. Kesler, and Helen Davis, "Melissa Jane Bigler Lambson," typescript, Church Archives; "Autobiographical Sketch of the Life of Alfred B. Lambson," typescript, Church Archives; "Alfred Boaz Lambson," in *Utah Genealogical and Historical Magazine* 6 (1915): 145–53.

The following biographies of Joseph F. Smith (the husband) and of Joseph Fielding Smith (the son) contain many references to Julina: Joseph Fielding Smith, *Life of Joseph F. Smith* (Salt Lake City: Deseret Book, 1938); Francis M. Gibbons, *Joseph F. Smith: Patriarch and Preacher, Prophet of God* (Salt Lake City: Deseret Book, 1984); Scott Kenney, "Joseph F. Smith," and Joseph Fielding McConkie, "Joseph Fielding Smith," in Leonard J. Arrington, ed., *The Presidents of the Church* (Salt Lake City: Deseret Book, 1986), pp. 179–209, 315–41; Joseph Fielding Smith Jr. and John J. Stewart, *The Life of Joseph Fielding Smith* (Salt Lake City: Deseret Book, 1972); and Dean May, "Joseph Fielding Smith" in Preston Nibley, *The Presidents of the Church* (Salt Lake City: Deseret Book, 1974), pp. 409–21. See also Hyrum M. Smith III and Scott G. Kenney, eds., *From Prophet to Son: Advice of Joseph F. Smith to His Missionary Sons* (Salt Lake City: Deseret Book, 1981).

Information about Julina's career as a midwife is given in Claire Noall, "Mormon Midwives," *Utah Historical Quarterly* 10 (1942): 84–144, esp. 139–42; Keith C. Terry, "The Contribution of Medical Women during the First Fifty Years in Utah" (Master's Thesis, Brigham Young University, 1964), esp. pp. 25–26; and Chris Rigby Arrington, "Pioneer Midwives," in Claudia L. Bushman, ed., *Mormon*

Sisters: Women in Early Utah (Cambridge, Massachusetts: Emmeline Press, 1976), pp. 43–65.

Julina's obituary and an editorial tribute to her are given in *Deseret News,* January 10 and 11, 1936.

In quoting from Julina's diary and personal history, we have corrected some misspellings and have supplied some changes in punctuation and capitalization.

Louisa Emeline
Bingham Lee

I have been blessed with . . . a grand and lovely mother,
one who didn't display her affection, but showed her
love in tangible ways that, as a child, I came early to
recognize as true mother love. As just a high school
boy I went away on a high school debating team. We
won the debate. I came back and called mother on the
telephone only to have her say, "Never mind, son, I
know all about it . . ." When I came home she took me
aside and said: "When I knew it was time for this performance to start I went out among the willows by the
creek side, and there, all by myself, I remembered you
and prayed God you would not fail." I have come to
know that that kind of love is necessary for every son
and daughter who seeks to achieve in this world.
—*Harold B. Lee*

At the time the pioneers established the settlement in the
Salt Lake Valley in 1847, 16,000 Saints were waiting on the
banks of the Missouri to make the journey to the Great
Basin. Several thousand Church members in New England, the
Middle Atlantic States, the Southeast, the Midwest, and Great
Britain were also expecting to join the Latter-day Saints in the
Rocky Mountain area as soon as places could be found for them to
settle. A prime task of the pioneers, therefore, was finding suitable
places for making a living. Many thousands could be settled in the

Louisa Emeline Bingham Lee

Salt Lake Valley, but locations would have to be found for thousands of others.

With this in mind, the early pioneers conducted a systematic program of exploration, beginning with the Salt Lake Valley and then proceeding to Tooele Valley to the west, Weber and Ogden valleys to the north, and Utah and Sanpete valleys to the south. One large exploring company was dispatched to southern Utah and across southern Nevada to California. They found oases and springs along their route and laid the basis for many future Latter-day Saint settlements.

Pioneering Saints pressed northward and settled on Box Elder Creek near the mouth of Box Elder Canyon in 1851, founding what was later called Brigham City. But trappers and other frontiersmen insisted that Cache Valley, still farther north and east between the Wellsville and Bear River ranges of the Wasatch Mountains, was too cold to grow crops. The Saints avoided it until 1856, when a year of drought forced them to try places with ample water. In 1856, therefore, Peter Maughan led a group of Saints from Tooele to settle Maughan's Fort, later renamed Wellsville. Other Saints colonized Logan, Hyrum, Providence, Mendon, Richmond, Smithfield, and Franklin. All told, eight villages were established in Cache Valley in 1859 and 1860. They were well-watered by mountain-fed streams, while sediments laid by the ancient Lake Bonneville extended from the mountains on each side in gentle slopes that were ideal for farming.

The principal problem facing further settlement in the northern end of Cache Valley was the periodic occupation of the area by a group of Shoshoni Indians. The Saints cultivated friendships with Indian leaders, treaties were made, and some of the more courageous Latter-day Saints gradually established ranches and residences further north.

In 1865 one of the settlers, Thomas C. D. Howells, once a member of the Mormon Battalion, with his four sons and others founded Clifton in southeastern Idaho. The village, with several hundred acres of good farming land, was located on Clifton Creek, a small tributary of Bear River, the large stream that flowed through much of Cache Valley and emptied into Great Salt Lake. As other settlers arrived, a branch of the Church was organized, a post office was established, and a meetinghouse was built in 1871. Ultimately, about 150 persons located in the village in the nineteenth century.

Among those attracted to Clifton in the early years were Levi Perry and Elizabeth Lusk Bingham and their children. They had crossed the Plains in the early 1850s and gone to Payson, Utah. Nine children were born in the family as they moved, in succession, to Pleasant Grove and Three-Mile, Utah, and on to Clifton, Idaho. Their oldest son was Perry Calvin Bingham, born in Payson

*Levi Perry Bingham and Elizabeth Lusk Bingham,
Louisa's paternal grandparents*

in 1857. He was still a boy when his parents moved to Clifton. In 1875, at age eighteen, he married Rachel Elvira Henderson, who was born in Kaysville, Utah, and whose parents were also early pioneers in Clifton. Perry and Rachel were married in Clifton and remained there until her death in 1907 at the age of forty-nine.

A daughter was born to Perry and Rachel in 1876, but she died at the age of two. On New Year's Day, January 1, 1879, Rachel gave birth to her second child, also a girl, whom she and Perry named Louisa Emeline Bingham. In succeeding years a boy and four additional girls were born, all of whom, except one daughter, died while they were still young. Thus, Louisa and her sister Effie, five years younger, were the only two children to survive to adulthood, out of seven births.

Because of the invalidism of her mother, Louisa was obliged, as early as age eight, to care for her mother and her younger brother and sisters. Because her father was away much of the time freighting into Montana, and later buying and selling cattle, she did the cooking, bathing, washing, ironing, sewing, and the outside chores as well—all this in addition to attending school. Independent and resourceful, Louisa helped to plow and plant the crops, cut and stack the hay, shear the sheep, and care for the chickens and milk the cow. Her son Harold, who must have heard her tell many times of this experience, wrote that she was so small as a girl that when she did the washing, she had to stand on a box so she could reach far enough down into the tub to scrub the clothes on a washboard. When she was sewing, her feet would barely reach the treadles on the sewing machine. He continued:

"They lived about a five-minute walk from school, and Mother would arise very early, fix breakfast, dress and care for her brother and sister, bathe and feed her mother, then dash off for school. When all the other children were enjoying their games at recess, Mother would run home to care for her mother and begin preparing lunch. At noon she would hurry home again to take care of the family responsibilities which came upon her early in her life. Mother owned a famous saddle pony named Maude, which she rode for the cows and on other errands."

Louisa attended church regularly. In those days Primary was held on Wednesdays, Young Women's Mutual Improvement Association meetings on Tuesdays, ward dances on Fridays, Sunday School on Sunday mornings and sacrament meetings on Sunday evenings. Louisa enjoyed the classes, gave two-and-a-half minute talks, read the scriptures, and, at the age of fourteen, began teaching a Sunday School class, which she continued to teach for four years.

When she was sixteen, dark-eyed, dark-haired Louisa met and married a nineteen-year-old newcomer to Clifton, Samuel Marion Lee Jr. They were married May 13, 1895, in the Logan Temple. Samuel was the son of pioneer settlers of Panaca, Nevada. His mother, Margaret McMurrin Lee, an emigrant from Scotland, had given birth to eleven children, each of whom had died shortly after birth. Then, upon the birth of her twelfth child, Margaret herself died. This last baby, Samuel Jr., weighed only three and a half pounds at birth and was so tiny that a large finger ring could be slipped over his arm. He was nursed for six months by his aunt and

Samuel Marion Lee and Louisa Bingham Lee

then taken by wagon to Salt Lake City to be raised by his grandparents, Joseph and Margaret McMurrin. Upon his grandmother's death of cancer in 1893, when he was seventeen, Samuel went to Clifton to live with his uncle and aunt, Riley and Jeannette McMurrin Davis. He had been in Clifton a year and a half before his marriage to Louisa.

Samuel and Louisa settled down to a life on the farm, although during the first year he taught at the local school. Fully aware of the burdens of farm life because of her experience running her father's household, Louisa prepared to help with the planting, cultivating, and harvesting of their farm crops. She did some of the hoeing and irrigating, put up hay, helped with the threshing, and often fed the stock. She was also active in the Clifton Ward. She served as counselor in the Young Women's MIA for six years; as president for seven years; and as a counselor in the Oneida Stake MIA presidency for several more years. She enjoyed music, the arts, sports, and the outdoors.

About a year and a half after their marriage, Samuel and Louisa had their first child, Samuel Perry Lee. Their second child, born March 28, 1899, was Harold Bingham Lee, who later became President of the Church. In the years that followed, Clyde, Waldo, Stella, and Verda were born, all in Clifton. All six children lived to marry and have families of their own. Samuel and Louisa saw to it that they were educated in the home as well as at school.

Louisa's first four children were boys, and she apparently became impatient to have a girl. Her oldest son, Perry, wrote that Harold had beautiful wavy black hair, and Louisa trained it into dangling ringlets that reached below his shoulders. The women of the neighborhood thought he was a beautiful boy, but his father and the neighborhood boys scoffed at him until one day Harold, about four, snipped off one of the danglers, forcing his mother to give him a short, boyish haircut. "The shorn curls were carefully preserved," however, wrote Perry, and later, "when Grandfather Bingham was deputy warden of the Idaho State Penitentiary, he prevailed upon one of the inmates to braid the curly locks into two watch chains, which our mother kept among her treasures."

Louisa's presence of mind in the face of potential disaster is suggested in two experiences described by Harold in his life's history:

"Mother was making soap and had a large tub of lye preparation stored on a high shelf to keep it out of the reach of the younger children. She wanted to take it down, and since I was the only one home she enlisted my help. We climbed up on a chair and began to steady it down. When it was exactly above my head, our hold slipped and the tub and its burning lye water dashed over my face, head, and arms. As quickly as she could act, Mother seized me so I wouldn't run and kicked off the lid from a jar of beet pickles she had just made, and with the right hand cupped, dipped out the reddened, pickle vinegar from the beets over my burning face, neck, and arms to stop the eating of the lye and save me from being badly scarred. What could have been a tragedy was averted because of her inspired action. Often she was intuitively led by the Spirit."

The second story is a vivid illustration of Louisa's possession of a heavenly gift:

"There was a severe thunderstorm raging near the mountain where our home was located. Our family, consisting of my grandmother, my mother, and two or three of the younger children, were seated in the kitchen before an open door, watching the great display of nature's fireworks. A flash of chain lightning followed by an immediate loud clap of thunder indicated that the lightning had struck very close. I was playing back and forth in the doorway when suddenly and without warning, my mother gave me a vigorous push that sent me sprawling backwards out of the doorway. At that instant, a bolt of lightning came down the chimney of the kitchen stove, out through the kitchen's open doorway, and split a huge gash from top to bottom in a large tree immediately in front of the house. Had it not been for Mother's intuitive action, and if I had remained in the door opening, I wouldn't be writing this story today."

In 1909, after Louisa's father had been in Boise for three years (her mother had died in Clifton in 1907), his health broke and he returned to Clifton, where, as had happened earlier with Rachel, he was an invalid dependent on Samuel and Louisa. He died in 1916 at age fifty-nine.

Her son Harold testified in his journal of Louisa's skill in caring for the sick:

"She always began with castor oil, and so successful was she that never was a doctor in our home excepting when the babies came. I recall the many weary days and nights when four of us were down in bed at the same time with scarlet fever. Father was away much of the time, and for several days, my brother Clyde, particularly, was at death's door. I remember also Mother's bitterly successful fight to save his life when he suffered with diphtheria. She swabbed his throat constantly for several days and nights to prevent its closing."

In later years Louisa assisted as a midwife, helping with the delivery of eight of her own grandchildren. She was also one of the finest cooks, seamstresses, and quilters in Clifton, which enabled her to be especially helpful to the members of the ward during the nine years (1914–1923) Samuel served as bishop. Indeed, there is a hint of evolution of the Church Welfare Program, which her son Harold later managed, in the way Samuel ran his own storehouse, the commodities coming from Louisa's pantry. In the late evening when no one was watching, Samuel would often take a sack of flour to a family in need.

Louisa's two daughters recall their childhood home with special fondness:

"The simple joys created by a loving mother of hot, homemade tomato soup after sacrament meeting on Sundays; the 'lumpy-dick' of which Harold was so fond; a very special evening when mother had made new flannel nightgowns for us little girls; and the nights when we couldn't sleep because the delicious aroma of baking bread cast its tantalizing aroma through the house to our nostrils in the bedroom. . . . We did have the sweetest childhood. . . . Though our family was poor for many years, we children were always well dressed and well fed because of Mother's thrifty efforts and talents."

One of the children characterized their growing-up years by declaring: "We had everything that money could not buy." One author told a story illustrating Louisa's method of disciplining her children (including Harold):

"She kept a little green willow handy, and when the children got out of line she would swish it around. One day a six-year-old son refused to do as he was asked and dashed off through the alfalfa field. Louisa couldn't see him and knew she couldn't catch him, so she just stood at the edge of the field, switch in hand, and called: 'Now, son, you think it over. You're going to get this little green willow whether you stay in there all day or fifteen minutes.

Samuel Marion Lee and Louisa Bingham Lee

So it's up to you. I'm going to stand here fifteen minutes and then I'm going back to the house. Now you just keep it in mind while you play today, that you are going to get this little green willow.'

"After fifteen minutes the errant little boy appeared; and though it was 'the hardest thing in the world to do' at the moment, she applied the little green willow—but very lightly! Those fifteen minutes of her precious time were spent waiting at the edge of eternity for a child to think it over, to repent, and to learn to obey."

In 1923 their son Harold moved to Salt Lake City, and one year later Samuel and Louisa moved there also. Two years later they were in Green River, Wyoming, where Samuel worked for ten months as manager of a Piggly Wiggly grocery store. They returned to Salt Lake City in 1927 and remained there until their deaths.

Samuel spent many years as a night supervisor for ZCMI. Louisa taught Primary, served in the Relief Society, was the choir "mascot" and visited with her children. Both were present when their son Harold was sustained as president of Pioneer Stake in 1930, when he was only thirty-one. In 1935 he became general manager of the Church Welfare Program. Harold was ordained an apostle in 1941, and Samuel and Louisa proudly listened to him speak many times in general conference. Samuel died in 1947 at age seventy-one. Louisa, who suffered with angina pains for many years, died on July 27, 1959, at age eighty.

Before his death, Samuel paid Louisa a tribute that would have been completely satisfying: "Her efforts have not been in vain, for she can look with honor and pride upon her children, realizing that they are monuments of her life's mission."

SOURCES

The best single source on the mother of President Harold B. Lee is L. Brent Goates, *Harold B. Lee: Prophet and Seer* (Salt Lake City: Bookcraft, 1985), a biography of President Lee, which contains extensive quotes from his diary and personal history, including memories of his parents and grandparents. Also excellent are Jaynann Morgan Payne, "Louisa Bingham Lee: Sacrifice and Spirit," *Ensign* 4 (February 1974): 80–85; and S. Perry Lee, "Prophet's Brother Recalls Early Days," *Church News*, December 29, 1973, pp. 5, 10.

The early history of Clifton is treated in Harold C. Bateman, "The History of Clifton, Idaho" (Master's Thesis, Brigham Young University, 1931). Cache Valley's history is given in Joel E. Ricks and Everett L. Cooley, eds., *The History of a Valley: Cache Valley, Utah-Idaho* (Logan, Utah: Cache Valley Centennial Commission, 1956); M. D. Beal, *A History of Southeastern Idaho* (Caldwell, Idaho: Caxton Printers, 1942); and Edward W. Tullidge, *Tullidge's Histories: Northern Utah and Southern Idaho* (Salt Lake City: Juvenile Instructor, 1889), pp. 480–86. Freighting to Montana is treated in Betty M. Madsen and Brigham D. Madsen, *North to*

Montana! Jehus, Bullwhackers, and Mule Skinners on the Montana Trail (Salt Lake City: University of Utah Press, 1980).

Other useful sources include S. Dilworth Young, "Having Been Born of Goodly Parents," *New Era* 3 (March 1973):4–8; "Harold B. Lee," in Leonard J. Arrington, ed., *The Presidents of the Church* (Salt Lake City: Deseret Book, 1986), pp. 343–71; and Gordon B. Hinckley, "President Harold B. Lee: An Appreciation" *Ensign* 2 (November 1972): 2–11.

OLIVE WOOLLEY
KIMBALL

> My mother was faultless. She was a saint . . . , the epit-
> ome of perfection. Who could even mention one virtue
> that she did not possess? She seemed especially angelic
> when the light shined through her light red hair and
> made a halo. . . . When others spoke in condemnation,
> her lips were always silent. . . . I liked being with my
> Ma. —*Spencer W. Kimball*

Settlers living in the Great Basin in the late nineteenth century used a variety of mostly uncomplimentary phrases to describe the territory of Arizona. It was "a desert wasteland," "hot and dry," "colorless." Missionaries returned home to Utah claiming that the water from the rivers was so full of minerals that one "had to bite it off." Still another person described the land in his journal as "a formation of lava rock and sand, with here and there a poor unfortunate cactus or desert weed." But one word that young Olive Woolley Kimball never expected to use in describing that supposed inhospitable land was "home."

As a young mother living in Salt Lake City, by now a well-established community, Olive literally held her breath at general conference as leaders announced from the pulpit names of dependable priesthood holders being asked to move their families to Arizona to supervise and strengthen the wards, stakes, and missionary work there. Knowing this, it was with a heavy heart that

Olive's husband, Andrew Kimball, returned home one evening in 1897, having just met with Church leaders in President Wilford Woodruff's office, to tell Olive that their fears had become reality. Christopher Layton, president of the St. Joseph Stake in Arizona, was soon to be released, and Andrew had been called to replace him.

Olive was stunned. She could think of a hundred reasons why they couldn't go. She and Andrew were paying off a home and rental house and were fifteen hundred dollars in debt. She had just recently given birth to their seventh child. Six were living; the first child had died in infancy. It was not an opportune time for the family to pull up deep roots and start over as pioneers. Then too, she enjoyed living in Salt Lake City within walking distance of her mother and other family members and friends.

Together, Olive and Andrew prayed for understanding and acceptance. Andrew later wrote, "That couple bowed before God trying to pray while their hearts were so swollen with grief. They bubbled over with scalding tears and after a long and hard struggle a petition was made to the throne of Grace while a flood of tears gushed forth. This over, nothing remained but to go to work." There was but one answer, and that was to go. Olive and Andrew had both come from prominent pioneer families in which tremendous sacrifice "for the building of Zion in the latter days" was simply a way of life.

Olive Woolley was born in Salt Lake City on June 1, 1860, the sixth of eleven children born to Bishop Edwin Dilworth Woolley and Mary Ann Olpin. A former Quaker, Edwin Woolley was a dynamic, energetic, stubborn pioneer merchant who became one of the outstanding civic and Church leaders in early Latter-day Saint history. He was a native of Chester County, Pennsylvania, where he was born in 1807 to John Woolley Jr. and Rachel Dilworth. Edwin and his first wife, Mary Wickersham, moved to Ohio in 1831 to be closer to her family and to locate where there were better opportunities for making a living.

Edwin and Mary Woolley were living in eastern Ohio, in

Edwin and Mary Olpin Woolley, Olive's parents

Columbiana County, when they heard the gospel preached in 1837 by two Latter-day Saint missionaries, George A. Smith and Lorenzo D. Barnes. Mary was baptized soon after, but Edwin was undecided. He wanted to meet the Prophet Joseph Smith. So impatient was Edwin to meet him that he and his wife traveled some eighty miles by horseback in one day to Kirtland, Ohio, where the Prophet was thought to be staying. This trip was later referred to affectionately by his family as "Ed Woolley's wild ride to see the Prophet Joseph Smith."

Unfortunately, the Prophet was in Missouri at the time, so the Woolleys were disappointed, but they did ride on to Portage, Ohio, where they met the Prophet's parents, Joseph Smith Sr. and Lucy Mack Smith. Edwin seemed to benefit greatly from meeting and associating with the elder Smiths, and he was baptized a month later, on Christmas Eve, 1837, by Elder Barnes.

Edwin became a close friend of the Prophet and of Brigham Young, whose business affairs he managed years later in the Salt Lake Valley. The Woolleys crossed the Plains in a company led by Brigham Young, arriving in the Salt Lake Valley in 1848. In 1850, at the request of President Young, Edwin went to New England to purchase merchandise for the Church. During a stopover in

St. Louis on his return trip, he hired a young English convert, Mary Ann Olpin, to cook for his company for the remainder of the journey to Utah. Sister Olpin was delighted, for she had been waiting for an opportunity to join her fellow Latter-day Saints in the West. Thus, the future parents of Olive Woolley first became acquainted.

Mary Ann Olpin, who was known as Ann by her family and friends, was born in Cam, near Dursley, Gloucestershire, England. Her village was only a few miles inland from the Bristol Channel, an arm of the Atlantic Ocean that lies between Wales and southwestern England. Cam lay between two major industrial and shipping centers: Gloucester, about fifteen miles to the north, where Robert Raikes founded the world's first Sunday school in 1790, and Bristol, about twenty miles to the south, where the family had access to a wide variety of merchandise in the numerous shops and stalls.

After joining the Church, Ann got permission from her parents, Henry Olpin and Sarah Ann White, to emigrate to America with her Aunt Eliza, and in 1849 they sailed for six weeks before arriving in New Orleans. It was either on the voyage from England or on the riverboat trip they took from New Orleans to St. Louis that Ann promised to marry another young convert from England, Edgar Jones. He, however, left her in St. Louis to seek employment up the river a few miles, and he died there of cholera during the epidemic of 1849. Soon after, Ann's Aunt Eliza also died of the dread disease, leaving Ann completely alone in America, hoping for a way to get to Utah. Being an expert seamstress, she was able to earn a considerable amount with her needle and thus earned her passage to Kanesville, Iowa, where she joined the pioneer company of Edwin Woolley.

After a long, hard journey, the Woolley caravan arrived in the Salt Lake Valley in October 1850. Two weeks after their arrival, Ann became the plural wife of Edwin, the ceremony being performed on November 10 by President Brigham Young in the Endowment House.

Ann first lived in a wagon box on the corner of Third East and

Third South streets, where Edwin later built a small cabin for her. After the birth of their first child, Henry Alberto (Bert), Ann moved into a home owned by Brigham Young at 19 East South Temple, where the Hotel Utah garage would later stand.

In May 1860, Bishop Woolley was making final preparations for a business trip to the East, but he was concerned about the health and well-being of Ann, who was expecting their sixth child in June. He promised Ann's younger sister, Ellen, who had come west with her parents in a handcart company in 1859, a nice, eastern-made gift if she would stay with Ann and help run the house until his return. Ellen stayed through the birth of Ann's baby on June 1 and an additional two weeks until her own marriage; then another sister, Sarah Ann, came to assist Ann until Edwin's return. The baby, a beauty, was named Olive. She would become the mother of Spencer Woolley Kimball, twelfth President of the Church.

The home in which Olive was born was located at 29 South State Street and was designed by Truman O. Angell, architect of the Salt Lake Temple. The Woolley home, with its large, spacious rooms, was considered one of the finest homes west of the Missouri River.

It was in this home that Olive spent her first nine years. Her father had launched a successful mercantile business, had been elected to serve in the Utah House of Representatives, and was bishop of the Salt Lake Thirteenth Ward. Hence, their home was constantly teeming with activity, with many of the prominent civic and church leaders of the territory entertained there. Olive's mother considered it her calling to keep the bishop's home ready for callers at all hours, be they General Authorities or members of the ward seeking advice or assistance. History shows that she responded to her assignment cheerfully and effectively.

Next door on the north of the Woolley home was the Social Hall, the center of social and theatrical activities for Salt Lake City. Among Olive's earliest memories were the wonderful parties held there. Often the fiddlers for the dances would head for the Woolley home during intermission for oyster suppers. Then they would return to the hall for several hours of post-midnight dancing. The Woolley children were thrilled to observe these activities from their upstairs bedroom windows, as their parents joined in the festivities. In 1862, when Olive was two, Brigham Young and the Church built the Salt Lake Theater, across the street and a few steps south of the Woolley home. Modeled after the Drury Lane Theater in London, the theater was compared with the finest in Boston and New York. The Woolleys were eager patrons and often took their children and encouraged them to play children's parts.

The prosperity and culture that the Woolleys enjoyed in their "haven in the West" are described with obvious pride in a letter Bishop Woolley wrote to his in-laws, the Wickershams, in Ohio. It was written in 1865, when Olive was five years old. Part of it reads:

> All is peace and plenty, prosperity strides forth with her gigantic step and this once desolate land is now teeming with the busy bustle of life. Altho it is winter, nevertheless, the noise of the hammer, the hatchet, the plane and chisel, is heard at almost every step in some portions of our city, and there is a great spirit of improvement in this country of late. Our theater is very hard to beat. When I was east, I saw nothing this side of Boston to equal it. . . . We have a play every Wednesday and Saturday evening. The play tonight is Shakespeare's Macbeth a good play and is patronized very well, a full house almost every night.
>
> When I come to speak of stores and storehouses I never have seen better, we are getting to have some very fine displays in show windows, I don't know that I ever saw better.

Olive has been described as being "a very lovely child" who was basically good natured and obedient. She and her sister Ruth, two years older than she, both had light red hair at a time when such hair color was often blamed for disagreeable behavior. So at least she had an excuse if the need arose. The Woolley family tended to be small in stature, and "Ollie," as her friends called her, measured 5 feet 1½ inches as an adult; she weighed about 135 pounds while rearing her family.

Olive loved music and learned to play the organ. Once she won five dollars from her two older brothers, Bert and Orson, for being the first in the family to be able to sing a song and play her own accompaniment.

Olive attended school in the Thirteenth Ward District School, where she and students of various other ages were taught by her older brother Bert in a one-room schoolhouse. Bert was nine years older than Olive, and she idolized him. When he went on a proselyting mission to the Hawaiian Islands in 1880, he collected many interesting shells and ferns, which he brought home to Olive and his other sisters and brothers.

Roberta Flake Clayton, a friend, repeated a story she had heard of Olive's youth. One evening as Olive and some friends were playing cards, her father came home and saw what they were doing. After the friends left he said to her, "Daughter, where did you get those cards?" She told him a friend had given them to her. He said, "Where do you keep them?" She replied she kept them in her dresser drawer. He concluded, "That is the best place for them." She never did play with them again.

When Olive was nine, her father sold their beautiful home to Brigham Young, after President Young suggested that the home was more the style for the President of the Church to be living in. The Woolleys moved into the much more modest home of Brigham Young's son-in-law Jacob Gates, who had been called on a mission to St. George and was happy to have a buyer. The home, on the southwest corner of Second South and Second East, was purchased for seven thousand dollars. An adobe and stucco structure, it was directly across the street from the Thirteenth Ward meetinghouse, which made it convenient for the family, and especially Bishop

Olive Woolley Kimball

Woolley, to simply cross the street for the many Church functions and meetings they attended.

The large, extended Woolley family gathered often for special occasions, such as birthdays and Christmases, and also at general conference time. In celebration of her father's seventy-first birthday, Olive helped with a gathering of approximately seventy-five of his descendants—children, grandchildren, and great-grandchildren—as well as other relatives and friends. It was a surprise party for Edwin. "Cheerfulness, good humor and happy remarks were freely indulged in and all enjoyed a sumptuous, three-hour meal spread over several large tables," the *Deseret News* reported. After eating, the group moved to a large room for musical treats. Songs both written and sung by Woolley children "awakened deep emotions in Bishop Woolley." Various family members rose and reminisced concerning the deep trials and abundant blessings through the years. Edwin blessed them as the patriarch of the Woolley family and expressed deep gratitude for their love and affection. Such were the joyous family gatherings Olive learned to love. Three years after this gathering, on October 14, 1881, Edwin D. Woolley died at the age of seventy-four, being survived by ninety-five descendants. Olive's mother, Ann, died September 30, 1894.

As Olive matured into a young woman, she was well-liked by her friends and had many admirers among the young men of the city. She tended to be somewhat shy, often to the point of avoiding some meetings or activities lest she be asked to speak or pray. Among her friends in the Thirteenth Ward was a young man by the name of Heber J. Grant, who was three years older than she. When young Heber seriously decided to become a good baseball player, he threw his ball against the Woolley barn for practice.

But the young man Olive was particularly attracted to was Andrew Kimball, a six-foot tall, slender man with a dark complexion. Immaculate in dress, Andrew had a reputation for being a hard worker and strictly honest. He was the son of Heber C. Kimball, one of the Prophet Joseph Smith's closest and most faithful friends, who later became a counselor to President Brigham Young in the First Presidency.

Andrew's mother was Ann Alice Gheen, who, like Edwin Woolley, was of Quaker parentage, born and raised in Chester County, Pennsylvania. She was described as being "a delicate and intensely spiritual woman, Quakerish in dress, shy in society, with a soft heart for the weak and sick." Andrew and a twin sister, Alice, were born in 1858 in Salt Lake City. By 1880, both of Andrew's parents had died. He was working as a fireman on the Utah Central Railroad when he fell in love with pretty, blue-eyed Olive Woolley.

The date of Olive and Andrew's wedding had to be postponed because of her father's final illness and death; they were eventually married February 2, 1882, when Olive was twenty-one and Andrew was twenty-three. Sadness came quickly to the young couple when their first child, Maude Woolley Kimball, died of pneumonia at the age of ten months. Olive was grief-stricken, and journal entries she made during this period report numerous visits to the baby's grave. For months, her thoughts centered around this child: "May 14, 1884: I ironed all morning and in the afternoon, being alone, felt quite bad over the loss of our Darling Maude."

Within a year of Maude's death, Olive and Andrew were blessed with another child, Olive Clare. The couple would eventually become the parents of eleven children.

While her husband was away on business or Church assignments, Olive busied herself doing the wash, playing the organ, making rugs, starching clothes, and visiting her mother, whom she frequently walked a mile and a half to see. She often arose at five in the morning to begin the day's chores. Her diary of 1884 includes such phrases as "made a Mother Hubbard dress of calico"; "had to bussle around to get everything done"; "helped my husband plant potatoes, plant fruit trees, and fix the fence along the corral"; "made root beer."

When her daughter Clare was only three months old, another trial came to Olive. Her husband was called to serve a mission in the Indian Territory in present-day Oklahoma. The Woolleys rented their home, and Olive and the baby lived with her mother while Andrew was on his mission for three years. The separation was hard for both Olive and Andrew. Without Andrew's companionship, Olive felt especially lonely. She had given birth to two babies in less than two years, so her health was not the best. She worried about burglars and felt uneasy some evenings not having a husband around. Remembering the illness that took Maude from her, she was understandably frightened whenever Clare took sick. She wrote frequently to Andrew, but news and expressions of affection traveled slowly, letters often taking several weeks to reach their destination.

Meanwhile, Andrew and his companion missionaries made contact with a variety of Indian peoples, particularly Cherokees, Choctaws, and Creeks. They traveled without purse or scrip, mostly on foot, from one settlement to the next. They stayed with friends whenever they could, earning their keep by whittling household items and fixing gates, repairing farm machinery, and planting crops. Often they slogged through miles of mud and snow, wading through streams, to get from farm to farm. Five weeks into his mission, the first letter from Olive finally caught up with Andrew. He burst into tears as he read it.

Sometimes the missionaries had roads to travel and sometimes just trails. "Sometimes we get lost," Andrew wrote, "but by the aid of a compass we travel in Indian style and are sure to come out somewhere." They were pestered by swarms of mosquitoes, which carried malaria. For weeks Andrew and his companions fought off daily chills, fever, and headaches, walking and sleeping in wet clothes and missing many meals. But still they stayed and preached to those who would listen.

Andrew developed a special love and admiration for Indian peoples that remained with him for the rest of his life, and that inevitably influenced Olive and their children. Whatever Olive's problems at home, she was completely supportive of what her husband was doing and was especially appreciative of his work with these "people of destiny," as the Book of Mormon refers to the American Indians. During one three-month period Andrew was confined to bed with malaria and was cared for by some Cherokees.

Andrew's letters home were not only replete with information about the Indians, particularly the Cherokees, but also the countryside, "a beautiful country, composed of rolling hills, covered with many kinds of timber, open grassy prairies, and rich bottom lands." His letters exhibit a sly humor. For example, "The country is well supplied with wild fruits, such as plums, persimmons, woodticks, strawberries, centipedes and poisonous chiggers, black fleas, bedbugs and hickory nuts, tarantulas, scorpions, pecan nuts, tree lizards, grapes, and acorns."

In 1887, after almost three years, Andrew was released from his mission. Olive wept as she once more held him in her arms. Although released from his "walking mission," however, he was soon appointed president of the Indian Territory Mission. For the most part he was able to take care of this responsibility from Salt Lake City, with only occasional visits to Indian Territory. Under his direction the mission continued to expand, new chapels were built or acquired and dedicated, conferences were held, and church activity increased.

When he was not on visits to the mission field, Andrew traveled in Utah and southern Idaho in the interests of several firms, including the Beaver woolen mills, the Cedar City tannery, the Spanish Fork shoe factory, and new reservoirs and land projects at Fillmore and Kanosh. He traveled in Cache Valley, Box Elder, Weber, Morgan, and Summit counties, all in the interests of various "home industries." After ten years of service he was released from his Indian mission presidency in 1897. He served as a member of the Deseret Sunday School Union board, a position he held until the time of his death in 1924.

Andrew had civic responsibilities as well. He was also a district school trustee and a member of the constitutional convention that preceded Utah's emergence as a state in 1896. All together, his many obligations took him away from his family almost every evening of the week. Hence, nearly all responsibility for the care and raising of the Kimball children fell to Olive. Gordon was born in 1888, and a typical diary entry for these years is one written while he was still a toddler:

"Thursday, May 30, 1889. It was a holiday for most folks as it was Decoration Day [Memorial Day]. But not for us. Andrew had to work the most of the day at the store. I took up the dining room carpet, scrubbed the floor, and then he [Andrew] came and lifted out the kitchen stove and I took up that carpet and I started to fix one, then picked over a pan of strawberries, and then went to bed, not at all dissatisfied with my day's work. The baby was quite restless all night."

Delbert W. was born in 1890 and Ruth in 1892.

On March 28, 1895, Andrew returned home from the constitutional convention to find Olive ready to deliver their sixth child. He went for Olive's sister, Rachel Woolley Simmons, who had delivered four of the others, and at 7:50 P.M. a nine-pound baby boy was born. Andrew recorded in his journal: "I took the children in to see him. Clare [ten years old] had made up her mind for a girl, was badly disappointed, and had a crying spell."

In their efforts to choose a suitable name, Andrew favored the name Roberts Kimball, in honor of Elder B. H. Roberts of the First Council of the Seventy. Olive, however, was much less enthusiastic, knowing that Elder Roberts was leading the opposition against women's suffrage at the constitutional convention currently in session. (She was an enthusiastic suffragist.) Thus they named the baby Spencer Woolley Kimball. He would become the twelfth President of the Church.

In 1898, when Spencer was three years old and his baby sister Alice just one, the Kimball family responded to the call from President Wilford Woodruff that made Andrew president of the St. Joseph Stake, and moved to that supposed desert wasteland, the Gila Valley, in southeast Arizona. The family's feelings as they packed the last of their belongings are well described by Edward and Andrew Kimball in their biography *Spencer W. Kimball, Twelfth President of the Church:* "Arizona was a life sentence, a prison, hot and dry, infested with savages and spiders and flies. A death in the home would have brought fewer mourners, less sorrow. To send a man to Arizona was to bury him alive, they thought." Olive paid one last visit to the grave of little Maude, and, with six children and a heavy heart, she boarded the train. On the platform stood a little group of well-wishers, standing under umbrellas in a steady rain. It was a sad parting.

Olive and Andrew Kimball and six of their children in 1897.
Spencer, the future prophet, is sitting on his father's knee.

After four days of travel through mostly colorless, dry landscape, the Kimballs entered the Gila Valley, which turned out to be
less of a desert than an oasis—a strip of fertile farmland two miles
wide along the river bottom. In Thatcher, which was too small to
have a depot, a crowd of adults and children met them with arms
full of roses, an omen of the blossoming that would take place in
the valley under the direction of Andrew Kimball.

Thatcher had been colonized in the 1880s when a wave of new
settlements took root in the Gila Valley and the St. Joseph Stake
was created. The first stake president, Christopher Layton, gave the
town of Thatcher its name, built the academy there, and designated
it as the stake center. It had not been an easy place to subdue. One
settler said of the plants and animals: "If you touch it, it stings you;
if you pet it, it bites you; and if you eat it, it kills you." In 1854
General William T. Sherman said of the territory: "We have had
one war with Mexico and took Arizona. We should have another
and compel them to take it back."

Nevertheless, the stake continued to grow and flourish in the

face of many hardships. Andrew's most significant achievement was
the strengthening of St. Joseph's Stake Academy, a high school that
was later known as the Gila Academy; still later it was upgraded as
Eastern Arizona College, the largest church school in Arizona. He
also participated in crusades to minimize the sale of alcohol and
tobacco and to promote the proper observance of the Sabbath.

Ever anxious to encourage Latter-day Saints from Utah to join
the community in Arizona, Andrew presented a favorable impression of the Gila Valley on his visits to Salt Lake City. On one occasion, he boasted of corn sixteen feet tall, Johnson grass eight feet
high, a sweet potato that weighed thirty-six pounds (he carried an
affidavit to prove it), peaches too big to go into the mouth of a pre-
serving jar, sunflower stalks that were used for fence poles, weeds
that had to be cut with an ax, and sugarcane that grew four years
from one planting. Having fully accepted their call with the desire
to magnify the land, Olive was very loyal to Arizona and confident
of its future. When she heard a certain person boast of "green
Oregon" and talk of California as a "true garden spot," Olive, normally a quiet person, spoke right up. "We are in a good country,"
she insisted, and she brought up her children to believe it.

The Kimball family spent their first years in Thatcher living in
a three-room adobe house with no sink, no bath, and no running
water. Then the stake bought the family ten acres of land on which
they built a more suitable home and ran a small farm. The brick
house, which was Olive's pride and joy, was made possible by the
inheritance she received from her father's estate. Nevertheless,
keeping her eight children fed and clothed taxed her meager
resources. Andrew did everything from selling Bible scrolls and
insurance to contracting to lay railroad ties to support the family
in a modest manner.

Olive made shirts, patched pants, and crocheted sweaters to
make ends meet. "Fancy foods" were purchased only to feed conference visitors, and Spencer would later remember patiently waiting while the guests ate, hoping something would be left for him. A

basket of plums and apples from a Sister Jones was, Olive gratefully wrote, "a very acceptable" gift. The children were taught to do their part too, by caring for the farm animals and helping with the planting, irrigating, and harvesting. Olive had been brought up to hate idleness, and this part of her character was passed on to her children. She also believed in plenty of schooling. Her children attended school in Thatcher, and then furthered their education at the Gila Academy.

As always, the Church and the gospel played a central role in the Kimball household. Olive regularly sat with her children on the fourth row of the Thatcher meetinghouse for Sunday meetings, and the family prayed together at family meals, their chairs turned with their backs to the table, and offered nightly prayers at Olive's knee. At home, on special occasions, the family knelt around the revolving piano stool to pray. Andrew put a hand on the seat, Olive covered it with hers, and so on till each hand in the family was touching. "We felt very close together on those occasions," wrote Spencer.

In spite of the beautiful and sweet moments the family shared, life was challenging for Olive. Year after year she was the "Church widow," shouldering much of the responsibility while Andrew traveled to outlying wards or worked on a variety of jobs to support the family. She read the children stories from the Bible and supervised their baths in an iron tub, heating buckets of water on the wood stove.

She poured out her griefs only in the privacy of her journal. In 1901 she wrote: "I was sick with a pain in my bowels all night. It just poured down with rain. . . . All the beds and bedding got wet. Our house leaked in every room. I felt discouraged as every place but our front room was so wet, but we got through the day alright."

Brought up in a faithful household, Olive was determined to teach her children gospel principles and values. She led the way in practicing proper observance of the Sabbath, cautioned her children about criticizing Church officials, and taught them the law

of tithing, emphasizing that they must always give a full tenth—
one-tenth of the eggs, one-tenth of the hay, and one-tenth of their
earnings. Above all, she taught of God's love and his heavenly presence. On one occasion her horses began a runaway, and she was
terrified that someone would be hurt. "We were frightened
awfully," she wrote, "but the Lord heard my silent prayers and we
got the horse stopped. Praise be to our Heavenly Father for His
goodness to us."

In 1900 the region suffered from a persistent dry spell. Olive
was among members of the stake who fasted and prayed for rain.
She wrote in her journal: "No breakfast. We are fasting." There was
a similar entry the next Sunday. When, a week later, it rained hard,
she was not surprised. "That," she wrote, "was in answer to the
prayers of the saints in this stake." On another occasion she prayed
with her children to find a lost child. After the prayer, one of the
children walked directly to the very spot where the child lay sleeping. "We thanked our Heavenly Father over and over," wrote Olive.
"We could think of nothing else all evening."

Olive took her children to sacrament meeting regularly from
the time they were babes. If they became tired and fussy, she
allowed them to doze in her lap, even when they were older. When
reminded later in life that he had done this many times, her son
Spencer drily replied: "I was just unconsciously absorbing the
sermons."

Her family responsibilities, important and onerous as they
were, did not exhaust her time or energy. She was inevitably a
leader in the Relief Society in Arizona, at first as an officer and
teacher in the Thatcher Ward, and later as a counselor in the stake
Relief Society. She always found time to help those who were sick,
and to sew burial clothes.

Andrew and Olive were cultural, intellectual, and spiritual
leaders of the Arizona Saints. They had a large library and were
knowledgeable about the scriptures. They participated in a "poly-
sophical" society in Thatcher, where he often lectured and she

sang. They were among the first in the valley to buy a piano, and young Spencer learned to play. Olive had a fine soprano voice and was asked often to sing in public. On one occasion Alexander Brodie, governor of Arizona Territory, visited Gila Valley with his wife and small son, and they were entertained at the Kimball home. Mrs. Brodie commented that she thought it remarkable that Olive should be able to do her own housework for a large family and at the same time entertain visitors so graciously. "She had a sweet and mild disposition and would go more than half way to avoid misunderstandings or feelings," wrote one who knew Olive. Olive particularly enjoyed hosting President Joseph F. Smith, who had married Alice, Andrew's twin sister, and was therefore her brother-in-law. Olive and her daughter Clare often sang duets for President Smith and other General Authorities who visited their home.

Part of the responsibility Andrew felt in the St. Joseph Stake— a stake that included a vast arid region in southeastern Arizona, southwestern New Mexico, and some border areas of Texas and Mexico—was to supervise the construction of canals and other works to make possible the irrigation and reclamation of the immense stretches of arid lands. He served on the board of directors of several canal companies; was a member of the Twenty-first Arizona Legislature; was a director of the Arizona Eastern Railway and Atchison, Topeka and Santa Fe Railroad; and represented Arizona at many national and international farm congresses. He was associated with the leading implement business in Gila Valley and was manager of the Thatcher Implement and Mercantile Company. He was widely known as a person of integrity and practicality, and his prestige among the businessmen in Arizona helped to strengthen the friendship of those interests for the Latter-day Saints.

The work of Andrew, Olive, and other Latter-day Saint leaders was effective in building a Latter-day Saint homeland in Arizona. A temple was built in Mesa in 1927, three years after Andrew's death. The Snowflake Arizona temple was announced April 2, 2000, by President Gordon B. Hinckley. By the end of 1999, there were over 249,000 members of the Church in Arizona.

A constant concern of the Kimballs was the relationship of Arizona settlers with native Americans. Of their Indian brothers and sisters Andrew stated: "They are investigating the principles and watching the example of the Elders. . . . After a little they will make a break like a flock of sheep. When one goes all will go, and there will be a bounteous harvest. . . . A foundation is slowly and firmly being laid for a great work amongst this people." Not the least of the contributions of the Kimballs was the establishment of a relationship of brotherhood and respect between Anglos and Indians—a relationship that blossomed as never before under their son Spencer.

The growth of the Church and the increase in good will, however, did not prevent personal grief for Olive and Andrew. In 1903 their tenth child, Mary, died shortly after her birth. As the tenth child, Andrew said, Mary had been the Lord's, and He had taken her back as a tithe. A month later, five-year-old Fannie became sick, and her heart, the doctor said, was damaged by inflammatory rheumatism. The suffering continued for weeks until she died in Olive's arms on Spencer's ninth birthday. "I remember the scene in our living room," he later remembered, "my beloved mother weeping with her little dying five-year-old child in her arms and all of us crowding around. I shall never forget the anguish and pain which she was suffering." Olive was overcome with grief. This was the third child she had buried. Friends cautioned her about grieving too much, and she accepted their counsel in humility. "I do not wish to grieve too much and displease my Heavenly Father," she wrote. But it was not something that went away quickly.

In the fall of 1906, Olive was pregnant for the twelfth time, having averaged a birth every two years for the previous twenty-four years. Andrew decided that perhaps a trip to Salt Lake City to be with her family would cheer her up and help make her well again. They had no idea how ill she really was. Andrew went only part way to Utah on the train with her and then returned to Arizona, sending her on to Salt Lake City. She seemed to be getting sicker "by the hour." At home in Thatcher, the Kimball children fasted and prayed for their mother's health. Eleven-year-old Spencer wrote her the following letter October 17:

> Dear Mamma:
>
> As Clare told me to write a few lines to you, I will try. Clare and Ruth are doing the house work. They have the house all cleaned but the kitchen. We are all well now. We are very lon[e]ly without you. Gordon has hauled all the corn fodder from Bro Branham's. We are very busy around here. We received the telegram and were very glad to know that mama was out of danger. . . . I think I will close for it is getting bed time. Sister Allen told us in Religion Class that we should go to bed at eight o'clock so we could have enough sleep. Now it is nearly half past eight. Goodbye. Your loving Son.
>
> > Spencer Kimball

A day later, on October 18, 1906, Olive was dead. The baby miscarried, and Olive died from a related infection. She was only forty-six.

The next day the Kimball children were called home from school. Bishop William A. Moody gathered them around him and said simply, "Your Ma is dead." Spencer recalled, "It came as a thunderbolt. I ran from the house out in the backyard to be alone in my deluge of tears. Out of sight and sound, away from everybody, I sobbed and sobbed. Each time I said the word 'Ma' fresh floods of tears gushed forth until I was drained dry. Ma—dead! But she couldn't be! Life couldn't go on for us. My eleven-year-old heart seemed to burst."

Five days later the train came from Salt Lake City carrying Olive's body. She lay in the parlor until the funeral. Spencer would slip into the parlor to gaze at her. Her red hair looked the same as always, but her blue eyes were closed and she was quiet. Spencer kissed her forehead.

Olive's funeral was held in Thatcher on October 28, 1906. After the services, which were attended by more than a thousand people, sixty-five carriages followed her coffin to the cemetery.

Though their mother was now gone, Olive's children kept a place for her in their hearts the rest of their lives. Their father was conscious of this. Nine years after her passing, Andrew inscribed a gift copy of the Pearl of Great Price: "Andrew and Olive Woolley Kimball to Spencer Woolley Kimball, January 25, 1916." Inside the book cover, Spencer attached a picture of his dear mother.

SOURCES

There are seven volumes of Olive Woolley Kimball holograph diaries in the LDS Church Archives, Salt Lake City. They cover the years 1884, 1889, 1895, and 1899–1903 and include an account of her trip to Independence, Missouri, in 1895.

A brief biographical sketch is in Roberta Flake Clayton, comp., *Pioneer Women of Arizona* (Mesa, Arizona: Privately published, 1969), pp. 312–15. Biographies of Andrew Kimball include Andrew Jenson, "Kimball, Andrew," in *Latter-day Saints' Biographical Encyclopedia,* 4 vols. (Salt Lake City: Andrew Jenson Historical Company, 1901–1936), 1:364–66, and Thomas C. Romney, "Andrew Kimball," in *The Gospel in Action* (Salt Lake City: Deseret Sunday School Union Board, 1949), pp. 93–98.

A splendid biography of Spencer W. Kimball that includes considerable treatment of his parentage, and which we have used extensively, is Edward L. Kimball and Andrew E. Kimball, Jr., *Spencer W. Kimball, Twelfth President of the Church* (Salt Lake City: Bookcraft, 1977).

Olive's ancestry is treated in Preston W. Parkinson, *The Utah Woolley Family* (Salt Lake City: Deseret News Press, 1967); Leonard J. Arrington, *From Quaker to Latter-day Saint: Bishop Edwin D. Woolley* (Salt Lake City: Deseret Book, 1976); Orson F. Whitney, *Life of Heber C. Kimball* (Salt Lake City, 1888); and Stanley B. Kimball, *Heber C. Kimball: Mormon Patriarch and Pioneer* (Urbana: University of Illinois Press, 1981).

The settlement of Arizona is described in James H. McClintock, *Mormon

Settlement in Arizona (Phoenix: Arizona Historical Department, 1921); Charles S. Peterson, *Take Up Your Mission: Mormon Colonizing along the Little Colorado River, 1870–1900* (Tucson: University of Arizona Press, 1973); and William A. Moody, *Years in the Sheaf* (Salt Lake City: Granite Publishing Company, 1959).

Kimball and Woolley family group sheets and pedigree charts are in the Family History Library, Salt Lake City.

The quotation from Spencer W. Kimball at the head of the chapter is a composite of several statements.

SARAH SOPHIA
DUNKLEY BENSON

We had great spiritual moments in our home, many of
them after Father left for his mission. In our prayers at
night [Mother] would pray and pray and pray that
Father would be successful, that he wouldn't worry
about home. She'd pray that our work might go well in
the fields, that we'd be kind to each other. . . . When
your mother prays with such fervor, night after night,
you think twice before you do something to disappoint
her. —*Ezra Taft Benson*

S arah Dunkley Benson, as a farm wife in Southern Idaho,
worked hard to tame the harshness of the new land that she
and her husband were pioneering. With unwavering love and
faith, she and her husband raised eleven children, all of whom
would serve missions for the Church and remain faithful Latter-day
Saints throughout their lives. In the process, Sarah came to have
strong and deeply felt convictions about America and about the
restored gospel of Jesus Christ. She was an ideal mother to raise a
son who would eventually serve the United States as Secretary of
Agriculture in President Dwight D. Eisenhower's Cabinet, and later
serve as the thirteenth President of The Church of Jesus Christ of
Latter-day Saints.

Sarah Sophia Dunkley was born June 29, 1878, in a small cabin
in the newly established colony of Franklin, Idaho. Franklin is

*Sarah Benson and seven of her children at the time of her husband's
call to serve a mission. Ezra, the future prophet, is
standing behind his mother's right shoulder.*

often referred to as "mother of the settlements" in Idaho, for it was
from here that the first comers to northern Cache Valley lived
before spreading out to form new communities farther north.
Sarah's parents, Joseph Dunkley and Margaret Wright, had found
separate ways to this southeastern part of Idaho before they met
there and married on November 12, 1868.

Margaret was born and raised in Scotland, where her parents
joined the Church in 1846. Margaret's father died during the great
cholera plague of 1854, and for several years thereafter she and her
siblings worked in cotton factories to earn enough money to join
the Saints in America.

In 1868, Margaret, her brothers and sisters, and their widowed
mother set sail from Liverpool, England, in a leaky packet ship, the
Constitution. They spent most of their time singing, dancing, praying,
and bailing out water. The ship sank on its return trip to England.

The Wright family crossed the Great Plains in 1868, in a trip
that Margaret enjoyed as somewhat of a lark. She remembered the

names of their oxen: Nig and Coly, Duck and Dime, Buck and Bawley, Lam and Lime. After their arrival in the Salt Lake Valley on September 15, the Wrights immediately went north to Franklin, where relatives had settled several years earlier.

Sarah's father, Joseph Dunkley, was born in 1824 in Stratford, England, where he helped his father in a calico block-printing factory. The youngest of eleven children, Joseph shocked his family when he announced in 1852 that he had received a testimony of the truthfulness of the restored gospel, had been baptized, and was planning to sail to America. He was twenty-eight and had married Margaret Leitch, with whom he had studied the gospel. His parents literally begged on their knees for the young couple to remain in England. His mother even said that she hoped Joseph would break his leg, thus preventing them from leaving. But their desire to be with their fellow Latter-day Saints was unyielding, and they left in 1854, arriving in the Salt Lake Valley in 1855.

By the spring of 1860, President Brigham Young had asked Joseph and Margaret, along with several other families, to move to and help strengthen the little colony of Franklin, twenty miles north of Logan, which had been settled the year before. Through the years, Joseph and Margaret remained childless. With Margaret's consent, Joseph took a second wife, Mary Ann Hobbs, who subsequently died in childbirth. Later, Joseph was sealed in the Endowment House to a third wife, Margaret Wright, and they became the parents of thirteen children. Sarah, who would later become the mother of a future prophet, was their sixth child and second daughter.

Sarah's father, like many of the first settlers in Franklin, probably lived temporarily in a wagon box placed on the ground. Later, the Saints built cabins surrounded by a protective fort. The pioneers in this area had numerous encounters with the Indians, who were fiercely protective of the land they had roamed for hundreds of years. The settlers wanted to live in peace with the Indians, but they also saw them as representing a threat to their livestock, crops, and even their own persons. Farmers were encouraged to work in groups out in the fields, and their firearms were kept as handy as the scythes and homemade rakes with which they harvested hay.

When Sarah was ten years old, the Dunkley family moved to Whitney, Idaho, five miles northwest of Franklin, where Joseph homesteaded 160 acres of land. Much of the land with productive and fertile soil had been taken by settlers lucky enough to arrive earlier, and the Dunkleys ended up farming acreage that was not the best because of the presence of alkali, a mineral salt detrimental to the growing of crops. The family often said, however, that it did furnish a setting for developing the qualities of industry, cooperation, and perseverance in their children.

These early years for the Dunkleys were often difficult, with many supplies available only in Salt Lake City, a distance of 110 miles to the south. Some people made the trip as many as four or five times during the spring and summer, often walking every step of the way, and occasionally returning with a fifty-pound sack of flour on their back. Men and women also walked to Salt Lake City to attend general conferences of the Church. Wages at the time were low, and girls went into homes and did housework for less than a dollar a week. One local girl worked fourteen weeks to pay for a homemade linsey-woolsey dress.

In spite of the difficulties, Sarah Dunkley was a happy girl who enjoyed good health and a vivacious and attractive personality. She had dark eyes and an abundance of thick black hair, about which she tended to be quite fussy. As an adult she had a special barrel in which she caught rain water to use in washing her hair because of the water's "soft feel." She liked to brush her hair thoroughly, braid it, wind it around on top of her head, and carefully pin it in place.

Sarah quickly earned the nickname of "little mother" because of her tendency to be a leader among her friends and an influence for good among her brothers and sisters. Her education began in the small Nashville School, across the Cub River from Franklin. In this log structure the children sat on long boards and used slates for writing. During the winter, Sarah and her friends and cousins who lived nearby were taken to school in a homemade horse-drawn sleigh that slid over ice and snow while the girls sang their merry songs.

When she wasn't in school or busy helping with the farm and housework, Sarah found plenty of time for skating, wading, swimming, sleigh riding, picnics, and outings in the canyon. She especially enjoyed playing with their Uncle George Wright's children, who lived nearby.

After graduating from the one-room schoolhouse in Whitney, Sarah attended and graduated from the Oneida Stake Academy in Preston, Idaho, where she then organized and taught a summer school. The Academy was established by the Church as a middle school and high school in which the teaching of the physical, biological, and social sciences, and the humanities could be combined with the teaching of scriptures and theology. The Church shouldered most of the burden of financing the school but solicited donations from local stake members and charged each student a modest tuition. Stake members were called on missions to haul rock from the local quarry to construct the school building, and they donated locally produced goods, such as eggs, molasses, flour, and broom corn, to help finance the project.

The building was finally completed in 1894 and was dedicated in 1895 by Elder Moses Thatcher of the Council of the Twelve Apostles. Subsequently, several additions were made to the original campus, including a mechanical arts building, recreational facilities (where Sarah's children would play many basketball and softball games), and a library that by 1914 had grown to twenty-five hundred volumes. The Academy had a profound influence on the people of southeastern Idaho and was a source of great pride, bringing them education, culture, and wholesome recreation. It was at the Academy in 1912 that Sarah's son, Ezra Taft, first met a classmate named Harold B. Lee, with whom he later associated in the Council of the Twelve. The closure of the Academy in 1922 was considered an irreplaceable and sentimental loss.

Much of Sarah's social life centered around activities at the Whitney Ward. She had a lovely voice and often sang vocal solos. She was also a member of the Whitney Ward Choir, which won first prize in a valley wide contest, and was active in the auxiliaries as a teacher and officer. At the age of seventeen, she took a special sewing class in Logan and soon became known as an excellent seamstress. This talent would serve her well throughout her life, for she later made virtually all the clothing for her large family.

During her adolescent years Sarah was especially fond of a pair of lively twin girls who lived close by—Addie and Florence Benson. Together with Sarah's sister Kate, they were the "popular four" of their ward, of which Addie and Florence's father, George Taft Benson Sr., was bishop. The girls spent many hours together, often had matching dresses, and styled their hair in the latest fashion. They made a tumbling mat on which they could work out regularly, laughing and keeping fit at the same time. The girls were together so much that they wore a regular path between the Dunkley and the Benson homes.

During these many fun-filled afternoons, the Benson twins' older brother, George Taft Benson Jr., began to take notice of Sarah, who by this time was blossoming into young womanhood. George was soon walking Sarah home from his family's house or from singing practice. Clearly, he was captivated by her charm and friendliness.

George Jr. was a grandson of Elder Ezra Taft Benson, an early apostle in the Church and leader of the Latter-day Saint settlements in Cache Valley from 1860 until his death in 1869. George Jr. had a reputation for being the best hay pitcher in the county and inherited his father's dedication to hard work and religious devotion. But he knew how to enjoy himself, too. He loved sports and participated actively. Every Wednesday night—and Friday, if there was a dance in Franklin or Preston—he would take the buggy to court Sarah Dunkley.

Sarah and George's courtship progressed naturally as they shared many buggy rides, picnics, outings to the Cub River Canyon, Church meetings and socials. Sarah often played the guitar while many of their young friends sang and danced.

As things began to look more serious for the couple, George busily brought logs from the canyon and had them cut at the sawmill to build their first home. Sarah and her mother made patchwork quilts, curtains, dish towels, and rugs for the home. After George and Sarah were married October 19, 1898, in the Logan Temple, they returned to Whitney to live in the two-room house George had built for his bride—with a shanty in back for washing. This was their home for thirty years, and in it their eleven children were born.

The arrival of their first child a year later was an event of considerable concern and anxiety, for the life of both mother and child seemed to hang in the balance as childbirth progressed. The attending doctor told George and the two grandmothers who were present that there was almost no chance Sarah would live and very little chance that the baby would survive. The three of them almost instantaneously fell to their knees and prayed to God for the preservation of these two precious lives. As the doctor worked quickly to try to save Sarah, Margaret Dunkley and Louisa Benson worked to save their grandchild. The black and blue, nearly eleven-pound baby boy was put first in a pan of cool water and then a pan of warm water until finally he began to breathe and let out a boisterous cry. Tears of joy were shed as it soon became clear that both mother and child would survive. The child was blessed and given the name of his great-grandfather: Ezra Taft Benson. Thus was ushered into the world the man who would be sustained as prophet and President of the Church in 1985.

Not only did Sarah survive, but she went on to give birth to ten more children over the next twenty-one years: Joseph, Margaret,

George and Sarah Dunkley Benson

Orval Dunkley, Louisa, Lera, Valdo Dunkley, George Taft III, Sarah, Ross Dean, and Volco Ballif.

Sarah and George raised their family on an eighty-acre farm in Whitney. By this time the town had grown to fifty families—about three hundred people, all of whom were members of the Church except one man. Even he finally converted. Numerous small businesses were established by now, making a wide variety of services available. Nephi McLeary, for instance, had a shoe-mending department in the corner of the local cooperative general store, where he mended shoes six days of the week and then led the choir on Sunday. Joseph Simons operated a blacksmith shop, J. W. Winward sold farming implements, and the Ballif family owned and operated a general merchandising store, which also included the Whitney Post Office for a time.

The Benson children were heavily involved in work on the farm. At the age of four, Ezra Taft (often called "T"), the oldest, was driving a team. At seven he began to thin sugar beets, and at fourteen he worked a team of eight horses on the dry wheat farm. The children all had turns pitching hay, thinning and topping sugar beets, canning fruit, driving wagons, milking cows, and feeding the chickens. The girls spent many hours with Sarah sewing, cleaning house, making jams, jellies, and pies, and helping tend younger members of the family. The sight of several hundred quart jars of applesauce and other fruit was enormously satisfying and comforting as the cool fall air signaled that winter was not far away.

Much of the family's food supply throughout the year came from a large garden, an excellent raspberry patch, a small dairy, and many fruit trees. Seeds for the garden were understandably precious and not always easy to obtain. Families would go to great lengths to protect and preserve their seeds. Consider the actions of Sarah's half-sister, Margaret Mary Ann Hansen, who lived nearby, as related by her daughter, Ida Colby:

"One spring morning Mother had worked hard preparing the soil for the planting of her annual crop of peas. She finished the last row, placed the seed bag over the stick at the end of the row and went into the house. A short while later she noticed a red-combed rooster strutting by her pea bed. When she examined the area she found that this cock had eaten all of her planted seeds. 'That villain will not get away with this,' Mother thought. Quick as a flash she grabbed the rooster, beheaded him, stuck him in boiling water, plucked off his feathers, cut him open, and, sure enough, there was her crop of precious seeds. Mother replanted the seeds and cooked the fowl for dinner."

At threshing time, Sarah and the girls baked bread, pies, cakes, and cookies for two or three days. It was an exciting day when the threshing machine pulled into the yard. The children enjoyed watching the large machine operate and took cookies and lemonade to the twenty or so men working in the fields. Afterwards the family enjoyed fresh, clean smelling straw in their bed ticks.

Not all activities on the farm were work-related. The Benson family enjoyed swimming in the creek, picking wildflowers, riding horses, and playing with newborn puppies and calves. Sarah could be counted on to cook fried chicken, potato salad, and lemon and pumpkin pies for a family picnic. The children especially looked forward to the July 4th and July 24th celebrations, when they romped and ate to their heart's content with their Benson and Dunkley cousins. These gatherings always included races, small rodeos, various contests, and plenty of homemade ice cream. During the winter months, the family frequently went sleigh riding, and had a pot of Sarah's oyster stew to warm them afterwards.

Knowing the hard work Sarah faced while feeding, clothing and nurturing their large family, George tried to bring modern conveniences to their farm house to lighten her load. Sarah cried happy tears, for example, when George completed the plumbing that enabled them to have running water from a tap. However, when George announced one day that he was going to make it possible for their family to have a indoor bathroom, Sarah put her hands on her hips (which was apparently a very serious stance) and said "Taft, are you talking about bringing the 'privy' inside? Not in my house, you don't!" The family laughed about that incident for years.

One day in 1912, George and Sarah went to Uncle Serge Benson's general store and post office. As the buggy returned, the children could see their parents had been crying. A letter had come from "Box B" in Salt Lake City. Missionary calls were mailed from "Box B." Their tears, they told the children, were tears of joy that their father had been found worthy to be called to serve as a missionary in the Midwest. Sarah was expecting their eighth child, but she felt the family would be blessed by having their husband and father in the mission field. To finance the mission, George sold their dry farm, leased eighty acres on half share, and left for Chicago. When Sarah gave birth to her eighth child, George Taft III, she and the baby were seriously ill, but she refused to tell her husband until they had both recovered, so the news would not interfere with his proselyting activity.

When the entire family came down with the measles, Grandmother Dunkley came to help with the sick and entertain the restless. On the front lawn she danced the Highland Fling, while her young audience gleefully watched from the windows above. Sarah's mother was adored by her Benson grandchildren, who remembered her as "a darling, vivacious little Scottish bundle of energy."

When a letter arrived from her missionary husband, Sarah would gather her children around her and, with a baby in her lap, read aloud his experiences in the mission field. The children must have caught the missionary spirit from these letters, for each of the eleven children later served missions for the Church.

George returned from his mission in 1914. The following year, Sarah's brother Joseph Dunkley was called as the new bishop, with George as his counselor. Sarah later supported her husband's call to the Oneida Stake high council, followed in 1927 by seven years in the stake presidency. During the years she was raising her family, Sarah served in the Relief Society as president and as an officer in other stake and ward organizations. She and George also went to choir practice every Wednesday night.

Sarah's love of singing carried over into her home. In times of work and relaxation, her lovely voice filled the home with warmth and pleasant melodies. She sang while she cooked, cleaned, and sewed on her treadle machine, and while she rocked her babies to sleep. One of her favorite songs was "Have I Done Any Good in the World Today?"

During the thirty years that George and Sarah lived in their first home, they made additions and remodeled to suit their growing family. The last five years of their marriage were spent in a new home that George built a mile and a half southwest of their farm, next to the Whitney Post Office and across the street from the ward chapel. They sold the farm to "T" and Orval, and George went to work securing contracts from the farmers for the beet-sugar factory.

A seemingly bright and comfortable future enjoying the fruits of their hard labors was cut short in 1932 when Sarah was diagnosed as having cancer. She underwent major surgery at LDS Hospital in Salt Lake City, but died a year later on June 1, 1933. She was fifty-four years old. Her youngest child was only thirteen years old, and her twenty-year-old son, George Taft III, was in the mission field at the time. Her last words to him as he left had been "George, no matter what happens at home, I want you to stay and finish your mission." In spite of the grief he felt at her passing, George honored his mother's request. Sarah's husband, George, died a year later of appendicitis.

With Sarah's death, her lovely voice was now missing from the home. But the children remembered the many songs she had sung, including this favorite, which became a tribute to Sarah, their own "angel mother":

> Oh, I had such a pretty dream, Mama,
> Such pleasant and beautiful things;
> Of a dear little nest, in the meadows of rest,
> Where the birdie her lullaby sings.
>
> A dear little stream full of lilies,
> Crept over the green mossy stones,
> And just where I lay, its thin sparkling spray
> Sang sweetly in delicate tones.
>
> And as it flowed on toward the ocean,
> Thro' shadows and pretty sunbeams,
> Each note grew more deep, and I soon fell asleep,
> And was off to the Island of Dreams.
>
> I saw there a beautiful angel,
> With crown all bespangled with dew:
> She touched me and spoke, and I quickly awoke:
> And found there, dear Mama, 'twas you.

Among the speakers at Sarah's funeral on June 4, 1933, was Elder David O. McKay of the Council of the Twelve Apostles, who had been the mission president of her son, Ezra Taft Benson. Elder McKay could sympathize completely with the family's grief. Jeanette Evans McKay had also died of cancer, at exactly the same age as Sarah Benson. He closed his remarks with these words: "With all my heart I say, God bless Brother Benson and those brothers and sisters who mourn. It is something to have known and to have lived with and loved such a noble person."

SOURCES

Books on the history of southeastern Idaho include Marie Danielsen, comp., *The Trail Blazer: History of the Development of Southeastern Idaho* (Preston, Idaho: Daughters of the Pioneers, 1930); M. D. Beal, *A History of Southeastern Idaho* (Caldwell, Idaho: Caxton Printers, 1942); Joel Ricks and Everett L. Cooley, eds., *The History of a Valley* (Salt Lake City: Deseret News Publishing Company, 1956); and A. J. Simmonds, "Southeast Idaho as a Pioneer Mormon Safety Valve" *Idaho Yesterdays, Winter 1980*. We have also profited from using *The Face of Rural America, 1976 Yearbook for the United States Department of Agriculture,* U.S. Government Printing Office.

Histories of the family include *Descendants of the George T. Benson Jr. Family,* privately published and circulated in 1968; Leonard J. Arrington, "Idaho's Bensons," and "Oral History of Ezra Taft Benson," *Idaho Heritage,* September 1977; and Richard P. Dunkley and K. Wright Dunkley, *History of Joseph Dunkley,* copy in the Family History Library, Salt Lake City, Utah; and *It Was Right Over There,* compiled by Richard Dunkley for the Whitney Ward Centennial, privately printed and distributed in 1989. We conducted oral interviews with Lera Benson Whittle, Provo, Utah, March 22, 1986; and Zetta Benson Peterson, Logan, Utah, March 23, 1986. "Oh, I Had Such A Pretty Dream, Mama" by J. S. Lewis is in *Deseret Sunday School Songbook,* p. 184. We have examined the family group sheets on the Joseph Dunkley family and the George Taft Benson Jr. family in the Family History Library, Salt Lake City, Utah. Also helpful were the Newell Hart Papers, Marie Eccles Caine Archives, Special Collections and Archives, Utah State University Merrill Library, Logan, Utah.

NELLIE MARIE
RASMUSSEN HUNTER

Mother has lived a long and useful life, and each one
of her posterity are active in the Church. . . . How
thankful I am to the Lord for my inheritance.
—*Howard W. Hunter*

A visit to Grandma Hunter's home in Los Angeles, California, was always a treat for her grandchildren. The hollow milk-glass chicken on the table in her living room was always filled with candy, usually butter mints with gummy centers. A slightly tropical-looking papier mâché parrot hung in the dining room. And Grandma's glass display case, filled with tempting little trinkets and keepsakes that the Hunter family had collected over the years, invited a sense of wonder. The Hunter grandchildren would forever remember looking at these treasures with intrigue and delight.

Nellie Marie Rasmussen Hunter was beloved by her children and grandchildren—and virtually everyone else who knew her. She had an electric personality. Within five minutes of entering a room crowded with people, Nellie would have the attention of the entire group. At any number of social gatherings, for instance, she would stand before a crowd, pause for dramatic effect, and launch into a recitation of a poem such as "The Curfew Must Not Ring Tonight."

With her quick wit, hearty laugh, marvelous conversation, and genuine love for people, Nellie was a pure joy to be around.

But her early life was not always so joyful. It would require great endurance and faith for her to become a powerful stabilizing force as wife and mother in her own home and to bear and nurture a son who would become the fourteenth President of The Church of Jesus Christ of Latter-day Saints.

Much of Nellie's vibrant strength came from her faithful and devoted pioneer forebears. Nellie's father, Martin Rasmussen, was the son of Morten and Karen Marie Christiansen Rasmussen. Both were Danish converts who had separately joined the Church in their native land, immigrated to America, and traveled in handcarts to Utah to be with their fellow Saints. They eventually met in Ephraim, a small town in the Sanpete Valley. They were married on April 1, 1859. Shortly thereafter, Nellie's grandparents were called by Brigham Young to participate in the building of a fort in what came to be known as Mount Pleasant and to help establish the new community. In a cave on the bank of the creek that ran through the fort, Martin, their first child was born in December of 1859.

As a young man, Martin met a woman by the name of Nicoline Christensen who had also grown up in the shadow of the fort at Mount Pleasant. Nicoline's parents, Anders and Nilla Torgersen Christensen, were Scandinavian converts to the Church and immigrants to Utah just as Martin's parents had been. Nicoline was born on October 24, 1861. Martin and Nicoline's similar backgrounds no doubt contributed to their mutual interest in each other. They courted and were later married in the Endowment House in Salt Lake City on May 27, 1880.

Following their marriage and sealing, Martin built a comfortable log cabin near his father Morten's home in Mount Pleasant. In this cabin, Nicoline gave birth to three children: Henry Arthur, Lawrence Martin, and Nellie Marie. Nellie, their youngest child and only daughter, was born on May 30, 1885.

The family's time together proved to be short and was soon

marred by heartbreak. Martin was working in Colorado in December of 1887 when he received word that Nicoline had suddenly fallen ill and was near death. He mounted his horse and rode for a day, a night, and a day to reach home as quickly as possible. He reached Mount Pleasant only to find that Nicoline had died three days earlier, on December 1, and had been buried just hours before his arrival. She was twenty-six years old.

Understandably, Nellie's life changed dramatically with the death of her mother. From this point onward through her teenage years, Nellie experienced a dizzying number of changes in her guardians and in her places of residence.

Just before Nicoline died, she had asked that two-year-old Nellie be cared for by Annie Cecelia, Nicoline's half-sister. Nellie lived with Annie Cecelia until the age of ten. During that time, Aunt Cecelia was married and she and her husband decided to move to Colorado. They intended to have Nellie go with them, but while the three of them stood waiting for their train to Colorado, Nellie's father Martin appeared and refused to allow her to go.

Nellie then went to live with her father and stepmother, Emma Elizabeth Jeffs, whom Martin had married two-and-a-half years after Nicoline's death. There, Nellie was expected to stay home from school most of the time in order to help with the young children and with work around the house.

Nellie had been living in these circumstances for about three years when Martin began to feel that she was being unfairly disciplined by her stepmother. Consequently, he allowed Nellie to go and live with his mother—Nellie's paternal grandmother—Karen Marie Christiansen Rasmussen. From the time of her grandmother Rasmussen's death in 1900, until 1906 when Nellie was twenty-one years old, she lived with four different families of relatives and friends, in five different homes in several towns and cities, including Mount Pleasant, Castle Dale, Salt Lake City, and Boise, Idaho. Nellie yearned for an enduring home and a stable family situation and her prayers were soon to be answered.

Nellie Marie Rasmussen Hunter at about age 19

At the end of this time, Nellie was living with her Aunt Christie and Uncle Fred Moore in Boise where she worked first as a waitress, then as a switchboard operator for the Idanha hotel, and finally as an operator for the Mountain States Telephone Company. It was during her employment with the telephone company that Nellie was introduced to John William Hunter, the brother of one of her co-workers. "Will," as he was commonly known, was working in the mines near Pearl, thirty miles north of Boise.

Evidently Nellie made an immediate good impression upon Will's parents. Shortly after having met Nellie, Will's mother Josephine declared, "Will, you'd be a fool to let that Nellie get away!" Will apparently agreed. Their courtship progressed primarily through letters as Will continued his work in the mines.

Will decided to move to Boise and began working as a motor-man on the interurban electric railroad. He proposed marriage to Nellie in the spring or early summer of 1906, but she was undecided. Although she cared deeply for Will, she was troubled that he was not a member of the Church. Will had been brought up in the Episcopal Church and had even served as an altar boy in his youth. However, by the time he met Nellie, he was not involved with any particular religious group.

Shortly after Will's proposal, Nellie left for Sanford, Colorado, to visit her Aunt Cecelia and to think things through. She did not, however, succeed in avoiding the attentions of eager suitors there; she was proposed to by another man while in Colorado. She declined his offer and traveled to Mount Pleasant, Utah, to visit family members and to consider her future even more carefully.

Nellie was visiting the home of one of her relatives in Mount Pleasant when she looked out the window and saw a young man walking up and down the street in front of the house. "If I didn't know better," she said, "I'd say that looks like Will Hunter!" Apparently Will, worried that Nellie's affection for him would grow lukewarm the longer she was away, had come to Mount Pleasant to find her. He professed his love then and there, and convinced her to marry him. The pair boarded a train to Manti where they regis-tered for a marriage license on December 3, 1906, and then took the return train to Mount Pleasant the same day.

That same evening, Nellie slipped into a wedding dress that her aunts had hurriedly sewn in her absence and was married to Will Hunter at the home of her aunt, Maria Sophia Rasmussen Madsen. The ceremony was performed by her uncle, Bishop Daniel Rasmussen. Friends and family, including her father, were in atten-dance. Nellie was twenty-one years of age, and Will was twenty-seven. The next day, the newlyweds traveled by train to Boise, Idaho, where they rented their first home at 1402 North 11th Street, on the northeast corner of 11th and Sherman Street.

In light of their different temperaments, Will and Nellie were

Will and Nellie Hunter

an intriguingly fitting match. While Nellie's exuberant, people-loving personality made her the center of attention, Will's markedly quiet manner made him more than happy to grant her all of the limelight. Will absolutely adored her.

Picture Nellie as Will knew her: She had blond hair, striking blue eyes, petite facial features, and stood about 5'2". She was meticulous about her appearance, had a particular love for hats, and had a characteristic way of cocking her head that made her a standout in any photograph.

Just a few months after their wedding, Nellie and Will discovered that they were expecting their first child. On November 4, 1907, they welcomed into their home a baby boy and named him Howard William Hunter.

Anxious for her new son to receive the blessings associated with the Church, Nellie brought five-month-old Howard to fast and testimony meeting on April 5, 1908, at the Boise Branch of the Northwestern Mission. There he was given his name and a blessing by the branch president. Although Will was not a member of the Church, he did attend such sacrament meetings on occasion with his family when his work schedule permitted.

Two years after the birth of their son, Will and Nellie moved to

Nellie Marie Rasmussen Hunter

another home owned by their landlord, situated at 1012 Sherman Street in Boise. In this roomier dwelling, Nellie gave birth to their second child, Dorothy Elaine, on November 1, 1909.

Will and Nellie were anxious to own their own home and, a few months after Dorothy's birth, they purchased a quarter-acre lot just outside the west city limits of Boise. By fall of 1910, their new three-room house was complete, and they excitedly moved in. Facing east, the house had a living room, a bedroom, and a kitchen. Nellie's kitchen amenities included a coal range for cooking and an icebox.

On the north side of the house was a spacious lawn where the children, Howard and Dorothy, entertained their childhood playmates. Approximately fifty paces from the back door on the west side of the house stood "a small, well-ventilated square building, placed over a hole in the ground, that was called the outhouse, a term much too dignified for the structure," her son Howard later recalled. The lot also had crab apple and plum trees, raspberry and gooseberry bushes, and a vegetable garden. Will was quite fussy about the state of his garden, and tenderly nurtured it throughout the growing season.

Later on, Will added an enclosed porch to the front of the house. It was on the south end of this porch that Howard and Dorothy often slept on cots throughout their growing up years.

Will's construction of the front porch for the family was an example of his rare gift of ingenuity and remarkable commitment to hard work. Always the handyman, he could fix literally anything. He even provided a way for water to be conveniently brought inside the house by placing a pipe down through a hole in the kitchen floor and attaching a hand pump to the top of the pipe. What a luxury this was for the little family!

Nellie's industrious nature clearly matched that of her husband. She busied herself during the summers canning quarts and quarts of beans, corn, and tomatoes. She regularly enlisted the help of her children in these projects. Howard and Dorothy recalled endlessly picking beans, gathering apples, and cleaning ears of corn in preparation for canning.

Nellie was also remarkably talented with needle and thread, and had mastered the delicate skills of tatting and embroidery. In addition, she crafted wonderful hooked rugs which always pictured roses, her favorite flower.

But Nellie's many skills were not always as tangible as cooking or sewing. Frugality, for instance, was one of her gifts, and nothing was ever wasted in her household. She would even go so far as to combine all of the "bottom of the jar" jelly remnants into one jar, assuring that it all would be used. Indeed, there were times when her "waste not" trait would clutter the house, as Nellie had difficulty throwing things away. "You never know when you might be able to use it!" she would exclaim.

Nellie's frugality turned creative as she worked to "make do."

Her ingenuity sparked her interest in a radio contest, which advertised that whoever could come up with the most creative use for the glass toothbrush covers that were "so wastefully thrown away" would receive a fifty-dollar prize. Nellie got right to work, crocheting a delightful jacket to go over the little glass cover, making it into a flower vase. Nellie won the prize.

Nellie's efforts extended beyond the walls of her own home. She often worked to supplement the family's modest income and was employed by a local dry-cleaning company to press suits. She also put her outgoing personality to work by demonstrating White King Soap in local stores.

Nellie was devoted to her community and country. She sold war bonds during World War II and avidly volunteered in the Boy Scout program. Her love for scouting rubbed off on Howard, who became the second boy in the state of Idaho to receive the rank of Eagle Scout. Nellie painstakingly stitched his merit badges onto a band of cloth, rightfully proud of her son's achievement.

Nellie also accepted Church responsibilities. She was called to serve in many capacities, including that of Sunday School teacher, Primary teacher, and counselor in the Primary presidency. She went on to serve as the Primary president and as president of the Young Women's organization in her ward. In addition to these callings, Nellie participated in the "singing mothers" choir and was very active in the Daughters of Utah Pioneers organization.

But first and foremost, Nellie was devoted to the welfare of her husband and two children. Her role in creating the happy and secure environment that characterized the Hunter home is particularly remarkable in light of her own experiences moving from home to home and family to family as a youth.

Gentle but firm in her parenting style, Nellie delighted in providing for her children many of the opportunities she had never had as a child. The family owned a piano, and Nellie made certain her children took music lessons. Both Will and Nellie loved books and read to their children often. Nellie also made sure Howard and

Dorothy had their own library cards, which became the gateway to adventures with Tom Sawyer, Pollyanna, and many others.

She also taught Howard and Dorothy to work. She assigned them various tasks including hauling in coal for the stove, chopping wood for kindling, and throwing grain to the chickens. She sent them to Anderson's Dairy in the evenings to pick up bottles of milk and carry them home in a canvas bag that she had made.

Day-to-day living made Nellie aware of how different her children were from each other in temperament and interests. Dorothy possessed a more spirited streak, while Howard was generally more reserved. Howard was fiercely protective of his younger sister, but there were occasions when Dorothy did the protecting. There was a period of time, for example, when a group of boys repeatedly teased Howard by putting his cap on the railroad tracks in front of an oncoming train. After Nellie expressed her exasperation at having to continually replace Howard's cap, Dorothy marched out the door, walked brazenly up to the group of boys and threatened that she would "beat them up" if they didn't "lay off."

Nellie met differently for each child the challenges of being a mother. On one occasion, as Christmas day approached, Dorothy fell in love with a beautiful porcelain doll that she had seen in a local shop. While Nellie was away one day, Dorothy was snooping in forbidden closets for hidden gifts and found that her mother had purchased the doll! She played with it for a time and, to her horror, broke it in several pieces. She hurriedly placed the doll back in its wrapping, hoping that her mother wouldn't notice. Christmas day arrived and Dorothy opened one of her gifts, discovering the beloved doll. She curiously checked the doll all over for evidence that it had been repaired, and while she was doing this her mother asked, "Dorothy, what are you looking for?" Dorothy answered, "Nothing!" Then Nellie went back into her room and brought out the broken version of the doll. No scolding was necessary, as little Dorothy humbly confessed her "snooping escapade" and thanked her mother profusely for having bought the replacement doll. It was a lesson Dorothy never forgot.

On another occasion, Howard had just rescued a small kitten from the cruel treatment of some neighborhood boys. The boys had been putting the kitten in a sack and throwing it into the canal. They would wait for the kitten to climb out, only to throw it back in again. When Howard brought the ragged little creature home, Nellie was convinced that it wouldn't live. But sensitive to Howard's feelings and the kitten's needs, she located a quilt and tenderly lined a box with it. Placing the small kitten in the box, she had Howard put it beneath the range to stay warm. The cat miraculously recovered and was a family pet for many years.

From the beginning, the relationship between Nellie's two children was something special. Boise provided endless opportunities for adventure, and Howard and Dorothy came home happily exhausted many an evening, after playing and swimming in the river and its attending canals and ditches.

Wintertime brought frozen ponds on which to ice-skate, and snow on the ground for the beloved activity known as "hooky-bobbing." Howard and Dorothy would attach a long rope to their sleds and wait anxiously by the side of the road. When a buggy or wagon drove by, they would run up behind it, loop the rope around the rear axle, and be pulled along on their sleds for as long as they wanted. They would then "hooky" a ride back to where they had begun.

The outdoors held great appeal for the Hunter children, but home was also a place full of wonderful memories. It became a Hunter family tradition to decorate the family Christmas tree on Christmas Eve. Howard recorded in his journal, "We used real candles which fit into holders that clipped onto the branches. Father kept two buckets filled with water, so that if the tree caught fire, he'd be able to put it out quickly. He always made sure the candles were out before he left home." The joy of the holiday season for the children is clear from Howard's journal writing, where he declares, "We had everything good there was."

Despite Will's good nature with regard to the rest of the family's involvement with the Church, there were disagreements, particularly with respect to baptism. Will felt strongly that his children should not be baptized at the age of eight, but should wait until they could decide for themselves. Nellie respected her husband's wishes, but Howard finally convinced his father to relent. Howard and Dorothy were both baptized on April 4, 1920, five months after Howard's twelfth birthday and Dorothy's tenth. Howard was elated to finally be ordained a deacon and to be able to pass the sacrament.

During these early years, Nellie was the driving force behind her children's involvement in the Church. Little did Nellie realize the joy that would follow approximately seven years later when her dear husband, Will, would himself enter the waters of baptism. Will's decision to be baptized was, no doubt, influenced by his observation over many years of the positive effect of the Church upon his wife and children.

Nellie's quick wit and lively personality were beautifully complemented by a deeply spiritual side. Her handwriting filled several small spiral notebooks in which she recorded hundreds of inspiring thoughts and quotations that she had either heard during the day from others or thought of herself. The majority of these passages focus on love for God and Jesus Christ.

Nellie also imparted to her son and daughter the elements of personal worship that would enable them to form a relationship with God. Howard tenderly wrote, "My mother had taught me to pray and to thank Heavenly Father for all the things that I enjoyed. I also learned to ask Him for the things that I wanted or needed." These lessons embedded themselves deeply in Howard's mind and set him on the path toward his own personal testimony of the restored gospel.

Shortly after Howard and Dorothy had both graduated from Boise High School, there was an abrupt change in Will's employment.

His work with the Boise Valley Traction Company, where he had labored for over twenty years, ended: railroad cars were being replaced by motor buses. In August of 1928, Will and Nellie sold their home and moved with Dorothy to Los Angeles where Howard was already working.

True to their practice of saving money whenever possible, Will and Nellie began working in Los Angeles as apartment managers, thereby receiving housing rent-free. The arrangement worked out quite nicely, with Nellie doing the managing, and Will using his many skills to serve as apartment handyman. The Hunters were managers for several different complexes, including Randolph Arms, Mayfair Manor, Casa Del Soul, and Mae Murray Apartments.

Following the marriage of their son Howard to Claire May Jeffs in June of 1931, and that of Dorothy to Marvin Rasmussen in December of 1935, a whole new experience dawned upon Nellie—grandmothering!

Nellie was soon affectionately known as "Omma Nell" because one little grandchild was unable to pronounce the word "grandma."

As providence would have it, Nellie lived only fifteen minutes away from Dorothy and her family, and just an hour away from Howard and his. With grandchildren so close to her home, she did all within her power to entice them there.

By this time in her life, Nellie had gathered quite a collection of curiosities that her grandchildren loved to see. But the greatest attraction at Grandmother's house was Nellie herself. Her warm personality and sense of humor did not dim with age. During one memorable family gathering, Nellie had a little grandbaby in her lap and was playing with his feet and kissing his toes. She suddenly looked up and brightly quipped, "They used to kiss my little toes, why don't they do it now?"

Nellie particularly relished telling the grandchildren the story behind a sizable scar on the end of her tongue—the result of having been accidentally dropped by her older brother as he was swinging her around. Her top teeth caused the scar that she would bear the rest of her life.

Nellie also made light of the fact that she wore dentures. Often, she would be leaving with the grandchildren for some activity and would realize that she hadn't put her "teeth" in. "Where are my dentures?" she would declare. After that she and the grandchildren would go on an all-out search for the missing teeth before leaving for the activity. The dentures became part of the fun of being at Grandma's house.

In her later years Nellie had a pet cat named "Blondie" which, her granddaughters recall, despised everyone but Nellie. Due to Blondie's hostile manner no other pets were kept in the home. The exception to this rule came one summer when Dorothy's family was going away on vacation and needed a "pet-sitter" for their cat, fish, and parakeet. Nellie took the job and the three additional pets came to visit. By the time Dorothy's family returned from their trip, the fish had died due to Nellie's good-intentioned cleaning of its bowl with bleach, and Blondie had made a meal of the bird and then chased away the children's cat. Needless to say, Nellie was as devastated by the tragic ordeal as were the tearful returning grandchildren.

Nellie was a prolific letter writer, sending out love and greetings to family and friends several times each week. She was particularly fond of cutting out figures and images from old greeting cards and postcards, and sending them into the delighted hands of her grandchildren. She was also well-known for signing birthday and Christmas cards, "Guess who?"

Holidays were a special treat in many ways. Nellie would always unveil a feast for the family—splendid meals the grandchildren would remember for years to come. During the Christmas holiday, the family tradition was to select one gift to be opened on Christmas Eve. Nellie was famous for egging on the children to open "just one more" gift, until there were very few left to be opened on Christmas morning.

These light and humorous moments of Nellie's later years were amplified by the spiritual growth in the family. A long hoped-for event was finally realized on November 14, 1953, the forty-sixth birthday of her son Howard. At this time, Howard was serving as president of the Pasadena California Stake, and was participating that day in the Pasadena stake trip to the Arizona Temple in Mesa. The members of the stake first assembled in the chapel for a brief worship service. Unknown to Howard, his parents elected to make this birthday one that he would never forget. Howard recalls, "My father and mother came into the chapel dressed in white. I had no idea my father was prepared for his temple blessings, although Mother had been anxious about it for some time. I was so overcome with emotion that I was unable to continue to speak. President Pierce came to my side and explained the reason for the interruption. This was a birthday I have never forgotten because on that day they were endowed and I had the privilege of witnessing their sealing, following which I was sealed to them."

In addition to this marvelous experience, other milestones were soon realized. One was in 1956, when Nellie and Will went to Hawaii in celebration of their fiftieth wedding anniversary. Having lived so frugally for their entire married lives, both of them were hesitant to spend money for this exotic trip. Will was particularly reluctant to go. But in a postcard home to family members Nellie declared that once he got to Hawaii, Will "didn't want to come home." This trip became one of Nellie's fondest lifetime memories.

Another milestone occurred just six years after the sealing of Nellie and Will in the Arizona Temple. On October 10, 1959, during the morning session of general conference, held in Salt Lake City, Nellie's son Howard W. Hunter was sustained as an Apostle in The Church of Jesus Christ of Latter-day Saints. Howard, overwhelmed by the magnitude of the call, accepted this new position with deep humility, trusting that the Lord would help him rise to the occasion.

Through this time of tremendous change for Howard and his family, Nellie was one of his biggest supporters. She was one of the first to contact him following his call to the Quorum of the Twelve. From her home in Southgate, California, she sent a telegram which read, "Proud of you. Speeches all wonderful. Such a thrill. I am covered with goose pimples. Most sincere. God be with you all. [signed] Mother."

In the years ahead, Nellie would need the strength and comfort of these powerful spiritual experiences. Her life unexpectedly took a turn towards sorrow when Will, who had been in good health up to this point, suffered a cerebral hemorrhage and died on February 1, 1963. He was eighty-three years of age. Nellie grieved deeply at the sudden loss of her lifetime companion. Nellie's granddaughter-in-law Louine Berry Hunter recalls that Nellie telephoned, "in a very heartbroken state and talked for quite awhile about her loss. This continued to be a very difficult adjustment for her."

Nellie enjoyed tremendously good health in her later years until she fell and broke her hip in 1967. The hip never fully mended, and her ability to move about freely was greatly reduced. She spent long periods of time confined to a hospital bed in a nursing home. Afterwards, her hospital bed was moved to the living room of her daughter Dorothy's home for a period of several months. Nellie's grandchildren recall how, despite her confinement to bed, Nellie never lost her sense of humor. In fact, Ron, the husband of her grandchild Kathy, recalls how he would bring his buddies over just to talk with Nellie, and she would manage to entertain these young men for hours with her sharp wit and stories.

In early September of 1971, Nellie became seriously ill and was taken to the hospital. She had suffered from heart problems and had developed pneumonia. Her condition rapidly declined, and on Thursday, November 11, 1971, Nellie died peacefully in her sleep at the age of eighty-six.

Nellie was recognized by many for her unique personality. The

Deseret News, in a 1983 Mother's Day article reflecting on her life, observed that Nellie, "had a strong personality, she had charisma, but she always loved people, and everyone loved her. She was not the show-off type, but they always said she was the life of the party at [Relief Society] working meetings; she always had a story to tell."

It is not surprising then that a woman like Nellie, who focused her life on loving God, her family, and her neighbors, would adopt the following as a favorite saying: "It's nice to be important, but it's more important to be nice."

Nellie's funeral and burial services were held in Los Angeles. Howard remarked in his journal, "This was a sad day for us, yet one of rejoicing. Mother has lived a long and useful life, and each one of her posterity are active in the Church. Her physical body has given out and it was time for her to go, her work accomplished. How thankful I am to the Lord for my inheritance."

SOURCES

The most helpful source in providing anecdotes and a sense of Nellie's personality was an interview conducted by the authors with two of Nellie Hunter's grandchildren, Susan R. Bagley and Kathy R. Rodda, held in Farmington, Utah, July 19, 2000.

Eleanor Knowles's biography, *Howard W. Hunter* (Salt Lake City: Deseret Book, 1994), was very useful in providing details of Nellie's ancestry, childhood, and family life. We also had access to a short biographical sketch of Nellie written about 1990 which is in possession of her grandchildren. Louine Berry Hunter, wife of Nellie's grandson, John, kindly provided her written reminiscences of Nellie to the coauthors.

ADA BITNER HINCKLEY

I am sure that I was a great worry to my Mother. I was
a spindly, frail little boy subject to considerable illness.
. . . When the influenza epidemic was raging in 1917,
some of us were ill. I was very sick, and I recall her
tenderly nursing me. I cannot adequately express my
gratitude and love for her care in bringing me through
those perilous years of childhood. —*Gordon B.
Hinckley*

Ada Bitner was twenty years old when she received her patriarchal blessing from John Smith in February 1901. Two sentences in that blessing are particularly intriguing and may have caught her attention a few years later during a careful reading: "The eye of the Lord has been upon thee from thy birth and a decree of the Father has gone forth that thou shalt have a mission to fill, a work to do. . . . Thy name shall be perpetuated and live in the memory of the Saints."

Nine years later, Ada had not yet married and was a successful and greatly admired faculty member at LDS Business College [originally named the Salt Lake Business College] in Salt Lake City. In thinking of her blessing, Ada may have wondered if her name was destined to "be perpetuated" as a memorable teacher or a well-educated grammarian. Was this her mission in life? Is this how she would "live in the memory of the Saints"?

Her acquaintance with and eventual marriage to fellow faculty member Bryant Hinckley on August 4, 1909, would change her life dramatically and begin the true fulfillment of those two sentences in Patriarch Smith's blessing. Yes, her name would be perpetuated for generations to come, and in many countries, but not because of her early professional life. Ada would be remembered and honored as the mother of a latter-day prophet, her first child, Gordon Bitner Hinckley.

Ada Bitner was born June 30, 1880, on a sprawling sixty-five-acre farm near the mouth of Big Cottonwood Canyon in Salt Lake County, Utah. She was the twelfth child of Breneman Barr Bitner, and the fifth child of Sarah Ann Osguthorpe Bitner, Breneman's third wife. Ada's ancestors on both sides of her family tree include courageous souls who sought a better life for their future posterity.

Breneman Barr Bitner, Ada's father

Breneman was born in Washington, Lancaster County, Pennsylvania, on December 15, 1837, to Abraham and Anna Barr Bitner. Abraham died in 1841, when Breneman was not quite four years of age, and Breneman's manhood was put to the test just a few years later at the tender age of eleven. His mother Anna, who converted to The Church of Jesus Christ of Latter-day Saints shortly after her husband's death, was determined to gather up her little family and join the Saints in the Salt Lake Valley. Young Breneman was a teamster throughout the entire journey. In his words: "I drove two yoke of oxen and a heavily laden wagon through heat and cold across the deserts and rivers and mountains. I have never performed a greater feat than that." Little did Breneman know an even greater accomplishment lay ahead—apostles and prophets would be among the fruit of his loins.

Breneman lived the law of plural marriage and had three wives. He married Mary Esther Benedict on December 10, 1864. She died a short time later, having no children. On April 10, 1866, he married Marjorie Martina Halseth (Martina). Through this marriage would come a grandson, Elder Joseph B. Wirthlin, who would become a member of the Quorum of the Twelve Apostles.

Later, on January 4, 1869, Breneman married Sarah Ann

Sarah Osguthorpe Bitner, Ada's mother

Osguthorpe. She was the daughter of English immigrants John and Lydia Roper Osguthorpe. Sarah was only eighteen months old in 1849 when she sailed with her parents from England to America. John and Lydia were converted to the Church shortly after their arrival in Philadelphia; they traveled to the Salt Lake Valley with the Charles Wilkin company in April of 1853, when Sarah was six years of age. Sarah spent her growing up years near the mouth of Mill Creek Canyon, not far from the Cottonwood area where Breneman had grown up.

Breneman, Martina, and Sarah and their families lived in a large adobe house in the Cottonwood area of the Salt Lake Valley (at present-day 4800 South and 1500 East). The two wives of the household shared a close relationship. Despite challenges, this sisterly kinship, combined with Breneman's reputation as a friendly and humble husband and father, made for a stable, generally harmonious household. Into this cooperative and hardworking environment, Ada Bitner was born.

It is certain that Ada never lacked for playmates in the bustling Bitner household. Her mother Sarah eventually had seven children, and Martina bore twelve. Ada's beloved friend during her growing up years was her half-sister Ardella or "Della." The two were inseparable. Della later remembered, "Ada and I didn't want anyone to walk home with us from high school. We really liked each other's company."

Everyone in the Bitner family, from the oldest down to the youngest, had work to do. Ada harvested vegetables, picked fruit, and fed the lambs, pigs, and chickens. She also learned the skills of a homemaker as she carded wool, sewed carpet rags, and helped cook meals. A woman of great faith, Ada's mother insisted upon regular family prayer every morning and evening. She would "ask the Lord to send guardian angels to watch over [the children] during the day and bring them home safely."

Ada's love of learning developed at an early age under the influence of her father Breneman. Della wrote that their father "was uncompromising with ignorance, with coarseness, and low standards. He was exacting with regard to learning." Ada acquired her father's deep love for good books which she would later pass on to her own children.

As a young girl, Ada likely attended one of the small public ward schools, then moved on to Oquirrh School, which opened its doors in September 1894, when Ada was fourteen years old. Family tradition assumes that Ada then attended the Salt Lake High School.

Ada Hinckley

But all was not hard work and formal learning during these years. Ada loved to swim with her siblings in Cottonwood Creek, which curved around the south border of the farm, where it washed out the creek bed and widened the banks to make an irresistible swimming hole. The girls would seek out a thicket of bushes for cover while they changed into their swimsuits and then would swim the afternoon away.

When Ada was seven years old, she moved with her mother Sarah and her siblings to Salt Lake City to be closer to good schools. They lived in a home located at present-day 274 East 400 South. Then, in 1901, Breneman purchased a home at 259 Center Street, a street just west of the Utah State Capitol building. Here, Sarah and her children lived until her sons, Milton and Hoffman, purchased a home for their mother on the northwest corner of 900 East and Garfield Avenue in Salt Lake City.

Ada lived in this home while she attended high school and college, and later while she worked downtown. Despite the hardships that came naturally in a crowded household, Ada's mother created such a pleasant atmosphere that the home became a gathering place for her children and their friends. Music and singing filled many an evening, and Ada's mother joined in and loved to sing and laugh with them.

In this loving and friendly environment, Ada blossomed into young womanhood. On a daily basis she absorbed her mother's personality and values, including Sarah's devotion as a wife, mother, and homemaker, and her deep love for the subtle beauties of nature and music. Ada also developed the humble commitment of her mother to the gospel of Jesus Christ.

Her father Breneman's love of learning had also taken root in Ada, and she was determined to continue her schooling. At one point she traveled with her sisters Lil (Sarah Lydia) and Ella to Chicago to learn the Gregg Shorthand Method. Following her return from Chicago, Ada was employed in 1899 by LDS Business College. She was the first teacher of the Gregg Method in Utah and also taught English and typing—a remarkable accomplishment for a nineteen-year-old woman in early Utah. The rarity of finding a young woman with such an excellent educational background at the end of the nineteenth century can be appreciated by reading a newspaper article of the day which declares that, "Girls in a commercial school were scarce as typewriters then." J. Reuben Clark Jr., head of the school's shorthand department at the time, and later a counselor in the First Presidency of the Church, enthusiastically attested to Ada's brilliance as a teacher. Her popularity among students added to the high praise.

About one year after Ada began her teaching career, Bryant Stringham Hinckley was offered the position of principal at the Salt Lake Business College. He had previously been a professor at Brigham Young Academy in Provo, but enthusiastically accepted this new position. He moved to Salt Lake City with his wife, Christine Johnson Hinckley, and their four children, and vigorously began to work on the challenges associated with his new assignment.

Bryant was the son of Ira Nathaniel and Angeline W. Noble Hinckley, who were charged by Brigham Young in 1867 to build a

Bryant Hinckley and Ada Bitner Hinckley

fort at Cove Creek in Millard County, Utah. Bryant spent some of his early years at Cove Fort, and in his veins ran the blood of pioneers and the spirit of ingenuity, hard work, and devotion to God.

About eight years after Bryant began his work at LDS Business College, tragedy struck his family. On July 11, 1908, Bryant's wife Christine fell ill and died quickly of appendicitis. Consumed by his grief, Bryant relied on his extended family for help as he sought to care for his eight motherless children—their ages ranging from fourteen years to two months. Two of his children, Carol, age six, and Christine, two months, went to live permanently with their mother's parents in Provo. The other six children stayed with their father, Bryant, in Salt Lake City.

By this time Ada and Bryant had been acquainted through their work at the college for at least eight years. Several months following Christine's death, their professional relationship became something more personal.

Bryant was about six feet tall, a slender and strikingly handsome man. A splendid speaker and orator, Bryant's classes were often filled to capacity. He began to court Ada, and they fell in love and were married in the Salt Lake Temple on August 5, 1909. Ada adored Bryant and made him the center of her life. It was plain to see Bryant's deep love and devotion for Ada as well. Standing five feet, four inches tall, Ada was a lovely and petite figure next to the towering Bryant. With beautiful hazel eyes, an oval face, fair skin, and long reddish-brown hair, Ada was the picture of grace, decorum, and dignity.

Bryant never hesitated to show his affection publicly for Ada; he would greet her warmly and throw his arms around her after having been away for an extended period of time. Ada sent letters to Bryant when they were apart which often began with, "My Darling Bryant," and concluded with, "Always know that I love you and wish you were here," or "Always and forever, your Ada."

The transition from life as a single woman and successful college teacher to that of a new wife with an instant family of six children in the home was, to say the least, a dramatic change. Bryant's children from his first marriage—Stanford, Lucile, Grant, Wendell, Waldo, and Venice—were greatly in need of a nurturing mother. Ada eagerly accepted her new responsibilities and immediately gave Bryant's large, two-story frame house at 840 East and 700 South in Salt Lake City, her own flavor. She brought with her a beautiful baby grand piano and a lovely collection of elegant dishes that she had gathered over the years.

But the coming of Ada to the family brought much more than a piano and fine china. Ada was a woman of tremendous industry and skill, and she brought order—as well as delicious cooking—to the Hinckley home. Ada's macaroni and cheese and her meat loaf were particular family favorites. The Sabbath was reason for celebration, and Ada's delicious "Sunday roast" with all of the trimmings became a tradition.

Ada also accepted responsibility for managing a good portion of the family's income. She paid most of the bills, kept a record of their finances, and saved scrupulously for the various needs of her husband and children.

Not long after their marriage, Bryant and Ada were expecting their first child. With joyful hearts they welcomed their firstborn son, Gordon Bitner Hinckley, into their home. Unbeknownst to them, a future prophet had been born. Ada would bear four more children within the next nine years; Sherman Bitner, Ruth, Ramona, and Sylvia Bitner.

Gordon's birth would soon significantly affect the family's way of life in unexpected ways. Physically small in build and vulnerable to allergies and infections, Gordon suffered from a variety of serious illnesses throughout his growing up years. At the age of two he came down with an acute case of whooping cough, and the doctor advised that he be taken away from the smoky air of the city to a place with clean, fresh air. Bryant immediately arranged to purchase a five-acre lot in the East Millcreek area of the Salt Lake Valley on which to build a small second home, complete with a rock fireplace built to Ada's specifications. A good portion of the down payment for the property was paid with money Ada had saved during her working years.

This location would serve as the family's "summer home" for four months of the year. The remaining eight months would be spent in the downtown home while the children were attending school. The farm in East Millcreek furnished an opportunity for the Hinckley children to work, and work hard. There was a large orchard bursting with fruit to be picked, a sizable garden to care for, and pigs, chickens, and two cows named "Babe" and "Polly" to supply the family with many necessities.

The family's early years at "The Farm" were spent without electricity or running water. Instead, Ada cooked on a coal range, used kerosene lamps for light, and carried water from a natural spring which ran south of the farmhouse. What a joyous occasion it was for her and the family when Bryant arranged for electric service from the power company. Later, he arranged for Smart Water Company to provide piped water to the farmhouse.

Ada was well known for bottling—some say a thousand quarts of fruit every summer, including applesauce and cherries. She cooked her famous strawberry jam in the heat of the sun, in pans, on the low-pitched tar roof of the farmhouse. She was expert in the art of bread making and produced eight loaves at least every other evening. Another beloved treat was Ada's famous "banana cream cake." All week long, she would save the cream from the top of the milk from the family cows, then serve it with a flourish atop a white cake with sliced bananas.

Because of Ada's constant use of the coal range, the heat inside the house was intolerable, and the children understandably spent a good share of the day outside working and playing. Their mother was known for letting her family know that dinner was on the table by calling out across the farm "Yoo-hoo!" She was even known to occasionally yodel, which was an absolute delight to her children.

Ada's voice could often be heard above the clinking and clanking of dishes in the kitchen, singing hymns and songs from her childhood as she worked. She would rock little Sylvia to sleep singing, "Baby's Boat's a Silver Moon," and "Kentucky Babe." The words to a favorite song she often sang to the children highlight the family's happy, though frugal, situation:

> We are a happy family, sitting on the floor galore.
> We haven't any chairs to sit on, so we have to sit on the
>   floor.

> They've taken all the chairs and the table.
> There's a mortgage on the rolling pin.
> And all we've got is a big round pot
> And a frying pan to wash the baby in.

Ada's talents went beyond her accomplishments in the kitchen. Gifted as an artist, she painted beautiful floral designs on dishes, which, when time permitted, she had fired to a final, permanent finish in a kiln. She was also a talented seamstress. One of her daughter Ramona's most treasured memories is that of her mother going into town just before the beginning of the school year and purchasing the patterns for new dresses, coats, and trousers along with yards of material and trim. If the children were lucky, Ada would also bring home a large bag of Keeley's Candy for their enjoyment. Ada would then take Ramona and her sisters to the home of "Aunt Minnie," a close family friend, where the two women would spend the day measuring, cutting, and fitting the girls' new school clothes. Ramona "could hardly contain [her] glee" at being able to wear such beautiful clothing to school each fall.

In addition to these projects, Ada's creative energies were used to teach her daughters how to shape handfuls of burrs into baskets, and how to cut and make doll furniture from the cardboard that came with Bryant's laundered shirts.

Life on the farm also provided the Hinckley family with a steady stream of adventure. Gordon and Sherman, who were inseparable, spent countless hours building carts and curious devices out of old wood and wheels. One afternoon, the pair constructed a "shower" in which the water was heated in a tank by the afternoon sun and provided a quick, though gloriously warm, rinsing. Their creation of a tire swing that swung out over the hollow located on the farm also provided hours of fun.

The girls had their share of excitement as well. One afternoon Bryant decided that it was just as important for his daughters to learn to shoot a rifle as it was for his sons. He took Ruth and Ramona out behind the farmhouse, instructed them in the fine points of marksmanship, and placed the gun in Ramona's hands. When she pulled the trigger, the kick knocked her backwards onto the ground. Ruth, terrified by her sister's experience, nonetheless took the gun in her hands. Just as she was about to shoot, Ada came out of the house and firmly expressed her displeasure at the thought of her little girls shooting a gun. That ended the shooting lesson.

Indeed, Ada believed in a woman maintaining her femininity. Somewhat meticulous about her own neat and clean appearance, she expected as much of her children and she was a stickler for baths. Ada possessed a gentle, generally quiet disposition, but was also quick to laugh. Her ways of disciplining the children were a product of this gentleness. Both Bryant and Ada steered clear of using physical force. Ada was said to employ "a look" which was enough to deter any wrongdoing on the part of her children. Sherman recalls, "You were expected to do what was right."

There was also a quiet discipline in the routine of home life. When the children were older, for example, Ada would place a chalkboard near the door with each child's name written on it. The children would come in one by one at night and erase their name off the board. The last person to erase their name was to lock the door.

Ada's even-tempered personality was put to the test when faced with what is said to have been her only phobia—lightning. This fear no doubt stemmed from an experience in the kitchen of the farmhouse when, during a fierce thunderstorm, a lightning bolt struck the electric stove. Ada was in the kitchen at the time, and the earsplitting "crack" of the bolt of lightning was so loud that young Ramona was knocked off the porch where she had been sitting. No one was hurt, but Ramona recalls that this experience was a rare moment when her mother "fell to pieces" out of fear for her family's safety.

Ada was an effective nursemaid when sickness periodically swept the household. Little Gordon once fell victim to a particularly terrible earache. Ada placed small bags of salt on the stove to heat, and then throughout the night held them tenderly against Gordon's throbbing ear to help relieve the pain. When Bryant, Venice, Gordon, and Ruth fell ill during the flu epidemic, Ada skillfully nursed them through the ordeal, despite the fact that she was expecting the birth of Sylvia.

Life at home was influenced by Bryant's callings in the Church, and the speaking and writing they required. He served as second counselor in the Liberty Stake presidency from 1907 to 1919 and was called in 1925 as stake president in the same stake, which by then was the largest in the Church. Bryant's abilities as a remarkably gifted speaker and writer led to his authorship of probably more Church manuals and teaching materials than any other single person in the history of the Church. Ada, skilled at shorthand and an expert grammarian, was the perfect helpmeet during this challenging endeavor. Many late nights were spent with the two working together, Bryant dictating and Ada pounding away on the old manual typewriter.

Ada's mastery of the English language gave her no patience with incorrect usage among her children. She would not tolerate the slightest laziness in their speech and was horrified by any slang words such as "nothin'" or "ain't" used by her children or their playmates.

Due to Bryant's callings in the Church, the Hinckleys also had a continual stream of visitors and enjoyed a busy social life. Ada's daughter Ramona recalls watching her mother go out for the evening dressed in a beautiful blue velvet dress with a coral beaded necklace. Oh, her mother was an elegant sight!

Ada loved having visitors in her home and was the perfect hostess. She took time to pass on this skill to her daughters, using her crystal tumblers, Haviland china, silver-plated silverware, and linens to demonstrate how to set an attractive table.

Each year, Ada invited her children's schoolteachers to the Hinckley home for a luncheon, sending handwritten invitations with each child. It was a gracious way to check on the progress of the children. This was long before the schools scheduled regular parent-teacher conferences. Ada's children were expected to walk their teachers to the home, which the children often said was the "longest walk of their lives."

Ada also hosted elaborate breakfast parties on the porch of the summer farm. Guests feasted on an array of food including bacon, eggs, sausage, peaches and cream, fried tomatoes, and pancakes with syrup.

Christmas was always a gala affair at the Hinckley household. Ada produced "pounds and pounds" of fondant, candy, and chocolates. She baked fruit cake and plum pudding, and sewed doll clothes for her daughters.

In addition to her responsibilities at home, Ada likewise served in many capacities in the Church. She served in the Young Women's Mutual Improvement Association (YWMIA), and served as second counselor in the stake Young Women's presidency for a period of time.

The year 1927 brought a dark cloud which cast a long shadow over the hustle and bustle of the Hinckley household. Ada's son Sherman recalls an alarming experience he had while working with his father, Bryant, in the orchard of the East Millcreek farmhouse: "[Father] broke down and started to sob uncontrollably. This really shook me because I had not ever seen Father this way before. When he gained some of his composure, he excused himself saying he was sorry but he had learned that Mother had a lump in her breast and they both feared it might be malignant." The tumor was indeed malignant, and at the age of forty-seven years, Ada underwent a radical mastectomy in an attempt to remove the cancer and keep it from spreading. Ada exhibited extraordinary serenity through this difficult period, a trait stemming from her desire not to alarm the children and her unquestioning trust in God.

For two and a half years, Ada's health seemed good. She was able to carry on her responsibilities as a wife and mother, and she accompanied her husband on many of his church- and work-related trips. Following a trip with Bryant to Chicago, however, Ada's arm became swollen and hard to move. A visit with a physician confirmed the family's worst fear—the cancer was back.

Ada began radium treatments, the side effects of which made her violently ill. Despite the terrible pain and discomfort associated with the cancer and treatments, Ada was determined to take advantage of a government-sponsored program known as the "Gold Star Mothers Pilgrimage." This program, the result of an Act of Congress passed on March 2, 1929, enabled the mothers and widows of American soldiers to make an all-expense paid journey to the final resting places of their beloved sons and husbands who had died while serving their country during World War I. Stanford, Bryant's oldest son from his first marriage, had died of pneumonia in Bordeaux, France, while serving in the army during the war. He was buried in the American military cemetery in Suresnes, overlooking Paris. Ada made the journey with Bulah, Stanford's widow, as her traveling companion. The first leg of the journey took the women by train to New York City. Despite her ill health, the humorous events of the train ride were not lost on Ada, who related the following story:

"Another woman didn't know how to turn off her light [in her sleeping compartment]. She pushed every hole, screw, and button but the right one and finally left the light burning all night, so that she had quite a pain across her eyes. Then her daughters had insisted on her getting a new Spirella corset—she's not in the habit of wearing a corset and is rather fleshy. This new corset reaches from her armpits down below her thighs. She went through all kinds of contortions trying to get it off and finally gave up and slept in it all night. So with the light and the corset [both on], she feels a wreck this morning. I laughed myself sick while she was telling it."

Ada kept detailed notes on her trip to France, notes which she would use to summarize the group's experience in an article which was published in the *Improvement Era* in December 1930. She was particularly enchanted by the Louvre, the national art museum located in Paris. In a letter to Bryant she declared, "I was simply speechless, the exhibition is so marvelous."

Ada's fascination with the art and history of France was overshadowed by her deteriorating health. For moral support, Ada carried with her a small book which contained the saying, "The God Power within me is stronger than my weakness." Her faith and courage throughout her quiet suffering is apparent in a letter to Bryant:

> Don't forget to pray for me. I need faith and prayer more than anything in the world. I haven't told a soul, not even Bulah, that I'm not well. I don't want any of them to know. I will get along better if they don't know, but I have to appeal to the Lord often. After all, He is the only one who can help me and I'm sure He will not forsake me at this time.

On Sunday, August 4, 1930, Ada visited the burial place of Bryant's oldest son, Stanford Hinckley. She poetically described the scene:

"There are no mounds, but rows and rows of Italian marble crosses standing with military precision in the graves—men from every state in the union, names denoting many nationalities. They marched as buddies to their death and now lie side by side, strangers in a strange land. The cemeteries are beautifully landscaped and beautifully kept. When we reached the cemetery there was ready for each grave a large and very beautiful wreath of roses, a gift of the government. One feels that it was best to let those who fell here be buried in France."

Upon Ada's return to Salt Lake City, Bryant and the children were there to greet her at the station. The cancer's toll on their mother was immediately apparent, and Ada's health rapidly declined from then on.

Bryant learned of two Los Angeles doctors who had developed a special cancer treatment and immediately sent Ada by train to

California with her sister Mary as caregiver. Although the treatment did much to relieve Ada of pain, the cancer continued its course. In early November Bryant received word from Mary that he should come as soon as possible. Despite Ada's request that Bryant wait until the less expensive train rates were available, he packed that very evening and left for Los Angeles.

A letter from Bryant to the children described the scene in Los Angeles:

> I stay at the house all the time so I can lift her, rub her feet, move her legs and help in any way I can. Mamma seems a little more weary otherwise not much change this morning. We are hoping for an improvement but are reconciled to what ever may come. Thus far we have done all that we could do and we seem powerless. She is in the hands of the Lord—He can spare her life and raise her and if it is his will, she will live. If not, all will be well. There is a very tranquil and sweet influence here. Mamma is just as calm and patient as an angel could be. Go about and do your work and do what is right and all will be well with us.

On the morning of November 9, 1930, Ada Bitner Hinckley died at fifty years of age. Her half-sister Della, who spent some moments with her in Los Angeles before her death, wrote, "She died as she had lived, calmly and bravely. I did not think such courage possible. She looked out on eternity with trust and perfect faith. He who had taught her how to live surely taught her how to die."

Bryant's arrival by train in Salt Lake City to greet his grief-stricken children was a scene that would always be remembered with soberness and reverence by the family. Ada's daughter Ruth wrote, "I think the evening we went to the depot to meet Father when he came home from California was the saddest day of my life. We could see the hearse waiting for the train and could not believe that it was there to pick up the mortal remains of our mother.

Father got off the train looking ashen and weary." Decades later, Ada's surviving children would still remember that day at the train station with tender hearts and great emotion.

Bryant wrote of Ada following her death, "There was a brilliancy of mind, a gentle resignation, a noble loyalty of heart about this dear little woman that will make her memory shine forever in the hearts of those who knew her. For twenty-one years she was the loving helpmate and companion of her husband, seeking as none else could, to forward him in every good he attempted. None miss her as he does and no one can cherish her memory as sacredly."

Even after her death, Ada's influence would still be felt in years to come. One act of service performed by her would have lasting implications. Three years following her death, her oldest son, Gordon, was desperately saving his money in order to serve a proselyting mission for the Church. The enormity of the sum needed to do so seemed hopelessly out of reach, since he had been called to the most expensive mission in the Church.

With humility and deep gratitude, it was discovered that Ada had set aside a small savings account with the money left over from her grocery purchases. She had designated the money to be used for her sons' missions. Such sacrifice and foresight enabled this son, Gordon Bitner Hinckley, whom the Lord would later call as the fifteenth President of the Church, to serve a mission in the British Isles. This young elder's service there would be the catalyst for spiritual experiences of profound importance in his life, which would forever commit him to the Lord and service in His Kingdom.

SOURCES

The most complete collection on the life of Ada Bitner Hinckley is a remarkable family scrapbook and history compiled by the husband of Ada's daughter, Ruth Hinckley Willes. This collection contains extensive information about Ada's forebears, a detailed chronology of the events of her life, photographs, copies of letters written between Ada and Bryant, reminiscences of those who knew Ada well, and a transcript of her funeral. It is Joseph Simmons Willes, *The Story of Ada Bitner Hinckley* as told by Ruth Hinckley Willes (privately distributed, 1980).

We are indebted to the late Judith Wirthlin Parker, of Salt Lake City, who, just a few days before her unexpected passing, provided us with a series of short biographical sketches on many of Ada's forebears. They are Lydia Osguthorpe Stillman, *History of John Osguthorpe* and *History of Lydia Roper Osguthorpe* (unpublished manuscripts, 1970), and Helen Bitner Wilcox, *A Lineal History of Breneman Barr Bitner* (unpublished). Mary O. Garret, of Salt Lake City, provided us with information on Ada's mother in the manuscript *Ella Bitner Bunbury, Sarah Ann Osguthorpe Bitner* (written in 1930, unpublished).

We are particularly grateful for the graciousness of Ramona Hinckley Sullivan and Sherman Hinckley for their willingness to share reminiscences of their mother through personal interviews conducted in their homes in Salt Lake City, May 26, 2000. Joan Willes Peterson, Ada's granddaughter, also provided valuable insights through interview and by providing research materials and photographs.

And, of course, Sheri L. Dew's excellent biography of Ada's oldest child, *Gordon B. Hinckley, Go Forward with Faith* (Salt Lake City: Deseret Book, 1996), was especially valuable.

LIST OF PHOTOGRAPHS
AND ILLUSTRATIONS

Page 2. Lucy Mack Smith. Courtesy of LDS Church Visual Resources Library.

Page 6. Joseph Smith Sr. Courtesy of LDS Church Visual Resources Library.

Page 23. Lucy Mack Smith's home in Nauvoo, Illinois. Courtesy of Kenneth and Audrey Godfrey.

Page 32. Abigail Young's five sons in 1856. Courtesy of LDS Church Visual Resources Library.

Page 41. Agnes Taylor Taylor. Courtesy of Archives Division, Historical Department, The Church of Jesus Christ of Latter-day Saints. Hereafter cited as LDS Church Archives.

Page 58. A church in Farmington, Connecticut. Courtesy of Family History Library, The Church of Jesus Christ of Latter-day Saints.

Page 80. Eliza Snow and Lorenzo Snow. Courtesy of LDS Visual Resources Library.

Page 94. David A. Smith and Joseph Fielding Smith at Black Creek, near Toronto, Canada. Courtesy of LDS Church Archives.

Page 99. Mary Fielding Smith and Hyrum Smith. Courtesy of LDS Church Visual Resources Library.

Page 111. Rachel Ridgeway Ivins Grant. Courtesy of LDS Church Archives.

Page 119. Jedediah Grant. Courtesy of LDS Church Visual Resources Library.

Page 120. Rachel Grant and young Heber J. Grant. Courtesy of LDS Church Visual Resources Library.

Page 123. Rachel Grant's home in Salt Lake City, Utah. Courtesy of LDS Church Archives.

Page 133. Sarah Farr and John Henry Smith. Courtesy of LDS Church Visual Resources Library.

Page 138. John Henry Smith. Courtesy of LDS Church Visual Resources Library.

Page 140. Sarah Farr Smith. Courtesy of LDS Church Visual Resources Library.

Page 143. Jeanette Eveline Evans McKay. Courtesy of LDS Church Visual Resources Library.

Page 150. David McKay. Courtesy of Margie Jacobsen.

Page 151. Jeanette Evans and her schoolmates in Ogden, Utah, in 1867. Courtesy of George and Melba Hill.

Page 152. Jeanette Evans McKay's four daughters. Courtesy of Margie Jacobsen.

Page 154. Jeanette Eveline Evans McKay. Courtesy of LDS Church Archives.

Page 160. Julina Lambson Smith. Courtesy of LDS Church Archives.

Page 167. Joseph F. Smith and Julina Smith in 1916 on their fiftieth wedding anniversary. Courtesy of LDS Church Visual Resources Library.

Page 178. Louisa Emeline Bingham Lee. Courtesy of LDS Church Archives.

Page 180. Levi Perry Bingham and Elizabeth Lusk Bingham. Courtesy of L. Brent Goates.

Page 182. Samuel Marion Lee and Louisa Bingham Lee. Courtesy of L. Brent Goates.

Page 186. Samuel Marion Lee and Louisa Bingham Lee. Courtesy of L. Brent Goates.

Page 191. Edwin Woolley and Mary Olpin Woolley. Courtesy of LDS Church Archives.

Page 196. Olive Woolley Kimball. Courtesy of LDS Church Archives.

Page 202. Olive and Andrew Kimball family in 1897. Courtesy of Edward L. Kimball.

Page 212. Sarah Benson and her children in 1912. Courtesy of LDS Church Visual Resources Library.

Page 218. George Benson and Sarah Dunkley Benson. Courtesy of LDS Church Archives.

Page 227. Nellie Marie Rasmussen Hunter. Courtesy of Kathy R. Rodda and Susan R. Bagley.

Page 229. Will and Nellie Hunter. Courtesy of Kathy R. Rodda and Susan R. Bagley.

Page 230. Nellie Marie Rasmussen Hunter. Courtesy of Kathy R. Rodda and Susan R. Bagley.

Page 242. Breneman Barr Bitner. Courtesy of Judith Wirthlin Parker.

Page 243. Sarah Osguthorpe Bitner. Courtesy of Judith Wirthlin Parker.

Page 245. Ada Hinckley. Courtesy of Ramona Hinckley Sullivan.

Page 247. Bryant Hinckley and Ada Bitner Hinckley in 1913. Courtesy of Joan Willes Peterson.

INDEX

Adam-ondi-Ahman, 84
Angell, Truman O., 193
Antipolygamy laws, 171
Arrington, Leonard James, vii

Barber, Lucius, 74–75
Barnes, Lorenzo D., 191
Barrows, Samuel, 76–77
Battle of Bunker Hill, 3
Beehive House, 173
Bennett, John C., 85
Benson, Addie, 216
Benson, Florence, 216
Benson, Ezra Taft: tribute of, to
    mother, 211; meets Harold B. Lee,
    215–16; birth of, 217; childhood
    responsibilities of, 218–19
Benson, George Taft, Jr., 216; marriage
    of, 217; mission call of, 220–21;
    death of, 222
Benson, George Taft, Sr., 216
Benson, George Taft, III, 220
Benson, Louisa, 217
Benson, Sarah Dunkley, vii–viii; son's
    tribute to, 211; birth of, 211, 213;
    parents of, 212; sails from
    England, 212; crosses plains,
    212–13; childhood of, 214;
    education of, 214–15; social life of,
    216; marriage of, 217; and near
    death in childbirth, 217; children
    of, 217–18; and work ethic, 218;
    responsibilities of, 219–20; and

missionary call of husband,
    220–21; death of, 221–22; David O.
    McKay speaks at funeral of,
    222–23; biographical sources
    concerning, 223
Benson, Serge, 220
Bible, 1
Bidamon, Emma Smith, 27. See also
    Emma Hale Smith
Bigler, Jacob G., 152
Bingham, Elizabeth Lusk, 179
Bingham, Levi Perry, 179
Bingham, Perry Calvin, 179–80
Bitner, Abraham, 242
Bitner, Anna Barr, 242
Bitner, Breneman Barr, 242, 246
Bitner, Marjorie Martina, 243
Bitner, Mary Esther Benedict, 243
Bitner, Sarah Ann, 242–43
Blair, Jacob, 73, 76
Boggs, Governor Lilburn W., 52, 99
Book of Mormon, 16; Young family
    introduced to, 38
Box B, 220
Boyes, George, 53
Breastplate, 14
Brigham City, founded by Saints,
    178–79
Brodie, Alexander, 206
Brown, Harriet Canfield, 132, 148
Bunker, Edward, 149
Buzzard, Philip, 148

Cahoon, Reynolds, 20
Campbell, Alexander, 80
Campbellite Christians, 81
Canfield, Rose, 148–49
Cannon, Annie Wells, 174
Cannon, George Q., 54
Cannon, Leonora, 51
Chase, Ezra, 129
Chase, Nancy, 133–34
Child, death of unbaptized, 112
Cholera, 147
Christensen, Anders, 225
Christensen, Nilla Torgersen, 225
Christensen, Nicoline, 225; death of,
    226
Church of Christ, 9; organization of,
    16–17
Church of Jesus Christ of Latter-day
    Saints, The: mothers of the
    prophets who led, ix; founding
    prophet of, 1; Welfare Program of,
    185
Clark, J. Reuben, Jr., 246
Clayton, Roberta Flake, 195
Cleaveland, Moses, 73
Cleveland, 73
Colby, Ida, 219
Connecticut, 56, 72; Land Company,
    72–73; Western Reserve of, 72
Coray, Martha Jane Knowlton, 25
Covey, Almira, 95

Davis, Jeannette McMurrin, 182
Davis, Riley, 182
Dead, salvation for, 115
Disciples of Christ, 90
Dort, David, 96
Dort, Fanny, 96
Dort, Mary (Polly), 96
Dunkley, Joseph, 212–13
Dunkley, Margaret Leitch, 213
Dunkley, Margaret Wright, 212–13,
    217, 220–21
Dunkley, Mary Ann Hobbs, 213

Dwight, Timothy, 59
Dyson, James, 89

Eastern Arizona College, 203
Edmund's Act, 171
Education, importance of, 148–49
Egan, Howard, 105
Evans, Margaret Powell, 144–45
Evans, Thomas, 144–45
Extermination order, 52

Family, early America and the, 1
Farr, John, 130
Farr, Lorin, 128–29, 131
Farr, Nancy Bailey Chase, 128–29
Farr's Fort, 129
Female Relief Society, 85, 128
Fielding, Ann, 92
Fielding, John, 88; marriage of, 90;
    children of, 90–92; death of, 91
Fielding, Joseph, 92–93, 104, 106; and
    Mormonism, 93–95; mission of, 95
Fielding, Mary, 93, 95
Fielding, Mercy, 92–95
Fielding, Rachel Ibbotson, 88;
    marriage of, 90; children of,
    90–92; spirituality of, 91; death of,
    91

Gates, Jacob, 195
Gathering, spirit of, 114–15
Gila Academy, 203
Gold, discovery of, 121–22
Gold Star Mothers Pilgrimage, 255
Golding, Reverend James, 91
Grant, George D., 121
Grant, Heber Jeddy, viii, 197; tribute
    of, to mother, 110; birth of, 120;
    called as apostle, 123–24; and
    Olive Woolley, 197
Grant, Jedediah M., 110–11, 117–18;
    birth of, 118; as missionary,
    118–19; responsibilities of,
    118–19; death of, 119–20
Grant, Rachel Ridgeway Ivins, viii–ix;

son's tribute to, 110; and missionaries, 111; conversion of, 112; birth of, 112–13; death of parents of, 113; upbringing of, 113–14; and love of music, 114; joins Baptist Church, 114; and Joseph Smith, 114, 115–16; moves to Nauvoo, 115; described by Emmeline Harris, 115; and malaria, 116; on Brigham Young's transfiguration, 116; migrates to Utah, 117; marriage of, 118; death of husband of, 119–20; gives birth to Heber Jeddy, 120; marriage of, to George Grant, 121; obtains divorce, 121; independence of, 121–23; Church activity of, 123; predicts apostleship for Heber, 123–24; health problems of, 124; death of, 124; biographical sources concerning, 125

Greene, John P., 36

Griffin, Charles, 108

Grinnels, "Aunty" Hannah, 98–99, 106

Hansen, Margaret Mary Ann, 219

Harris, William J., 107

Haws, Alex G., 122

Hess, Emeline Bigler, 162

Hinckley, Ada Bitner, vii, ix; son's tribute to, 241; patriarchal blessing of, 241; marriage of, 241–42, 248; birth of, 242, 244; responsibilities of, 244, 248–49; love of learning of, 144; moves to Salt Lake City, 245; work ethic of, 249–50, 253; talents of, 250–51, 253; appearance of, 252; and discipline, 252; as nursemaid, 252–53; social life of, 253–54; holiday traditions of, 254; contracts cancer, 254–55; and Gold Star Mothers Pilgrimage, 255; travels to France, 255–56;

letter of, to Bryant, 256; seeks treatment in Los Angeles, 256–57; death of, 257–58; biographical sources concerning, 258–59

Hinckley, Bryant Stringham, 241–42, 246; marries Ada Bitner, 248; receives letter from Ada, 256; sends Ada to Los Angeles for treatment, 256–57; writes children, 257; and Ada's death, 257–58

Hinckley, Christine Johnson, 246; death of, 247

Hinckley, Gordon B.: announces Snowflake Arizona Temple, 208; tribute of, to mother, 241; birth of, 242, 249; youth of, 251; receives mission call, 258; called as president of the Church, 258

Hinckley, Angeline W., 246–47

Hinckley, Ira Nathaniel, 246–47

Hinckley, Ruth, 257–58

Hinckley, Stanford, 255–56

Hoaglund, Abraham, 54

Howard, Caleb, 9–11

Howe, Elias, Jr., 30

Howe, Julia Ward, 30

Howe, Phineas and Susanna, 30–31

Howe, Samuel Gridley, 30

Howells, Thomas C. D., 179

Hunter, Claire May Jeffs, 236

Hunter, Howard W.: tribute of, to mother, 224; birth of, 229; baptism of, 235; marriage of, 236; and sealing of parents, 238; sustained as apostle, 238; on death of his mother, 240

Hunter, John William, 227; marriage of, 228; characteristics of, 230–31; baptism of, 235; sealing of, 238; death of, 239

Hunter, Louine Berry, 239

Hunter, Nellie Marie Rasmussen, vii–ix; son's tribute to, 224; as beloved grandmother, 224–25,

236–37; birth of, 225; marriage of,
228; characteristics of, 229;
children of, 229–30; talents of,
231; community service of, 232;
Church responsibilities of, 232;
parenting techniques of, 232–33;
family traditions of, 234–35, 237;
spiritualality of, 235; later years of,
238; sealing in temple of, 238;
sense of humor of, 239; death of,
239; biographical sources
concerning, 240
Hyde, Orson, 95, 112

Indian Territory Mission, 200
Indians, American, 199–200; Saints'
relations with, 149–50, 207;
encounters with, 213–14
Israel, gathering of, 18
Ivins, Anna Lowrie, 111, 117–18
Ivins, Caleb, Jr., 113
Ivins, Caleb, Sr., 113
Ivins, Edith Ridgeway, 113
Ivins, Esrael, 117–18

Jeffs, Emma Elizabeth, 226
Johnson, Lyman, 128
Johnston's army, 161–62

Kimball, Andrew, 190, 197; marriage
of, 197–98; serves mission, 198;
appointed president of Indian
Territory Mission, 200;
responsibilities of, 200; moves
family to Arizona, 201; and the
gospel, 204; and canal
construction, 206; death of
children of, 207
Kimball, Ann Alice Gheen, 197
Kimball, Heber C., 95, 104–5, 107,
197
Kimball, Olive Woolley, ix, 122; son's
tribute to, 189; in Arizona,
189–90, 201; birth of, 190, 193;
and family gatherings, 196–97;

marriage of, 197–98; children of,
198; responsibilities of, 198,
200–201, 203–4; Church activities
of, 204–5; and the gospel, 204–5;
as hostess, 206; death of children
of, 207; death of, 208–9;
biographical sources concerning,
209–10
Kimball, Spencer W.: tribute of, to
mother, 189; birth of, 201; letter to
mother, 208; death of mother,
208–9
Kimball, Vilate, 96
Kirtland, Turhand, 81
Kirtland Temple, 20, 83
Knight, Newel, 17
Knight, Sally, 17

Lambson, Alfred Boaz, 159–60; is
healed by Joseph Smith, 159;
called as missionary, 161
Lambson, Melissa Jane Bigler, 160
Latter-day Saints Millennial Star, 25–26
Law, Wilson, 52
Lawson, James, 105–6
Lawson, Joseph, 105–6
Layton, Christopher, 190, 202
Lee, Harold B.: tribute of, to mother,
177; on mother's childhood, 181;
birth of, 183; and haircut, 183; and
lye accident, 183–84; and
lightning incident, 184; on
mother's care of sick, 184–85;
moves to Salt Lake City, 186;
ordained an apostle, 187; meets
Ezra Taft Benson, 215–16
Lee, Louisa Emeline Bingham, viii;
son's tribute to, 177; birth of, 180;
childhood responsibilities of,
180–81; Church responsibilities of,
181, 183; marriage of, 181;
children of, 183; cares for invalid
father, 184; as midwife, 185;
homemaking skills of, 185; and

discipline of children, 186; moves to Salt Lake City, 186; moves to Green River, 187; death of, 197; biographical sources concerning, 187–88

Lee, Margaret McMurrin, 181

Lee, Samuel Marion, Jr., 181–83, 186–87

Lott, Captain Peter, 104

Lyman, Richard R., 139

Mack, Almira, 19, 24

Mack, Lovina, 4

Mack, Lovisa, 4

Mack, Lucy, 8–9, 10. See also Lucy Mack Smith

Mack, Lydia Gates, 2–3

Mack, Solomon, 2–4

Mack, Stephen, 4–5, 19

Mack, Temperance, 19, 24, 96

Madsen, Maria Sophia Rasmussen, 228

Martin, Edward, 147

Matthews, T. R., 92

Maughan, Peter, 179

Maughan's Fort, 179

McKay, David, 142, 148–49; tribute of, to wife, 143; marriage of, 149; accepts mission call, 142–44; emigrates to Utah, 147–48

McKay, David O.: tribute of, to mother, 142, 155; birth of, 150; and "The Old Home," 150–51; visits mother's birthplace, 155–57; speaks at Sarah Benson's funeral, 222–23

McKay, Jeanette Eveline Evans, viii; son's tribute to, 142, 155; sends husband on mission, 142–44; birth of, 144–45; parents of, 146–47; emigrates to Utah, 147–48; education of, 148–49; marriage of, 149; encounters with Indians, 149–50; children of, 150–53; and

motherhood, 151; and importance of education, 152; responsibilities of, 153–54; death of, 154; plaque inscribed for, 156–57; eulogy for, 57–58; biographical sources concerning, 158

McKay, Ellen Oman, 147

McKay, William, 147

McLeary, Nephi, 218

McMurrin, Joseph, 182

McMurrin, Margaret, 182

Merrill, Bathsheba Smith, 164

Merrill, Clarence, 164

Mesa Arizona Temple, 206–7

Milliken, Lucy, 27

Mills, George, 99

Milton, John, 44

Moody, William A., 208

Morgan, Ann, 156

Morley, Isaac, 86

Mormonism, 37, 93–95

Moroni, Angel, 13–14

Morrell, Jeanette McKay, 155–56

Murdock, John, 53–54

Nauvoo, 84; Temple

Nauvoo Female Relief Society, 23–24

Nauvoo Temple, 102

New Connecticut, 72

Olpin, Henry, 192

Olpin, Sarah Ann White, 192

Oneida Stake Academy, 215–16

Osguthorpe, John, 243

Osguthorpe, Lydia, 243

Parker, John D., 52

Penny Subscription, Sisters, 102

Pettibone, Jacob, Jr., 74

Pettibone, Jacob, Sr., 74

Pettibone, Jacob W., 76–77

Pettibone, Rosetta Barber, 74

Pierce, William, 107

Pratt, Orson, 25–26, 128

Pratt, Parley P., 51, 53; conversion of, 81–82; preaching of, 93

Quakers, 113–14

Rasmussen, Daniel, 228
Rasmussen, Karen Marie Christiansen, 225–26
Rasmussen, Martin, 225
Rasmussen, Morten, 225
Rees, Thomas, 145
Reiser, A. Hamer, 155–56
Reorganized Church of Jesus Christ of Latter Day Saints, 83–84
Retrenchment Society, 168
Revolutionary War, 2
Richards, Willard, 52, 95
Ridgeway, Richard, 114
Rigdon, Sidney, 80–82, 84, 96; arrest of, 99; and right of presidency, 116
Roxey, Eliza. *See* Eliza R. Snow

Saints: gathering of, 18–19; flee to Missouri, 21–22; gather at Adam-ondi-Ahman, 84; in Salt Lake Valley, 177–79
Salt Lake Theater, 194
Sherman, General William T., 202
Shoshoni Indians, 179
Simons, Joseph, 218
Simmons, Rachel Woolley, 201
Smith, Agnes Coolbrith, 165
Smith, Alvin, 5, 10, 12
Smith, Asael, 5
Smith, Bathsheba, 161, 163–64, 168
Smith, Don Carlos, 17, 22–23, 98, 101
Smith, Emma Hale, 15, 24. *See also* Emma Smith Bidamon, 27
Smith, George A., 107, 132, 161, 163; constructs home for family, 163; death of, 171; as missionary, 191
Smith, George Albert: tribute of, to mother, 126; life of saved, 127; prays for mother, 135; letter of, to mother, 139–40

Smith, Hyrum, 5, 10, 17, 115; and cholera, 20; arrest of, 22; martyrdom of, 24–25; wife of, dies, 98; marries Mary Fielding, 98; leaves Kirtland, 98; arrest of, 99; assassination of, 102
Smith, Jerusha, 98, 107–8
Smith, John Henry, 126–27, 134, 137–38
Smith, Joseph, Jr.: tribute of, to mother, 1; leg infection of, 7–8; and trip to New York, 10; visions of, 12–14; receives gold plates, 14–15; marriage of, 15; and translation of gold plates, 15–16; and cholera, 20; arrest of, 22; martyrdom of, 24–25; at Taylors's home, 52–53; meets Parley P. Pratt, 81–82; meets Rosetta Snow, 82; at Kirtland Temple, 83; and Nauvoo, 84; and Female Relief Society, 85; arrest of, 99; assassination of, 102; and Rachel Ivins, 115–16; and Chase family, 128; heals Alfred Lambson, 159; Edwin Woolley meets, 191
Smith, Joseph, Sr., 1, 96; marriage of, 5; financial ruin of, 5–6; dreams of, 9, 12; moves to New York, 9; and Joseph Jr.'s vision, 14; baptism of, 17; illness of, 17; arrest and imprisonment of, 17–18; ordained patriarch of the Church, 20–21; sustained as counselor, 21; blesses family, 22; death of, 22, 101; patriarchal blessing by, 65; Edwin Woolley meets, 191
Smith, Joseph F.: tribute of, to mother, 88; leaves Illinois, 102–3; describes tithing incident, 106; ordained an apostle, 107; birth of, 165; mission of, 165; marries Levira, 165–68; marries Julina Lambson, 165, 167; Church

service of, 165, 170–71; mission of, to Hawaii, 165; moves to Hawaii, 171; becomes president of the Church, 173; at Kimballs's home, 206

Smith, Joseph Fielding: tribute of, to mother, 159; birth of, 169; and St. George Temple dedication, 169–70; and mother's midwifery, 170–71; mission of, 173; marriage of, 173; on his mother, 173; ordained president of the Church, 174

Smith, Josephine Groesbeck, 137

Smith, Julina Lambson, viii–ix, 174; son's tribute to, 159; birth of, 159, 161; father of, leaves on mission, 161; and Johnston's army, 161–62; returns to Provo, 162; childhood responsibilities of, 164; marries Joseph F. Smith, 165–67; children of, 168–69, 171–72; Church activity of, 168, 172, 174; social life of, 168–69; and St. George Temple dedication, 169; as midwife, 170–71; moves to Hawaii, 171–72; visits mother, 172–73; moves into Beehive House, 173; death of, 174; biographical sources concerning, 175–76

Smith, Levira, 165–68

Smith, Lucy Mack, vii–ix, 103; son Joseph's tribute to, 1; birth of, 1–2; cares for sisters, 4; and religion, 4; marries Joseph Smith Sr., 5; hardships of, 5–6; children of, 6; and typhoid epidemic, 7; health problems of, 8; covenants with God, 8–9; baptism of, 9; impoverishment of, 9; moves family to New York, 9–11; joins Presbyterian church, 12; on Joseph's stories, 14–15; on Book of

Mormon, 16; baptism of, 17; moves to Kirtland, Ohio, 29; prophesy of, 19; and funds for schoolhouse, 20; prays for sick sons, 20–21; accidental fall of, 21; blessing restores sight of, 21; moves to Missouri, 21–22; at Joseph's imprisonment, 22; establishes museum, 23; and Nauvoo Female Relief Society, 23–24; and martyrdom of sons, 24–25; reminiscences of, 25–26; acknowledged as a Mother in Israel, 26–27; death of, 27; biographical sources concerning, 27–28; Edwin Woolley meets, 191

Smith, Martha Ann, 101, 103, 107

Smith, Mary Fielding, viii, 20; son's tribute to, 88; children of, 88; birth of, 90–91; religious upbringing of, 92; meets John Taylor, 94; moves to Canada, 93; baptism of, 95; arrives in Kirtland, 95; lives with Vilate Kimball, 96; on Joseph Smith, 96; receives patriarchal blessing, 97; marries Hyrum Smith, 98; leaves Kirtland, 98; stepchildren of, 98; delivers Joseph F., 100; visits Hyrum in jail, 100; moves to Nauvoo, 101; and death of Hyrum, 102; leaves Illinois, 102–3; and oxen, 103–5; westward trek of, 104; in Salt Lake Valley, 105–7; and tithing incident, 106; death of, 107; biographical sources concerning, 108–9

Smith, Samuel, 17–18, 25

Smith, Sarah, 108

Smith, Sarah Ann Libby, 132

Smith, Sarah Farr: son's tribute to, 126; experience with stranger, 126–27; and divine intervention, 127; patriarchal blessing of, 127; birth of, 127–28; responsibilities of, 130–31; schooling of, 131–32; marriage of, 132; children of, 132–33, 138–39; character of, 134–35; cupboard falls on, 135; letters by, 136; travels of, 136; health problems of, 136; and husband's plural wife, 137; death of husband of, 137–38; and death, 139; Mother's Day letter to, 139–40; biographical sources concerning, 140

Snow, Eliza R., 82, 85–86; as father's secretary, 78; and love of literature, 79; sews uniform for Lorenzo, 79; meets Sidney Rigdon, 80; meets Joseph Smith, 82; teaches school, 84; on her parents's disaffection from the Saints, 85; achievements of, 86; tribute of, to mother, 86

Snow, Franklin, 76

Snow, Leonora, 82, 86

Snow, Lorenzo: tribute of, to mother, 72; characteristics of, 79; military ambitions of, 79; attends college, 79; Church service of, 82–83; founds Brigham City, 86

Snow, Oliver, 73, 76, 85

Snow, Rosetta Leonora Pettibone, ix; son's tribute to, 72; birth of, 73–74; childhood of, 74–75; schooling of, 75; children of, 75–77; skills of, 78–79; teaches children, 79; joins Baptist church, 79; meets Sidney Rigdon, 80–82; meets Joseph Smith, 82; conversion and baptism of, 82; and the Female Relief Society, 85; death of, 85–86; biographical sources concerning, 86–87

Snowflake Arizona Temple, 207

Social Hall, 193–94

St. Joseph's Stake Academy, 203

Taylor, Agnes Taylor, viii; birth of, 40;

parents of, 40–42; marriage of, 40, 47–48; childhood of, 43–46; religious upbringing of, 46; possible work of, as a domestic, 46–47; children of, 48–49; emigrates to Canada, 50; conversion of, 51; and Joseph Smith, 52–53; travels to Salt Lake Valley, 53; death of, 54; eulogy for, 54; biographical sources concerning, 54–55

Taylor, Christopher, 42

Taylor, Elizabeth, 53

Taylor, James: marries Agnes Taylor, 40, 47; family of, 47; receives government appointment, 48; emigrates to Canada, 50; conversion of, 51; death of, 54

Taylor, Agnes Whittington, 40–42, 44

Taylor, John, 40–42, 44; birth of, 48; apprenticeship of, 49; conversion of, to Methodism, 49; emigrates to Canada, 50; marriage of, 51; conversion of, to Church, 51; called as apostle, 51; mission call of, 51; calls Heber J. Grant as apostle, 124

Taylor, Leonora Cannon, 54, 93

Taylor, Sarah, 162

Taylor, William, 53

Thatcher, Moses, 215

Thompson, Anna Hart, 57

Thompson, Bulah, 57

Thompson, Lot, 57

Thompson, Mercy, 106, 166

Thompson, Robert, 95, 101

Thompson, William, 106

Times and Seasons, 67

Treaty of Paris, 2

Urim and Thummim, 14

Walton, Izabella, 93

Washington, George, 3, 57

Webster, Dwight, 66, 68
Webster, Noah, 59
Wells, Daniel H., 122
Wells, Emmeline B., 115, 172
Western Reserve, 92
Whitmer, Mary, 16, 19
Whitmer, Peter, 16, 19
Whitney, Orson F., 118–19
Whittington, Richard (Dick), 42
Winward, J. W., 218
Wirthlin, Joseph B., 243
Wood, Park, 122
Woodruff, Aphek, 60–70
Woodruff, Azubah Hart, 56; son's
    tribute to, 56; marriage of, 61;
    children of, 61; responsibilities of,
    62–63; travels to Winter Quarters,
    69; returns to Iowa, 70; death of,
    70; biographical sources
    concerning, 70–71
Woodruff, Bulah Thompson, viii–ix,
    56; son's tribute to, 56; birth of,
    57; childhood of, 57–58; schooling
    of, 59; marriage of, 59–60;
    children of, 60; death of, 50–61;
    appears in dream, 67; biographical
    sources concerning, 70–71
Woodruff, Phebe Carter, 65
Woodruff, Wilford, viii, 52, 53; tribute
    of, 56; birth of, 60; chores of, 52;
    accidents of, 63–64; conversion
    and baptism of, 64–65; marriage
    of, 65; converts family, 65–67;
    called as apostle, 67; missions of,
    67; sees mother in a dream, 67;
    manages Times and Seasons, 67;
    moves to Nauvoo, 67–68; and
    Winter Quarters, 68–69; in Salt
    Lake Valley, 70; performs McKays'
    marriage, 149; calls Kimballs to
    Arizona, 190
Woolley, Edwin D., 122, 190; hires

Mary Ann Olpin, 192; marriage of,
    192; sells home to BrighamYoung,
    195; party for, 196–97; death of,
    197
Woolley, Mary Ann Olpin, 190;
    marriage of, 192; children of, 193;
    death of, 197
Wordsworth, William, 42
Works, Miriam, 37
Wright, George, 215
Wright, Joshua, 113
Wright, Theodosia, 113

Young, Abigail (Nabby) Howe, ix;
    son's tribute to, 29, 38; description
    of, 29–30; marriage of, 30; birth of,
    30–31; parents of, 30–31; children
    of, 31–33; teaches children, 32–33,
    37–38; health problems of, 33,
    36–37; converts to Methodism, 33;
    death of, 38; and conversion of
    family to Church, 38; biographical
    sources concerning, 39
Young, Brigham, 98; on Mother Smith,
    27; tribute of, to mother, 29, 38;
    birth of, 34; responsibilities of, 36;
    cares for invalid wife, 37;
    conversion of, 37–38; some Saints
    refuse to follow, 68; transfiguration
    of, 116; and Indians, 149–50; and
    Johnston's Army, 161–62; advises
    plural marriage for Joseph F.
    Smith, 166; death of, 171; and
    Beehive House, 173; and Edwin
    Woolley, 191; and Salt Lake
    Theater, 194; purchases Woolley
    home, 195; and colonists, 213
Young, Fanny, 34–35
Young, John, 29–30, 35, 37–38
Young, Rhoda, 36

ABOUT THE AUTHORS

The late Leonard J. Arrington was a prolific and respected author of many books and hundreds of articles relating to LDS Church history. He served as Church Historian, 1972–82, and was director of the Joseph Fielding Smith Institute for Church History at Brigham Young University. He and his wife, Grace, have three children and ten grandchildren. Leonard passed away February 11, 1999.

Susan Arrington Madsen is a graduate of Utah State University and a former adjunct faculty member at the Logan LDS Institute. She is the author or coauthor of eight books relating to LDS Church history. She and her husband, Dean, have four daughters and one son-in-law, and live in Hyde Park, Utah.

Emily Madsen Jones is a graduate of Utah State University and has published in LDS Church magazines. She is an assistant librarian at the Orem Public Library. She and her husband, David, live in Lehi, Utah.